OBEDIENT REBELS

OBEDIENT REBELS

Catholic Substance and Protestant Principle in Luther's Reformation

JAROSLAV PELIKAN

Professor at Yale University

HARPER & ROW, PUBLISHERS

NEW YORK AND EVANSTON

FIRST EDITION
LIBRARY OF CONGRESS CATALOG CARD NUMBER: 64-20200

CONTENTS

ABBREVIATIONS

BC   *The Book of Concord*, translated by Theodore G. Tappert, Jaroslav Pelikan, Robert H. Fischer, and Arthur C. Piepkorn. Philadelphia, 1959.

Bek.   *Die Bekenntnisschriften der evangelisch-lutherischen Kirche.* 2nd ed.; Göttingen, 1952.

CC   'Corpus Catholicorum'

CR   'Corpus Reformatorum'

DTC   *Dictionnaire de Théologie Catholique*

LW   *Luther's Works* (American Edition). Saint Louis and Philadelphia, 1955 ff.

NDL   'Neudrucke Deutscher Literaturwerke des XVI. und XVII. Jahrhunderts'

StL   *Dr Martin Luthers Sämmtliche Schriften.* Saint Louis, 1880 ff.

WA   *D. Martin Luthers Werke.* Weimar, 1883 ff. *Briefe (WA Br). Tischreden (WA Ti).*

WML   *Works of Martin Luther.* Philadelphia, 1915 ff.

ZHT   *Zeitschrift für die historische Theologie*

ZKG   *Zeitschrift für Kirchengeschichte*

PREFACE

THIS volume unites two of the deepest concerns of my thought and scholarship, the Reformation of the sixteenth century and the ecumenical movement of the twentieth, and studies each in the light of the other. It originated twenty years ago, when I began my doctoral dissertation at the University of Chicago under Wilhelm Pauck; the first half of the dissertation, in revised form, is included here. Since then I have published several chapters of this book in various journals and symposia, to whose publishers I am grateful for permission to revise and reprint them here. I am grateful, too, to my professors and to my colleagues, many of whom read portions of this monograph and gave it their constructive criticism.

I dedicate this book to one who was neither my professor nor my colleague, but who is none the less my teacher, the theologian who taught me to speak of 'Catholic substance and Protestant principle', Paul Tillich.

JAROSLAV PELIKAN

Yale University
Feast Day of SS.
Cyril and Methodius
July 7, 1964

I

THE PARADOX OF LUTHER'S REFORMATION

MARTIN LUTHER was the first Protestant, and yet he was more Catholic than many of his Roman Catholic opponents. This paradox lies at the very centre of Luther's Reformation. He claimed that his theology was derived from the Scriptures, as though the church fathers had never lived; still the theology that he claimed to derive from 'Scripture alone' bore a striking family resemblance to the tradition of the church fathers. He spoke of 'hating' the abstract theological terms in traditional dogmatic language about the Trinity and the person of Christ,[1] but the traditional dogma of the Trinity was in fact basic to his entire theology. He could attack the distinction between clergy and laity as a distortion of the institution of Christ; nevertheless, he exalted the ministry of preaching as 'the highest office in Christendom'.[2] He could sound utterly individualistic in his pronouncements on moral questions, asking Christians to be on their own when they made their ethical choices; at the same time he could also recognize that most Christians were not very heroic in their ethical choices and needed the moral support and discipline of both church and state. Sometimes he sounded like an iconoclast, sometimes he sounded like a traditionalist.

THE 'REAL LUTHER'?

Which Luther was the real Luther? Was it the Protestant Luther, who defied the authority of the church in the name of the word of God as he interpreted it? Or was it the Catholic Luther,

[1] *Against Latomus, WA* 8, 117-118 (*LW* 32, 244).
[2] *The Right and Power of a Christian Congregation or Community to Judge All Teaching and to Call, Appoint, and Dismiss Teachers, Established and Proved from Scripture, WA* 11, 415 (*WML* 4, 84).

who withstood the defiance and the private interpretations of other
Protestants in the name of the word of God as the tradition of the
church had interpreted it? Or was it some *via media* between these
two, who taught exactly what later Protestants (of whatever stripe)
have taught on every question? This third way of interpreting the
Catholic-Protestant Luther and his Reformation is the way followed
by most generations of Luther scholars. Thus there was an
orthodox Luther in the seventeenth century, a pietistic and a
rationalistic Luther in the eighteenth, a liberal and a confessional
Luther in the nineteenth, a Barthian and even a Nazi Luther in the
twentieth. The history of Protestant theology on the Continent
could be written on the basis of its picture of Luther's Reformation,
as recent books by Bornkamm, Carlson, and Dillenberger have
shown.[1] Only rarely, however, have these schools of interpretation
attempted to explain or expound the juxtaposition of Catholic
substance and Protestant principle in Luther's Reformation. In
some ways the critics of Luther have been more discerning than
have his disciples. Roman Catholic critics beginning with John
Cochlaeus have explained him as the seed plot of all later Protestant
heresies,[2] while the left wing of the Reformation and of Protestant
theology has continually expressed amazement that 'the same man
who delivered the gospel of Jesus Christ from ecclesiasticism and
moralism strengthened its authority in the forms of the Old
Catholic theology'.[3]

The most striking illustrations of the juxtaposition of Catholic
substance and Protestant principle in Luther's Reformation are
probably his doctrines of the eucharist and of the church. An
earlier monograph has probed the correlation of Protestant and
Catholic motifs in Luther's exegesis of the principal biblical passages on the Lord's Supper.[4] In the present volume it is Luther's
doctrine of the church that comes in for consideration as the point

[1] Heinrich Bornkamm, *Luther im Spiegel der deutschen Geistesgeschichte*
(Heidelberg, 1955); Edgar M. Carlson, *The Reinterpretation of Luther* (Philadelphia, 1948); John Dillenberger, *God Hidden and Revealed* (Philadelphia,
1953).
[2] The influence of Cochlaeus on subsequent Roman Catholic treatments of
Luther is assessed by Adolf Herte, *Das katholische Lutherbild im Banne der
Lutherkommentare des Cochläus* (3 vols.; Münster, 1943).
[3] Adolf Harnack, *History of Dogma*, tr. Neil Buchanan (7 vols.; New York,
and London, 1961), VII, 173.
[4] Jaroslav Pelikan, *Luther the Expositor* (Saint Louis, 1959), especially Part
Two.

of intersection between Catholic substance and Protestant principle. 'Catholic substance' in this context means the body of tradition, liturgy, dogma, and churchmanship developed chiefly by the ancient church and embodied (but not exhausted) for Luther in the Roman Catholic Church of his day. 'Protestant principle' is a summary term for the criticism and reconstruction of this Catholic substance which Luther and his Reformation carried out in the name of the Christian gospel and with the authority of the Bible.[1] To make sense of Catholic substance and Protestant principle in Luther's Reformation, three areas of inquiry will be examined on the basis of Luther's writings and of the confessions that emerged from his Reformation: Part One of this volume discusses the attitude of Luther's Reformation toward tradition and church history as 'critical reverence'; Part Two gives an account of some of the efforts of Luther's Reformation to achieve 'unity despite separation'; Part Three evaluates the relevance of 'Catholic substance and Protestant principle' today.

THE DOCTRINE OF THE CHURCH

The context for this investigation is the paradox of Luther's doctrine of the church. From Luther's writings it is possible to construct an ultra-Protestant view of the church as the product of the believers who made it up, deriving its just powers from their individual priestly authority.[2] Statements in support of this view were usually part of Luther's attack upon the entrenched authority of Rome, with its priesthood and its institutions. Faced by this array, Luther pointed men away from any trust in the church to the faith which the Holy Spirit had created in them personally through the word of God. Simultaneously he spoke in Catholic tones and called the church his mother, the source of his spiritual life.[3] Moreover, the church was not a Platonic republic, existing only in the mind of God and in the hope of the believers.[4] The church was a reality for Luther, and he knew himself to be part of its continuing life and tradition. And there were not two churches

[1] Cf. Paul Tillich, *The Protestant Era*, tr. James Luther Adams (Chicago, 1948; London, 1951), p. 163.

[2] So especially from his treatise of 1523, *On the Ministry*, *WA* 12, 169-195 (*LW* 40, 7-44); on the backgrounds of this treatise, see pp. 124-125 below.

[3] See p. 39 note 3, below.

[4] Cf. Apology of the Augsburg Confession, VII, 20, *Bek.* 238 (*BC* 171); and, p. 34, note 2, below.

according to Luther, one visible and the other invisible, but one church which was both visible and invisible.[1] Catholic substance and Protestant principle were inextricably combined in Luther's view of the church.

Hence Luther's Reformation sought to establish the church once more upon the foundation of the gospel, and so to root the unity of the church in the redemptive action of God rather than in human merit and human organizations. But an examination of the concrete results will reveal that the Reformation, which was intended to reform the church, issued instead in a divided Christendom, with dozens of separate groups and denominations. Not even the church that bore the name of Luther and claimed his message was united. Because of this situation, it is urgent that Luther's Reformation be examined as a church movement, as an action which was performed in the name of one holy catholic and apostolic church.

THE BREAK WITH ROME

Only from this point of view does Luther's break with Rome come into proper perspective.[2] The grounds for that break were churchly grounds, and Luther's break was basically a Catholic criticism of Roman Catholicism. Indeed, nothing else would have been possible in the light of Luther's doctrine of the church. According to Luther, the church's life is rooted in the gospel. What calls the church into being is the word of God in the gospel. That word, communicated through preaching and through the sacraments, is the 'constitutive element' in the church's life.[3] Where the word is being proclaimed and the sacraments are being administered, there the church is present. Organizational and liturgical order are a good thing for the church, but they do not make the church and it may be present where they are absent. But without the creative word of the gospel there is no church, regardless of what else may be present.

As long as the gospel is being proclaimed through the spoken

---

[1] Still a standard discussion of the problem is Ernest Rietschel, *Das Problem der sichtbar-unsichtbaren Kirche bei Luther* (Leipzig, 1932).

[2] For a masterful summary of the issues, see Wilhelm Pauck, *The Heritage of the Reformation* (2nd ed.; Glencoe, Illinois, 1961), pp. 3-17.

[3] Gustaf Aulén, *The Faith of the Christian Church*, tr. Eric H. Wahlstrom and G. Everett Arden (Philadelphia, 1948; London, 1954), pp. 353ff.

word and the sacraments, the church continues. And it does so in spite of doctrinal and theological aberrations that may be present at a given time. These are not good for the church; in time, they may even destroy the church—if they destroy the gospel, but only then. For the presence of the church is not dependent upon purity of doctrine, important as that is. The presence of the church is dependent upon the gospel, and the church can continue despite error. In fact, Luther knew from history that the church has never been without its error and its errorists,[1] but that it had nevertheless continued wherever and whenever the gospel was proclaimed and the sacraments were administered.

From this profound understanding of the basic nature of the church's life, Luther developed an equally profound interpretation of the meaning of the church's unity. The unity of the church is to be sought, first of all, in the gospel, and not in anything external or human. Not what a man thinks about the gospel (theology) or what he wears when he proclaims it (ritual) or how he organizes a church to proclaim it (polity), but God proclaiming the gospel through word and sacraments brings about the unity of the church. And Luther pronounced a 'Woe' upon the man who would interject himself between the Holy Spirit and this process—the man who would substitute an artificial, human unity for the unity which God alone creates; and the man who would tear asunder that which God has joined together and frustrate the unifying work of the Holy Spirit by his own pride.[2]

In the light of this doctrine of the church it is understandable why Luther maintained throughout his life that the church had always continued, even under the papacy. To be sure, the shadow of human works had frequently obscured the light of the gospel, and the machinations of an ecclesiastical organization had frequently replaced the power of God. But, like the leaven, the gospel was still there; and where the gospel is, there the church is, too. Against this church, preserved even under the medieval papacy, the gates of hell had never prevailed, and could never prevail; for it was founded on the rock of God's promise in Christ.[3] In the

[1] See especially the discussion in Chapter IV below.
[2] See the passage quoted on pp. 142-143.
[3] This was Luther's exegesis of the familiar words of Jesus to Peter in Matt. 16. 18; see p. 199, note 2 below.

continuity of Christianity despite medieval error Luther saw that promise fulfilled. There he saw the church.

SUCCESSION OF THE FAITHFUL

Of this church, corrupt and weak though it may often have been, Luther regarded himself as a member. For with all its frailties this church had baptized him with a baptism that was his comfort in all temptation.[1] Since he saw himself as standing in the 'succession of the faithful'[2] of all ages, including the Middle Ages, he was highly reluctant to break with the church which had mothered him. He did not take this lightly, this separation from the body of Western Christendom. The protests he voiced were based upon his responsibility as a priest and theological professor. He voiced them not as a revolutionary, nor even as a protesting critic, but primarily as a member of the church, as one of its doctors and professors.[3] He addressed his appeal from one member of the church to other members of the church for a consideration of that gospel which creates the church. Others may have left the church in order to find greater purity of doctrine or life elsewhere, but not Luther. He stayed where he believed his calling had placed him, and from that calling he spoke to the church of the peril which he saw threatening it. That peril he sought to correct, not by separation but by proclamation, not by schism but by the word.

How long he would have continued to do this is a matter that is open to conjecture. The fact is that the papacy as then constituted could not tolerate such a proclamation of the gospel in its midst. And therefore, after several warnings, the pope excommunicated Luther.[4] Luther maintained that by this action the pope was declaring his unwillingness to put up with the gospel for which Luther was contending. To Luther this meant that the pope had condemned not merely Luther but the gospel itself. He had spoken the gospel to a church that was supposedly built upon the gospel. Now that church had forbidden him to speak that gospel, and

---

[1] *Sermons on the Gospel of St John, WA* 33, 408-409 (*LW* 23, 257); *On the Councils and the Church, WA* 50, 563 (*WML* 5, 192).

[2] *Lectures on the Psalms, WA* 4, 165.

[3] See the passage quoted on p. 201; also Hermann Steinlein, *Luthers Doktorat* (Leipzig, 1912).

[4] Cf. Paul Kalkoff, *Forschungen zu Luthers römischem Prozesz* (Rome, 1905); Kalkoff's researches are summarized in Ernest G. Schwiebert, *Luther and His Times* (Saint Louis and London, 1950), pp. 481ff.

when he refused to be restrained, had expelled him. There seemed
to be no room any longer in that church for this kind of gospel.

THE IRONY OF LUTHER'S EXCOMMUNICATION

From this situation the true irony of Luther's work in relation
to the unity of the church becomes apparent. There seems to
have been room in the Roman Church for almost anyone and
anything except Luther and the gospel he was proclaiming. In
the very Italy from which Pope Leo X issued his decree of excommunication there were men whose scepticism denied basic
Christian tenets; but they were not excommunicated.[1] Whatever
may have been the status of Leo's own religious life—and our
reports on this vary somewhat[2]—some of his predecessors on the
throne of St Peter had been no more pious, and a good deal less
virtuous, than Cicero or Plato; but they were not excommunicated.
Luther's own contemporary, Erasmus, certainly disagreed with
much of what Roman Catholicism represented, and he made his
disagreement exceedingly vocal; but Erasmus was not excommunicated.[3] Yet Luther was. Why?

The answer to that question is exceedingly complex. Its roots
lie in the situation of imperial and papal politics in the first half
of the sixteenth century, and in that triangle of pope, emperor,
and princes that is the framework for so much of Luther's Reformation. In addition, there is a theological answer to the question,
lying at the very foundation of Reformation theology. Irritating
and troublesome as these other men and movements may have
been to the Roman Church, the Reformation alone constituted a
basic threat to the medieval theological and ecclesiastical system.
For the Reformation had as its central Protestant principle the
doctrine of justification by faith alone, the uselessness of human
or ecclesiastical merit in the process of salvation, the free forgiveness of sins for the sake of Jesus Christ. If all this were true, then
the traffic in merit and grace dispensed by the hierarchy was worse

---

[1] As Paul Oskar Kristeller and John Herman Randall Jr. have observed, 'the
fifteenth-century Italian Aristotelians . . . were not enough concerned with
Christianity to be violently anticlerical'. 'Introduction' to *The Renaissance Philosophy of Man* (Chicago, 1948), p. 10.

[2] Cf. G. Mollat, 'Léon X,' *DTC* IX-1, 329-332.

[3] On the relation between Erasmus and Luther, cf. Craig R. Thompson,
'Introduction' to Erasmus, *Inquisitio de Fide* (New Haven, 1950); and Jean
Boisset, *Erasmus et Luther* (Paris, 1962).

than useless. This was the threat of the Protestant principle to the ecclesiastical establishment, and against this threat the pope reacted when he excommunicated Luther.

Yet by his teaching of justification by faith, Luther stood in the continuity of the faithful in all generations.[1] He was proclaiming the gospel by which and for which the church lives. The pope excommunicated him and condemned justification by faith alone. As far as Luther was concerned, the pope had thereby also condemned the gospel. And so, in Luther's eyes, it was Rome that had left Luther, and not Luther that had left Rome. As long as the Roman Church would tolerate the gospel it remained the church for Luther, despite its error. But when it condemned the gospel and forced Luther out, it became sectarian. If, as Luther maintained, the church is where the gospel is, then it followed that by condemning the gospel Rome was condemning the church. It was in this spirit, and not primarily in a spirit of boasting, that Luther said of Worms: 'Then I was the church!' Because he was contending for the gospel and the gospel made the church and Rome condemned the gospel, Rome had condemned the church as represented in this case by the church's loyal servant, Martin Luther. Luther believed he was standing for the same gospel for which the church had stood before it became corrupt and condemned him. When it condemned him, so he believed, it was forsaking the gospel to which it had previously been loyal, while he continued in his loyalty. Thus Rome turned its back on the church, while Luther remained with the church. Such was Luther's interpretation of what happened when he severed his relations with Rome.

'HOLY APOSTATES'

This interpretation is of great importance in the determination of Luther's responsibility for a divided Christendom. He was convinced that as there was no church without the gospel, there was no church unity without the gospel either. Therefore, the gospel was the only valid basis for true church unity. It is inaccurate, then, to maintain that Luther left the Roman Church

[1] Cf. Karl Holl, 'Der Begriff der iustitia dei in der vorlutherischen Bibel-auslegung', *Gesammelte Aufsätze zur Kirchengeschichte*, III, *Der Westen* (Tübingen, 1928), 171ff.; also Heiko A. Oberman, *The Harvest of Medieval Theology* (Cambridge, Mass., 1963), pp. 146ff.

because he was dissatisfied with this or that in its doctrine or practice. For he was an obedient rebel; or, as he put it, 'By the grace of God, we are holy apostates.'[1]

A failure to understand Luther's Reformation as the work of 'holy apostates' and obedient rebels has caused various interpreters, some of them sympathetic and some of them critical, to attribute Luther's Reformation to false grounds and to evaluate it on the basis of a false assessment. One serious charge against the Reformation is the claim that it helped to destroy not only the unity of the church but also the influence of the church upon Western culture and life. Beginning with a churchly protest against the medieval church, Luther has apparently produced the great apostasy of modern times. This interpretation of the Reformation was almost standard in Roman Catholic textbooks until the scholarship of men like Lortz, Herte, and Hessen.[2] The older accounts saw the Middle Ages as the golden age of Christian civilization and Luther's Reformation as the vulgarization and paganization of the West.[3] In this judgment Roman Catholic interpreters have sometimes been joined by liberal students of the Reformation, who interpreted it as the beginning of the liberation of the human mind from the authority of revelation. Thus Ralph Waldo Emerson is quoted as saying that if Luther had known his ninety-five theses would lead to Boston Unitarianism he would rather have cut his arm off than have posted them.[4]

Nor are Roman Catholics and liberals alone in this view. More than once, American Protestants have stated that Luther's Reformation brought on the Declaration of Independence, and that there is a direct line of descent from Luther's doctrine of the liberty of the Christian man to the Jeffersonian doctrine that all men are created free and equal.[5] Actually, there is a great gulf

---

[1] *Lectures on Genesis*, WA 42, 412 (*LW* 2, 213).

[2] Cf. Jaroslav Pelikan, *The Riddle of Roman Catholicism* (New York, 1959; London, 1960), pp. 196-198.

[3] Thus for James Cardinal Gibbons, the 'barbaric warfare [of "the Reformers", not otherwise specified] against religious memorials was not only a grievous sacrilege, but an outrage against the fine arts'. *The Faith of Our Fathers* (83rd ed.; New York, 1917), p. 198.

[4] Cf. Preserved Smith, *The Life and Letters of Martin Luther* (2nd ed.; Boston, 1911), p. xvi.

[5] The classic critique of this view is Ernest Troeltsch, *Protestantism and Progress. A Historical Study of the Relation of Protestantism to the Modern World*, tr. W. Montgomery (Boston, 1958), esp. pp. 117ff.

fixed between the two doctrines. Luther maintained that the only freedom that mattered was the freedom from sin, death, and hell available in Christ to men who otherwise were enslaved;[1] Jefferson maintained that freedom in political and economic affairs was provided, but also limited, by the natural law, and that is was the function of historical religions to teach and support this natural law. It has been argued that Jefferson's ideas are closer to those of other Protestant leaders or to those of certain Roman Catholic thinkers than they are to Luther's conception of freedom.[2]

LUTHER AN INDIVIDUALIST?

Another charge frequently heard even from sympathetic historians is the view that Luther's break with Rome was motivated by his individualism.[3] He developed some private ideas that he insisted upon carrying out. And when Rome refused permission, he left the church in a fit of pique and took some of his followers along. The entire Reformation, with its theology, was nothing more than the extension of the individualism of one man, whose spirit refused to bow to the supreme authority of the Holy Father.

Such an interpretation of the thought and work of Luther is obviously a superficial one. But since it has received such wide circulation, it needs examination. The fundamental assumption of this interpretation is the claim that Luther was a schismatic, who was willing to divide the church in order to retain his private notions. Even a cursory study of Luther's writings will show that this assumption is wrong. Luther sought to subject his private notions to the gospel; and as he said at Worms, his conscience was bound by the word of God.[4] We have pointed out the reluctance with which he came out against the prevailing religious views of his time and his efforts to stay with the church of his day. As Part Two of this book will show, he always remained willing, at least in principle, to discuss the controverted points and to consider

---

[1] Cf. Karl Holl, *The Cultural Significance of the Reformation*, tr. Karl and Barbara Hertz and John H. Lichtblau (New York, 1959; London, 1961), pp. 30ff.; on Calvin, see p. 72. Holl's essay was a critique of the work of Troeltsch referred to in the previous note.

[2] On Jefferson's religious thought, cf. Daniel J. Boorstin, *The Lost World of Thomas Jefferson* (Boston, 1960; London, 1961), pp. 151-166.

[3] This is true even of the sympathetic Roman Catholic historian, Joseph Lortz; cf. Pauck, *op. cit.*, pp. 241-244.

[4] *Luther at the Diet of Worms, WA* 7, 838 (*LW* 32, 112).

the re-establishment of church unity in his time. Luther's entire life and thought stand as a refutation of the claim that the Reformation was motivated by individualism.

Another interpretation of the Reformation that appears frequently is the thesis that the essence of the Reformation consisted in the recovery of the authority of the Bible, and that Luther's historic achievement was the fact that he replaced the authority of the church with the authority of the Bible.[1] Like many pat statements, this view can be true and it can be false. In a sense, it is true that Luther's achievement did consist in the recovery of the Bible —but of the Bible as the bearer of the gospel. He had been loyal to the Bible even before he discovered the meaning of justification by faith alone, but it was only with that discovery that, as he himself said, the Scriptures were opened to him.[2] For that matter, the Middle Ages were quite articulate in their views of biblical authority, as well as of biblical inspiration. In Luther's day there were several theories of biblical inspiration being taught by various theologians, and the doctrine of the supreme authority, if not the sole authority, of the Scriptures was widely acknowledged by medieval scholastic theologians.[3] The church did not need a Luther to tell it that the Bible was true.

But it did need a Luther to tell it what the truth of the Bible is. The distinctive contribution of the Reformation to the Christian understanding of the Bible was its discovery that all theology is related to the gospel, and that the purpose of the Bible is not merely to provide sacred information but to communicate the gospel of the forgiveness of sins. The Bible must be understood in the light of God's redemption in Christ, or it is not understood at all, regardless of how one thinks of biblical authority or biblical inspiration. From this insight Luther developed his characteristic

[1] To be sure, certain statements of Luther himself tend in the direction of this interpretation; cf. Karl August Meissinger, *Der katholische Luther* (München, 1952), p. 43.
[2] *Preface to the Complete Edition of Luther's Latin Writings, WA* 54, 186 (*LW* 34, 337).
[3] Much material on medieval attitudes toward the Bible is assembled in Friedrich Kropatschek, *Das Schriftprinzip der lutherischen Kirche*, I, *Die Vorgeschichte. Das Erbe des Mittelalters* (Leipzig, 1904); Kropatschek's work was, unfortunately, never completed or translated. See also Beryl Smalley, *The Study of the Bible in the Middle Ages* (Oxford, 1941); and Jean Leclercq, *The Love of Learning and the Desire for God*, tr. Catharine Misrahi (New York and London, 1962), pp. 76-93.

views of biblical authority and biblical inspiration, and, as we have shown elsewhere, his characteristic method of biblical interpretation.[1] But it is inaccurate to designate his work as that of restoring the Bible to the church. It would be more accurate perhaps to interpret it as the task of restoring the gospel to the Bible. For he did not seek to repristinate New Testament Christianity. When he thought that Zwingli was trying to do something like that in his mode of celebrating the Lord's Supper, Luther repudiated this mode as irrelevant.[2] What was always relevant in New Testament Christianity was its gospel.

RECONSTRUCTION OF MORALITY

There is another misconception of the Reformation that has gained currency from time to time, especially in so-called 'evangelical' circles. This is the claim that the basis of Luther's protest was the low level of morality in the church of his time.[3] The morals of fifteenth- and sixteenth-century Roman Catholicism were indeed nothing to be proud of, although sober scholarship does not emerge with as black a picture as is sometimes painted by Protestant writers and preachers. It is a simple procedure, though not a completely honest one, to describe moral conditions in the pre-Reformation church with such vividness as to shock the reader, then to portray the Reformation as the awakening of a new moral consciousness, the abolition of clerical celibacy with its attendant evils, and the creation of a healthy, normal, respectable morality.

The Reformation was indeed responsible for a 'reconstruction of morality', as Karl Holl has called it,[4] but this cannot be regarded as the basis of Luther's break. There had been groups throughout the Middle Ages who protested against the moral decline of the church and who separated themselves from the church because of it.[5] Perhaps the most notable among them were the Donatists of the time of St Augustine, who refused to

[1] Pelikan, *Luther the Expositor*, Part One, with extensive bibliographical notes.
[2] See the passages quoted on p. 82, notes 2-3.
[3] Cf. Hermann Sasse, *Here We Stand*, tr. Theodore G. Tappert (New York, 1938), pp. 53ff., for a careful study of this problem.
[4] Karl Holl, 'Der Neubau der Sittlichkeit', *Luther*, pp. 155-287.
[5] Cf. Herbert Grundmann, *Religiöse Bewegungen im Mittelalter* (2nd ed.; Darmstadt, 1961), especially the interesting new material on *vita apostolica*, pp. 503ff.

acknowledge the validity of the ministry of evil men in the church.[1] But Luther was no Donatist,[2] and any interpretation of the Reformation on this basis fails to strike at the core of the problem. Moral conditions in the Roman Church after Trent were not what they had been in the heyday of the Renaissance, and it is neither fair nor honest to describe them as though they were. Nor dare the Protestant observer forget that the moral level of the Reformation often left much to be desired. For example, a comparison of moral conditions in Lutheran courts and Roman Catholic courts of Germany during the sixteenth century reveals no appreciable moral superiority on either side.[3] It was not moral degradation that brought on Luther's protest and the split, and no amount of moral improvement would have healed the split.

IMPLICATIONS

Only if the heirs of a divided Christendom are as serious about the church as Luther's Reformation was, can they draw the implications of this history. For the paradox of Catholic substance and Protestant principle in Luther's Reformation is matched by the need of both Protestantism and Roman Catholicism for this very combination. Liturgical reform in Roman Catholicism cannot get its mind off Martin Luther; Protestant studies of worship continually inquire whether the loss of Catholic substance has not impoverished Protestant spirituality since the Reformation.[4] Paul Tillich has made the terms 'Catholic substance' and 'Protestant principle' basic to the vocabulary of systematic theology; Karl Barth has found himself obliged to look more closely at the

[1] See G. G. Willis, *Saint Augustine and the Donatist Controversy* (London, 1950); W. H. C. Frend, *The Donatist Church* (Oxford, 1952); F. Van der Meer, *Augustine the Bishop*, tr. Brian Battershaw and G. R. Lamb (London, 1961), pp. 79ff.; and Gerald Bonner, *St Augustine of Hippo. Life and Controversies* (London and Philadelphia, 1963), pp. 237-311. Prof. Oberman speaks significantly of a 'pan-European Donatist upsurge' in the fifteenth century, *op. cit.*, p. 221.

[2] See the passages cited in Werner Elert, *The Structure of Lutheranism*, tr. Walter A. Hansen, with a Foreword by Jaroslav Pelikan (Saint Louis, 1962), p. 267, note 17.

[3] The most notorious *cause célèbre* in this connection was, of course, the bigamy of Philip of Hesse; cf. Smith, *Martin Luther*, pp. 373-386 and the accompanying bibliography.

[4] Cf., for example, Ernest B. Koenker, *The Liturgical Renaissance in the Roman Catholic Church* (Chicago, 1954), pp. 151-152; and Hans Asmussen *et al.*, *The Unfinished Reformation*, tr. Robert J. Olsen (Notre Dame, 1961).

Catholic substance behind his thought.[1] And an ecumenical movement that began as a Protestant solution to a Protestant problem
now includes not only the Catholic substance of Eastern Orthodoxy in its discussions of the church and its unity, but Roman
Catholicism as well. Thus Luther, the obedient rebel, and the
Reformation he inaugurated set forth both Catholic heritage and
Protestant reconstruction in a form that continues to be relevant
to the life and thought of the entire Christian community.

[1] Paul Tillich, *Systematic Theology* (3 vols.; Chicago, 1951-1963; London,
1953-1964), III, 6, on 'Catholic substance and Protestant principle'; on Karl
Barth, cf. his surprised and surprising comments in the Introduction to Hans
Küng, *Rechtfertigung. Die Lehre Karl Barths und eine katholische Besinnung*
(Einsiedeln, 1957).

PART ONE

CRITICAL REVERENCE TOWARDS TRADITION

To probe the paradox of Catholic substance and Protestant principle in Luther's Reformation, this study will first examine its relation to the Christian past. It has been said that there is an ecumenicity in time and an ecumenicity in space.[1] Hence the ecumenical movement of the twentieth century has moved simultaneously toward a 'renewal of the Christian tradition'[2] and toward the removal of the barriers that separate Christians today. These two directions sometimes seem to be in contradiction, as when spokesmen for Eastern Orthodoxy are accused of elevating the authority of tradition over the urgency of removing the scandal of Christian division. But in fact the only sound basis for such urgency is a critical reverence for 'our common history as Christians'.[3] Therefore the quest for Christian unity could not move very far without raising the question of Christian tradition.

For the same reasons, Luther's Reformation manifested an evangelical Catholicity in time and an evangelical Catholicity in space. Evangelical Catholicity in time expressed itself in a distinctive interpretation of the dogmatic, conciliar, and liturgical development of Christian history. Evangelical Catholicity in space took the form of efforts to achieve the reunion of Christians —or at least of some Christians—after the separations that emerged from the Reformation. Part One of this book assembles evidence on 'evangelical Catholicity in time' and explores in succession the theory of church history, the sense of tradition, the

[1] Cf. Georges Florovsky, 'The Quest for Christian Unity and the Orthodox Church', *Theology and Life*, IV (1961), 201.
[2] Albert C. Outler, 'The Renewal of the Christian Tradition', *The Report of the Theological Commissions on Tradition and Traditions* (Faith and Order Paper, No. 40; Geneva, 1963), pp. 5-27.
[3] *The Third World Conference on Faith and Order* (Geneva, 1952, London, 1953), p. 27.

attitude toward church councils, and the interpretation of liturgy that characterized Luther and 'the confessional generation'[1] of Luther's Reformation. For history, dogma, council, and liturgy were the chief forms in which the Reformation confronted the Catholic substance of the tradition; from its treatment of these themes the contours of its critical reverence toward the tradition may become visible. And as Edward Gibbon observed, a modern observer 'will rather be surprised at the timidity than scandalized by the freedom of our first Reformers'.[2] With this attitude toward tradition in view, Part Two will go on to 'evangelical Catholicity in space' and the irenic efforts of Luther's Reformation.

[1] This is my term for the theologians of the three decades between Luther's death in 1546 and the Formula of Concord in 1576-1577; Jaroslav Pelikan, *From Luther to Kierkegaard* (2nd ed.; Saint Louis, 1963), pp. 24-48.

[2] Edward Gibbon, *The Decline and Fall of the Roman Empire*, Ch. LIV (Modern Library Edition), II, 890.

II

CHURCH AND CHURCH HISTORY

A s Luther's Reformation sought to articulate the doctrine of the church in a way that was faithful to both Catholic substance and Protestant principle, it was forced especially to clarify its understanding of the history of the church.[1] The antitheses against which its view of the church was directed involved basic assumptions about historical interpretation. Luther himself participated vigorously in the debates over historical interpretation, even preparing a chronicle of world history.[2] His most thorough historical scholarship, as Chapter IV will point out, came in the course of an examination of the history of ecumenical councils. Not in Luther's own writings, however, but in the confessions that were based upon his thought, Luther's Reformation systematized its characteristic and profound insights into the history of the church. For here both fronts of its theological war, Roman Catholicism and the spiritualism of the left wing Reformers, compelled a clarification of its critical reverence toward the Church Catholic and toward the history of the church.

CHURCH HISTORY IN ROMAN CATHOLICISM

The principal target of Reformation polemics on the church was the Roman Catholic doctrine of the church, as formulated by theologians like Eck and Cochlaeus and as summarized in the Roman Catholic Confutation of the Augsburg Confession. According to this doctrine, the church which Christ established was coterminous with the institution which the pope heads. All the rights, privileges, and attributes that the New Testament ascribed to the church were assigned to the papal institution, and properly to it

[1] Cf. John M. Headley, *Luther's View of Church History* (New Haven, 1963), with an extensive bibliography.
[2] *Reckoning of the Years of the World, WA* 53, 1-184.

alone; thus this doctrine 'transfers to the popes what is the prerogative of the true church'.[1] As Chapter VII will show, this meant to Eck that if anyone wished to find the church, he needed only to look for the presence of the Roman Catholic organization, its bishops and its hierarchy; for Christ had committed to Peter, and through him to his successors, sovereignty over the church. The church was, then, essentially a sociological entity, like the family, the state, or any other social grouping in which men banded together for certain specific purposes. And to be a member of the church meant to be associated with that sociological entity, regardless of conviction or conversion. Thus for Cochlaeus, the church was merely an 'outward government',[2] differing from other forms of social organization principally by virtue of its divine validation. Good and evil men both belonged to it, bound together by their external membership in the ecclesiastical organization, even though the objects of their religious loyalty were as divergent as Christ and Belial.[3]

Against this institutional interpretation of the nature of the church the Apology of the Augsburg Confession directed very vigorous criticism. If the church was a sociological entity among sociological entities, what was the qualitative difference between the church and Israel of old, in which good and evil were held together by their external association with the Israelitic people rather than by a common bond of faith? In Israel there were those whom the Apology termed 'the physical descendants',[4] carried along by the external promises given the entire nation, but not sharing in the blessings of the everlasting covenant. If the Confutation's definition of the church held, there was no difference between the old and the new Israel on this point. But then the substance was no better than the shadow,[5] and membership in the

[1] Apology of the Augsburg Confession, VII, 27, *Bek.* 240 (*BC* 173); henceforth referred to simply as 'Apology'.

[2] The phrase occurs several times in Article VII of the Apology: 'an outward government of certain nations', par. 10, *Bek.* 235-236 (*BC* 170); 'an outward organization embracing both the good and the wicked', par. 13, *ibid.* In preparation for my translation of the Apology in *The Book of Concord*, I discovered the same Latin phrase, *externa politia*, in Caspar Cruciger, *In epistolam ad Timotheum priorem commentarius* (Strasbourg, 1540), p. 114.

[3] Apology, VII, 16-19, *Bek.* 236-237 (*BC* 170-171). See Luther's strong answer to this theory: *On the Papacy in Rome*, *WA* 6, 301.

[4] Apology, VII, 14, *Bek.* 236 (*BC* 170). This had been Luther's argument already in his early *Lectures on the Psalms*. *WA* 3, 632; 4, 24.

[5] Apology, VII, 15, *Bek.* 237 (*BC* 170).

church had no greater spiritual significance than did citizenship in Israel. It was a purely sociological function.

According to the Reformation confessions, this doctrine of the church had its source in a rationalization of the politico-ecclesiastical situation rather than in a primarily theological concern. It was intended to provide divine validation for the political involvement of the Roman bishop, and the exegetical and doctrinal support for it was supplied after the fact. The theory of papal sovereignty had appeared in its most extreme form during the medieval controversies between church and state.[1] It was at times like these that the papacy had defined the church as a 'supreme outward monarchy of the whole world in which the Roman pontiff must have unlimited power beyond question or censure. . . . Therefore the pope must be lord of the whole world, of all the kingdoms of the world . . and must have . . . both swords, the temporal and the spiritual.'[2] Characterizing this desire for organizational prestige and power as the source for the Roman Catholic doctrine of the church, Luther explained sarcastically that 'the holy see of Rome came to the aid of the poor church', and he accused the papacy of having drawn its viewpoints 'from the imperial, pagan law'.[3]

Because, according to the Reformation confessions, Roman Catholic theology, as represented by the Confutation, falsely identified the church with its own ecclesiastical institution, it inevitably fell into the same fallacy in its interpretation of church history. Compelled to validate its divine right by reference to precedent and example, this theology had to find support even where there was none. And because it endowed a human institution with divine right, it also endowed that institution's history with a divine quality which it did not possess. This need to find

[1] Cf. Gerd Tellenbach, *Church, State, and Christian Society at the Time of the Investiture Contest*, tr. R. F. Bennett (Oxford, 1940), esp. pp. 28-60 on 'The Medieval Conception of the Hierarchy'.

[2] Apology, VII, 23, *Bek.* 239 (*BC* 172). On the origins of this idea, cf. P. Lecler, 'L'argument des deuz glaives', *Recherches de science religieuse*, 21 (1931), 293-399; XXII (1932), 151-177, 281-303; and H. X. Arquillière, 'Origines de la théorie des deuz glaives', *Studi Gregoriani*, I (Rome, 1947), 501-521. I have been led to these discussions by *A Scholastic Miscellany: Anselm to Ockham*, ed. Eugene R. Fairweather, 'The Library of Christian Classics', X (Philadelphia and London, 1956), 253, note 43.

[3] Smalcald Articles, Part III, Art. III, par. 24, *Bek.* 442 (*BC* 307); Part II, Art. IV, par. 14, *Bek.* 431 (*BC* 301).

historical legitimation for the ecclesiastical institution and its patterns of thought and action caused the defenders of the *status quo* to attribute to the history of the church an absolute character which could not stand up under the impact of historical criticism. Without such historical legitimation the Roman claim to superiority seemed to lose basis in given fact; hence the desperate insistence upon historical absolutes on the part of the Roman Catholic theologians and historians who opposed the Reformation.[1]

In an effort to supply this historical legitimation, the historical theology of Cochlaeus and Eck was first of all concerned to demonstrate the historicity of its theory of organizational continuity. It answered the question of the church's continuity through the ages by pointing to the supposedly unbroken succession which its organization had maintained since apostolic days, and it proposed to assure the believer that the church would never perish by reference to the integrity of the Roman institution through the ages.[2] This it did in the face of the historical record, which showed that often the church had come to such a state 'as if there were no church, as happened under the papacy',[3] and in the face of scriptural warnings 'that there will be ungodly teachers and wolves'.[4] The assurance of the church's continuity could not come, therefore, from a hypothetical and non-existent organizational succession; for it was a matter of historical fact 'that the holy church was without a pope for more than five hundred years at least'.[5] If the guarantee of the church's historical continuity was to be derived from the historical continuity of the papal institution, it could not withstand the scrutiny of honest historical research.

One feature of this theory which attracted particular attention in the Reformation discussions was the claim of the polemicists that not only the organization as such, but also its rites, had been uniformly maintained through the centuries. To the Reformation thesis that 'it is not necessary for the true unity of the Christian

---

[1] Cf. Harry Elmer Barnes, *A History of Historical Writing* (2nd ed.; New York, 1962), pp. 126-128; see also G. P. Gooch, *History and Historians in the Nineteenth Century* (2nd ed.; London, 1952; Boston, 1959), pp. 513-522.

[2] See Holl, *Luther*, pp. 298-299.

[3] Apology, VII, 9, *Bek.* 235 (German text); see also XXIV, 97, *Bek.* 276 (German text).

[4] Apology, VII, 22, *Bek.* 238 (*BC* 172).

[5] Smalcald Articles, Part II, Art. IV, par. 4, *Bek.* 428 (*BC* 299); Treatise on the Power and Primacy of the Pope, 12-21, *Bek.* 474-477 (*BC* 321-323).

church that ceremonies, instituted by men, should be observed uniformly in all places',[1] they had replied with the insistence that such ceremonial uniformity was indeed necessary for the church's unity and that it was historically demonstrable.[2] The lengthy and penetrating refutation which the Apology of the Augsburg Confession offered to this insistence was based not only upon such biblical evidence as Col. 2. 16ff.,[3] but also upon historical evidence assembled from the fathers and councils of the ancient church, as well as from the churches of Eastern Christendom,[4] proving 'that a difference in human observances does not harm the unity of faith'.[5]

But the most far-reaching claim to historical absoluteness made by the defenders of the papacy was neither organizational continuity nor ceremonial uniformity, but theological infallibility. Claiming to embody all the attributes of the church, the popes put themselves forward as 'pillars of truth'.[6] Although the dogma of papal infallibility did not become official until the nineteenth century and had a rather chequered history in the Middle Ages,[7] there was general agreement on the notion that the church, whether represented by pope or council or the two in conjunction, was the pillar of truth and that therefore its theological development was a source of religious truth. The polemics of Luther's Reformation took this to mean that, according to papal claims, 'all laws are in the shrine of his heart, and he claims that whatever he decides and commands in his churches is spirit and law, even when it is above and contrary to the Scriptures or spoken word'.[8] As a view of church history, this theory meant that what the popes, councils, and churches had said since the close of the New Testament was not only uniform, but true and binding.

It did not require profound or extensive historical knowledge

---

[1] Augsburg Confession, VII, 3, *Bek.* 61 (*BC* 32); cf. Pauck, *op. cit.*, pp. 56-57.
[2] *Confutatio pontificia* in M. Reu, *The Augsburg Confession* (Chicago, 1930), II, 353-354.
[3] Apology, VII, 35, *Bek.* 243 (*BC* 175).
[4] Apology, XXIV, 6, *Bek.* 350 (*BC* 250).
[5] Apology, VII, 45, *Bek.* 245 (*BC* 177), also Apology, XV, 49-52, *Bek.* 306-307 (*BC* 221-222).
[6] Apology, VII, 27, *Bek.* 240 (*BC* 173); see also par. 20, *Bek.* 238 (*BC* 171) for the Apology's own interpretation of 1 Tim. 3. 15.
[7] See the interesting compilation of data on the patristic and medieval development in W. J. Sparrow Simpson, *Roman Catholic Opposition to Papal Infallibility* (Milwaukee, 1910), pp. 9-65.
[8] Smalcald Articles, Part III, Art, VIII, par. 4, *Bek.* 454 (*BC* 312); also Luther's *An Open Letter to the Christian Nobility*, *WA* 6, 459 (*WML* 2, 148).

to demonstrate that this assumption was not warranted by the facts of history. For one thing, there was no uniformity in the theological development, for 'the writings of the holy fathers show that sometimes even they built stubble on the foundation'.[1] After all, the fathers were men, too.[2] Even if there were a uniformity in the church's theological tradition, this would not be binding; for 'it will not do to make articles of faith out of the holy fathers' words or works'.[3] And for that matter, the fathers had not intended their actions and words to become normative in the church.[4] On both counts, uniformity and authority, the Reformation confessions made use of historical insights to refute the historical claims of Roman Catholicism.

Because of their doctrine of the church, Roman Catholic theologians from Eck to Caesar Baronius were compelled to interpret church history on the basis of a preconceived system and to explain away the many stubborn and embarrassing facts that could not be accommodated to that system. Having absolutized the ecclesiastical organization, they had to go on to absolutize that organization's history by ascribing to it an organizational continuity, ceremonial uniformity, and theological infallibility that had no substantiation from historical evidence. The Protestant principle in Luther's Reformation enabled it to be critical in dealing with the historical assumptions in the inherited Catholic substance, and thus to make room for the exercise of objective, critical historical methodology in the study of church history.

CHURCH HISTORY IN THE LEFT WING REFORMERS

But the historical assumptions in the Roman Catholic version of Catholic substance were not the only axis of the Reformation's concern with the church and with church history. Luther's doctrine of the church, like his doctrine of the word[5] and of the

---

[1] Apology, VII, 21, *Bek.* 238 (*BC* 172); on the lack of uniformity among the fathers in the matter of terminology, cf. Apology, XIII, 2, *Bek.* 292 (*BC* 211).
[2] 'Thus the fathers were men, too, who often made concessions to the customs and opinions of their times'; Martin Chemnitz, *Examen Concilii Tridentini* (1565-1573), ed. E. Preuss (Leipzig, 1915), p. 624.
[3] Smalcald Articles, Part II, Art. II, par. 15, *Bek.* 421 (*BC* 295).
[4] Apology, XV, 13, *Bek.* 299 (*BC* 216); cf. also Pelikan, *Luther the Expositor*, pp. 80-81.
[5] Cf. R. H. Gruetzmacher, *Wort und Geist*. Eine historische Untersuchung zum Gnadenmittel des Wortes (Leipzig, 1902).

Lord's Supper,[1] was developed in simultaneous conflict on two fronts. Luther's Reformation rejected with equal vigour the heteronomy of Eck and Cochlaeus, whose institutionalism caused them to ascribe absolute authority to the empirical church, and the autonomy of Münzer and Carlstadt, whose biblicism and individualism caused them to think that each man is his own authority in religious matters.[2]

Only in the context of this ambivalence can the doctrine of the church in Luther's Reformation, and therefore its interpretation and use of church history, be adequately understood. Faced by the power of the tradition and sensing the loneliness of one who believed that God had called him to a task, Luther had sometimes given voice to an individualistic view of the church.[3] On the other hand, when the 'enthusiasts' sought to carry out a thorough individualism, he stoutly insisted that no man makes the church and that membership in the church is necessary for salvation.[4] The Reformation confessions took account of both these fronts—the Roman Catholic and the radical Protestant—when they articulated both Catholic substance and Protestant principle in their view of church history. And as they felt compelled to take issue with the Roman Catholic institutionalization of the church, so they had to defend the reality of the church, and therefore the value of its history, against the radical individualism of the left wing Reformers.

Believing that they were carrying out in consistent practice what Luther had asserted in theory but had been unwilling or unable to carry out because of his political ties,[5] the radicals espoused just such an individualism. These 'fanatics'[6] changed Luther's criticism of the institutional church into a deprecation

---

[1] Pelikan, *Luther the Expositor*, pp. 109-134.

[2] The standard interpretation of Luther's relation to the left wing of the Reformation is Karl Holl's essay, 'Luther und die Schwärmer', *Luther*, pp. 420-467.

[3] See pp. 13-14 above.

[4] 'Outside it [the church] no one can come to the Lord Christ': Large Catechism, Part II, par. 45, *Bek.* 655 (*BC* 416); 'outside the Christian church (that is, where the Gospel is not) there is no forgiveness', *ibid.*, par. 56, *Bek.* 658 (*BC* 418); cf. also Apology, IX, 2, *Bek.* 247 (*BC* 178): 'It [the promise of salvation] does not apply to those who are outside of Christ's church, where there is neither Word nor sacrament'.

[5] Cf. Holl, *Luther*, p. 423, note 1.

[6] Apology, XIII, 13, *Bek.* 294 (*BC* 212-213). Luther used the word *fanatici* as the Latin equivalent for his more familiar term *Schwärmer*; cf. my note *LW* 13, 368, note 26.

and ultimately a rejection of the empirical church as such. Their deprecation of the empirical church was particularly evident in their attitude toward the ministry. They held that 'the ministry of the church, the word proclaimed and heard, is not a means whereby God the Holy Spirit teaches men' and that therefore 'a minister of the church who is himself not truly renewed, righteous, and pious cannot teach profitably nor administer genuine and true sacraments'.[1] Luther and his supporters argued that such a spiritualization of the church led to the conclusion that the church has no concrete reality, but is merely an idea, a 'Platonic republic', 'an imaginary church, which is nowhere to be found'.[2] Only the individual mattered, not the church, for by his decision the individual created the church. For this reason the Anabaptists were consistent with their view of faith and of the church when they rejected the validity of the church's baptism of infants.[3]

To defend the reality of the church against the radicals and to avoid being classified with them, Luther's Reformation made its antithesis to this spiritualism very explicit. The two points on which the radicals had concentrated in their attack upon the church, the ministry and baptism, were also the points of the confessions' defence. They wanted to defend the ministry 'in opposition to the fanatics who dream that the Holy Spirit does not come through the word'[4] and who therefore despised the ministry and the empirical church. For this reason the Apology wanted to retain ordination and was even willing to have it called a sacrament.[5] And in antithesis to the individualism of the Anabaptists, the confessions stressed the idea that in the sacraments of the church, specifically in baptism, it was not man and his decision, but God

[1] Formula of Concord, Solid Declaration, XII, 30, 35, *Bek.* 1097-1098 (*BC* 635).
[2] Apology, VII, 20, *Bek.* 238 (*BC* 171). Significantly, Cruciger (see p. 28, note 2) immediately follows his rejection of the notion of an *externa politia* with the warning, *op. cit.*, p. 115: 'We do not speak of the church as a Platonic republic, which does not exist anywhere'. Cf. also Luther's reply to this charge, *WA* 7, 683.
[3] On the conflict over this issue, cf. Jaroslav Pelikan, 'The Relation of Faith and Knowledge in the Lutheran Confessions', *Concordia Theological Monthly*, XXI (1950), 327-328.
[4] Apology, XIII, 13, *Bek.* 294 (*BC* 212-213).
[5] On ordination, Apology, XIV, I, *Bek.* 296 (*BC* 214); on ordination as a sacrament, Apology, XIII, 11, *Bek*, 293 (*BC* 212) and R. H. Gruetzmacher, 'Beiträge zur Geschichte der Ordination in der evangelischen Kirche', *Neue Kirchliche Zeitschrift*, XXIII (1912), 363-379.

and his condescension that had the initiative; for 'baptism is not an act which we offer to God but one in which God baptizes us through a minister functioning in his place'.[1] Underlying the spiritualists' opposition to the empirical church was their insistence on purity and their refusal to accept anything less than absolute purity in the church. From its proponents in the ancient church this viewpoint had derived the name 'Donatism', but it was by no means restricted to the day of St Augustine.[2] In the era of the Reformation, too, some had arisen who maintained 'that that is no truly Christian assembly or congregation in the midst of which sinners are still found'.[3] Only that was the church which was absolutely pure, and a group where such absolute purity did not exist they would not call the church. On the basis of this approach, they made of excommunication, that is, of the process of purification, an essential mark of the church, and 'offended by the personal conduct of priests or people', they withdrew from the fellowship of the empirical church.[4]

Because Luther's Reformation, by contrast, wanted to take the empirical church and its ministrations seriously, it wanted also to take account of the weaknesses that afflicted the church. The Reformation confessions acknowledged that there were 'tyrants *who rule the church*. Under the pretext of religion they usurp the kingdom of the world. . . . They have instituted new worship *in the church*.'[5] They admitted that wolves and false teachers 'become rampant *in the church*' and that 'there is an infinite number of ungodly *within the church* who oppress it'.[6] But the church did not live by its purity; it lived by the forgiveness of sins. And as all life in the forgiveness of sins was the life of one who was at the same time righteous and a sinner, so it was with the church; 'for what he quickens by his Spirit is always the same kingdom of Christ, whether it be revealed or hidden under the cross . . . and he teaches that the church is hidden under a crowd of wicked

---

[1] Apology, XXIV, 18, *Bek.* 354 (*BC* 252).
[2] See p. 23 above and the accompanying notes; also Augsburg Confession, VIII, 3, *Bek.* 62 (*BC* 33), and Apology, VII, 29, *Bek.* 241 (*BC* 173).
[3] Formula of Concord, Solid Declaration, XII, 14, *Bek.* 1095 (*BC* 634).
[4] Apology, VII, 49, *Bek.* 246 (*BC* 178); on excommunication, see also Formula of Concord, Solid Declaration, XII, 34, *Bek.* 1098 (*BC* 635).
[5] Apology, XXIV, 41, *Bek* 362 (*BC* 257); italics my own.
[6] Apology, VII, 22, *Bek.* 238 (*BC* 172); *ibid.*, par. 9, *Bek.* 235 (*BC* 169). Italics are my own.

men so that this stumbling block may not offend the faithful.'[1] Thus also Luther warned his contemporaries: 'That is the true church which prays seriously and in faith: "Forgive us our trespasses as we forgive those who trespass against us." That is the church which grows day by day, which day by day puts on the new man and puts off the old man. That is the church which receives the first fruits of the Spirit: not the tithe, much less the fullness. We are not yet fully rid of the flesh but are in the process of shedding it and of going forward or growing. Whatever is left of sin, therefore, offends the spiritual Donatists, Manicheans, and Papists; but it does not offend God, for because of faith in Christ he overlooks and forgives it.'[2]

An insistence upon absolute purity seemed to Luther to make the left wing Reformers contemptuous of the liturgical and theological heritage received from the ancient, albeit impure, church of previous centuries. Thus the left wing Reformers maintained that pure Christians ought not attend services 'in those temples in which the papistic mass has formerly been read'.[3] In their theology, as in their liturgy, they proceeded as though the tradition of past centuries were irrelevant to the theological task and as though they could think theologically without reference to what the church had thought in the past.[4] The confessions of Luther's Reformation were anxious to prove that they did not share this contempt for tradition. In fact, Article VIII of the Augsburg Confession was added for this very reason, to avoid the impression that the Lutherans were Donatists.[5] Against the charge that they were abolishing the mass or clerical vestments or other ancient liturgical usages, the Reformation confessions insisted that the Lutherans retained all of these, indeed, they

---

[1] Apology, VII, 18-19, *Bek.* 237-238 (*BC* 171). On the backgrounds of this idea, cf. Rudolf Hermann, *Luthers These 'Gerecht und Sünder zugleich'* (2nd ed.; Gütersloh, 1960); on the idea of the kingdom hidden by the cross, see Tileman Hesshusius, *Examen theologicum* (2nd ed.; Frankfort, 1578), p. 230.

[2] *Commentary on Psalm* 90, *WA* 40-III, 506 (*LW* 13, 89-90).But see already his early *Lectures on the Psalms, WA* 4, 400.

[3] Formula of Concord, XII, 15, *Bek.* 1095 (*BC* 634).

[4] The contrast between Luther and the left wing of the Reformation on this point is well brought out by Karl Ecke, *Schwenckfeld, Luther und der Gedanke einer apostolischen Reformation* (Berlin, 1911).

[5] 'That was why we added the eighth article, to avoid the impression that we separate evil men and hypocrites from the outward fellowship of the church or deny efficacy to the sacraments which evil men or hypocrites administer', Apology, VII, 3, *Bek.* 234 (*BC* 168).

claimed to be more faithful in their liturgical observance than their Roman Catholic opponents.[1]

The attitude of the radicals toward tradition showed their general disregard for the past. That disregard of the past, in turn, was the product of their view of the church as a Platonic republic; for being a timeless, abstract idea, a Platonic republic had no history.[2] History is of time and space and of the concreteness that is the basic feature of spatial and temporal reality. If the church was a *civitas Platonica*, its reality could not be discerned under the forms of space and time. In short, there could be no such thing as church history. The only thing that had a history was empirical Christendom with its errors, impurities, and mistakes; and this empirical Christendom was not the church.

The history of Christianity since apostolic days, consequently, emerged as a series of apostasies, in which heresy followed heresy until now, for the first time since the days of the New Testament, a pure Christianity had emerged once more.[3] The principal value of the history of Christianity, then, was a negative one, to show how far from the truth previous generations had strayed. Luther's Reformation accused the radicals of assuming that they could dispense with all that previous generations had thought or done and could read the Scriptures as though no one had ever read them before. These Scriptures they interpreted legalistically, even to the point of 'imposing on us the judicial laws of Moses'.[4] Between the Scriptures and the present there was very little that was worthwhile, for only that was church which was pure. The history of Christianity was not pure, and therefore the history of Christianity was not the history of the church.

[1] Apology, XV, 38-44, Bek. 304-305 (BC 220-221); *ibid.*, par. 51-52, *Bek.* 307 (BC 222); XXIV, 1-3, *Bek.* 349-350 (BC 249-250); VII, 33, *Bek.* 242-243 (BC 174-175).

[2] It is noteworthy that at the end of (the seventeenth century, in the conflicts over Pietism and Rationalism, critics of the ecclesiasical establishment such as Philip Spener and Gottfried Arnold had to defend themselves against the charge of spiritualizing the church into a *civitas Platonica;* cf. Hermann Dörries, *Geist und Geschichte bei Gottfried Arnold* (Göttingen, 1963), p. 136, note 161.

[3] To cite an extreme instance, Sebastian Franck said: 'I believe that the outward church of Christ, including all its gifts and sacraments, because of the breaking in and laying waste by Antichrist right after the death of the apostles, went up into heaven and lies concealed in the Spirit and in truth'. 'A Letter to John Campanus', *Spiritual and Anabaptist Writers,* ed. George Huntston Williams 'The Library of Christian Classics', XXV (Philadelphia and London, 1957) 149.

[4] Apology XVI, 3, *Bek.*, 308 (BC 223); cf. also Luther, *Against the Heavenly Prophets, WA* 18, 75-76 (*LW* 40, 92-93).

Carried to its logical conclusion, this Protestant principle without Catholic substance, with its disregard of tradition and its insistence upon absolute purity, seemed to Luther's Reformation to end in a hyper-criticism which supposed that because it could discern the errors of the past, it had been released from the errors of the present and inoculated against the errors of the future. Indeed, since it did not regard the historical church as the church, it could deal with this historical and empirical church as though it were purely a secular thing. There was no need to take the history of the church seriously, for the church lived as a Platonic republic, which no one had ever seen. There is a direct analogy between this attitude toward church history and historical relativism; therefore it is significant that Ernst Troeltsch found the left wing of the Reformation so congenial.[1] For if all the systems of the history of Christian thought are to be explained on the basis of their environment, of the ideological backgrounds of their originators, and of the tradition which they inherited from their past, then none of them can lay claim to the truth, since, in Troeltsch's famous phrase, to be historical is to be relative.[2] And so the history of dogma could be read as the record of a process which issued in the dissolution of dogma.[3] Viewed in this light, the work of the church historian is to debunk the work of his predecessors and to destroy the golden calves of historical tradition. Thus the history of the church ultimately becomes merely a part of secular history, while the church as a Platonic republic remains abstracted from the historical process in a realm of super-historical purity.

THE DISTINCTIVE VIEW OF LUTHER'S REFORMATION

From what has been said thus far, the distinctive view of the church and of church history characteristic of Luther's Reformation should become clear. For in their articulation of the doctrine of the church, and hence in their use of church history, the con-

---

[1] Ernst Troeltsch, *The Social Teaching of the Christian Churches*, tr. Olive Wyon, with an Introduction by H. Richard Niebuhr (2 vols.; London, 1931, New York, 1960), II, 691 ff.

[2] See Wilhelm F. Kasch, *Die Sozialphilosophie von Ernest Troeltsch* (Tübingen, 1963), pp. 172-175, on the implications of historical relativism.

[3] Werner Elert, *Der Ausgang der altkirchlichen Christologie* (Berlin, 1957), pp. 313-333, is a recent discussion of the problem.

fessions of Luther's Reformation strove to come to terms with the valid emphases of both Catholic substance and Protestant principle, without involving themselves in the extremes of either. An oversimplified solution of the dilemma would have been to assert the existence of two churches: one of them, the church visible, possessing all the attributes which Roman Catholicism ascribed to the church; the other, the church invisible, characterized by all the qualities which spiritualism assigned to the church. Such a solution would have meant a position between the two alternatives. But as a later theologian succinctly summarized the Reformation's position, 'we do not posit two churches'.[1] Rather than taking the stand between the two alternatives, Luther's Reformation sought to go beyond them both to the biblical view of the church as the 'body of Christ',[2] of which institutionalism and spiritualism, as well as a combination of the two, were misinterpretations.

In relation to Catholic substance, therefore, the confessions of Luther's Reformation wanted to take the empirical church seriously. They shared the deep concern of Roman Catholicism for the church as it is, since there is no other. It is this church which through baptism and preaching had become 'the mother that begets and bears every Christian'.[3] It would be crass ingratitude to despise this church; for, as a modern interpreter of the Reformation has put it, 'we recognize the church as our mother, through whom has come, whether we like it or not, our spiritual life. It is wise to admit the human weaknesses of our parents; it is unwise to suppose that we can dispense with our particular parents now that we have achieved the abstract conception of parenthood.'[4] The concluding paragraphs of the Formula of Concord, therefore, enunciated their testimony 'in the presence of God and of all

[1] Johann Gerhard, 'Disputatio de Ecclesia', *Disputationes theologicae* (Jena, 1655), p. 1533, where he continues: 'We believe and confess one church, and assert that this is treated in Scripture in a double way [*bifariam*]'.

[2] Apology, VII, 5, *Bek.* 234-235 (*BC* 169); but see the trenchant comments of Paul S. Minear, *Images of the Church in the New Testament* (Philadelphia, 1960; London, 1961), pp. 173-174.

[3] Large Catechism, Part II, Art. III, par. 42, *Bek.* 655 (*BC* 416). On the origins of this metaphor see Joseph C. Plumpe, *Mater Ecclesia*. An Inquiry into the Concept of the Church as Mother in Early Christianity (Washington, 1943), particularly the illuminating discussion of Cyprian, pp. 81-106.

[4] James Hastings Nichols, 'History in the Theological Curriculum', *Journal of Religion*, XXVI (1946), 185.

Christendom'[1]—no less. But in its profound regard for the empirical church, Luther's Reformation refused to follow Eck and Cochlaeus by equating the church with a human, historical institution. Indeed, it saw such an equation as an expression of the pride with which churches attempt to absolutize themselves and as a mark of Antichrist.[2]

In rejecting Roman Catholic institutionalism, Luther's Reformation affirmed the correctness of a basic spiritualist emphasis, namely, the insistence upon purity. Repeatedly the Apology of the Augsburg Confession asserted that the church is holy,[3] and that this holiness could not be predicated of any institution, and especially not of the Roman Catholic institution. With the radicals, Luther's Reformation insisted that the church must be holy and that this holiness dare not be taken lightly. But it rejected the conclusion drawn from this insistence upon holiness: since the empirical church is not holy, since indeed no one has ever experienced a pure and holy church, the church must be an abstraction, a Platonic republic. Rather, Luther emphasized at the same time the holiness and the reality of the church, and saw in this paradox another example of the 'already—not yet' that marked the entire Christian life.[4]

The interpretation of church history flowing from this we have sought to summarize thus: 'According to Lutheran theology, it would seem that history is the conditioned bearer of the activity of God. This applies alike to the church and to the church's witness. For this reason, Lutheranism is not fearful of historical criticism, for it does not pin its faith on the infallibility of the historical church. But when such criticism discovers that the historical church is indeed historical and that it has not managed to escape the corruption that affects all things historical, Lutheran theology does not discard its regard for the historical church. . . . It devotes itself to the study of patristic theology, not with authoritarian reverence, nor yet with supercilious contempt, but with a

[1] Formula of Concord, Solid Declaration, XII, 40, *Bek.* 1099 (*BC* 40)—actually the peroration of the entire Formula rather than of Article XII alone.
[2] Apology, VII, 24, *Bek.* 239-240 (*BC* 172), especially the German text; XV, 19-21, *Bek.* 300-301 (*BC* 217-218).
[3] Most expressly in Apology, VII, 7-8, *Bek.* 235 (*BC* 169); *ibid.*, par. 16, *Bek.* 237 (*BC* 170-171).
[4] Cf. Werner Elert, *The Structure of Lutheranism*, pp. 495-497.

deep regard and a healthy suspicion.'[1] Thus the attitude of Luther's Reformation toward church history is an epitome of the critical reverence that strove to combine Catholic substance and Protestant principle.

[1] Jaroslav Pelikan, 'Form and Tradition in Worship. A Theological Interpretation', *Essays Presented at the First Liturgical Institute* [1949] (Valparaiso, 1950), pp. 22-23.

III

THE MEANING OF TRADITION

IN a series of sermons delivered for the tercentenary of the Augsburg Confession in 1830, Friedrich Schleiermacher voiced objections both to the traditional Catholic substance and to the particular Protestant principle in the polemical and condemnatory clauses of the confession. On the one hand, it seemed to him that 'there were less than adequate grounds for uncritically incorporating into the new confession of faith all the traditional doctrinal definitions and all the terminology of centuries long since past'.[1] In other words, the confession was too Catholic and traditional. At the same time, he asked the rhetorical question: 'Would it not be presumptuous if we imagined we had found the truth in such a way as to make us perfectly certain, both that no one else could condemn us this same way and that we can gain nothing further from associating with those who think otherwise and whom we condemn?'[2] In other words, the confession was too particular and exclusive. The contradiction which these two objections reveal helps make it clear how Schleiermacher could discuss the relation of theology and the church as he did in *The Christian Faith*,[3] but it also reflects the fundamental paradox between Catholic substance and Protestant principle in the Reformation as Luther carried it out and as it was codified in the confessions of his colleagues and pupils of 'the confessional generation'. A study of two such codifications—the Augsburg

---

[1] Friedrich Schleiermacher, *Predigten*, VI (Berlin, 1831), 149.
[2] *Ibid.*, pp. 160-161. In an earlier sermon he makes the characteristic suggestion that any such condemnatory clause had to be a dead letter 'for any one who could not live through all the controversies upon which the definitions of doctrine rest' (*ibid.*, p. 57).
[3] Friedrich Schleiermacher, *Der christliche Glaube nach den Grundsätzen der evangelischen Kirche im Zusammenhange dargestellt*, ed. Martin Redeker (2 vols.; Berlin, 1960), I, 119-125, 148-154 (Theses 19 and 27).

Confession and the *Examen* of Martin Chemnitz—will indicate the dual role of tradition in the theology of Luther's Reformation.

THE AUGSBURG CONFESSION

When the Augsburg Confession is examined for evidence of its attitude toward tradition, the dual character of that attitude becomes apparent very quickly. The word *traditio* is used in the plural to translate *Menschensatzungen*, 'human traditions, instituted to placate God, to merit grace, and to make satisfaction for sins;'[1] therefore the term has a predominantly pejorative connotation and is used to express the Protestant principle of biblical authority. But if the examination goes beyond a concordance study of the word *traditio* to a consideration of how the Augsburg Confession treats the received Catholic substance of the past, the traditionalism of the confession is its striking feature. It makes its protestations of loyalty to tradition abundant and explicit. One feature of this loyalty was the acceptance of the ancient creeds, which were expressly included in the *Book of Concord* and cited in the confessions. Indeed, the ordination formulas of sixteenth-century Lutheranism suggest that the Augsburg Confession was viewed as a commentary upon the ecumenical creeds, just as later Lutheran symbols, in turn, were commentaries upon it.[2]

There were, to be sure, good political reasons for affirming the tradition as represented by the Trinitarian and the Christological dogmas, and it would be historically dishonest to ignore these. Viewed politically, the Augsburg Confession is the defence offered by the protesting German estates, princes, and free cities as a validation of their right to reform the churches within their own principalities. This right had been contested by leaders of both church and empire, who maintained that by their defection from Rome the Protestant estates had lost their right to rule. For under the law of the empire, all nations and rulers were compelled to accept the 'apostolic discipline' of the Trinitarian tradition as inherited from the ancient church.[3] A violation of this Trinitarian

[1] Augsburg Confession, XV, 4, *Bek.* 70 (*BC* 37).
[2] Cf. Otto Ritschl, *Dogmengeschichte des Protestantismus*, I (Leipzig, 1908), 380-389.
[3] Werner Elert, *The Structure of Lutheranism*, pp. 274ff. is a discussion of the relation between the political and the theological grounds for the evangelical Catholicity of the Reformers.

tradition constituted not merely heresy in the theological realm but sedition in the political realm, and any ruler who was disloyal to this Catholic tradition could be deposed. To forestall any attempt at deposing the Protestant princes and estates for their support of Luther, Melanchthon made the Augsburg Confession a demonstration of their continued loyalty to the Catholic tradition despite their defection from Rome.

But it would be a mistake to emphasize the political element in this loyalty at the expense of the religious and theological, as was fashionable in the nineteenth century. For one thing, the content of the tradition, as the Augsburg Confession interprets it, is principally the dogma of the Trinity. Despite his occasional aspersions upon Trinitarian terminology, Luther's theology was more explicitly grounded in the doctrine of the Trinity than that of many among his predecessors. In addition, the declaration of loyalty to the tradition was important to the confessors because they still clung to the ideal of one religion in one state. Therefore they tried to interpret the conflict as a contention between two parties in a single church, rather than as a conflict between churches. In keeping with this desire to 'embrace and adhere to a single, true religion and live together in unity and in one fellowship and church',[1] they saw in the tradition both a symbol of the existing unity and a means for restoring the lost unity. What they designated by the pejorative *traditio*, then, was not the creedal and liturgical substance of Catholic Christendom, especially of ancient Christendom, but 'the opinion which holds that they justify',[2] that is, the use of traditions as human law rather than as testimony to the divine gospel.

A symbol of the existing unity and a means for restoring the lost unity were also the condemnatory clauses of the confessions, which afford an interesting insight into the attitude toward tradition underlying Luther's Reformation.[3] These clauses had a twofold purpose: to disavow any affinity with the heresies condemned by the tradition, and to point out features of the Roman Catholic position that were a betrayal of the tradition. Thus the

[1] Augsburg Confession, 'Preface', 4, *Bek.* 44-45 (*BC* 25), a direct quotation from the imperial summons to the Diet of Augsburg.
[2] Apology, XV, 38, *Bek.* 304 (*BC* 220).
[3] Hans-Werner Gensichen, *Damnamus*. Die Verwerfung von Irrlehre bei Luther und im Luthertum des 16. Jahrhunderts (Berlin, 1955).

first and the nineteenth articles of the Augsburg Confession condemned the Manichaean heresy, apparently because the interpretation of God's relation to evil espoused in Luther's *Bondage of the Will* had been accused of Manichaean tendencies.[1] Even more significant are the condemnations of heresy which explicitly refer to the matter of church and tradition. From the past, it was Donatism which Roman Catholic polemics claimed to find reincarnate in the Reformation; from the present, critics were trying to interpret Anabaptism as the logical and consistent outcome of Luther's work.[2] As Chapter II has pointed out, the Augsburg Confession condemned 'the Donatists and all others'[3] like them and thus affirmed the correctness of the tradition by which they were condemned. Likewise, it repeatedly dissociated itself from Anabaptism,[4] not only because of the political implications of the question, but because its attitude toward the tradition and that of the Anabaptists were fundamentally different. It refused to be identified with those movements, past and present, which accepted the identification between Roman and Catholic and then proceeded to reject both. Rather, the Augsburg Confession sought to root its protest against Rome in the Catholic tradition.

The conclusion of the confession therefore made the claim that 'in our circles nothing has been accepted in doctrine or in ceremonies that is opposed to Scripture or the Catholic Church, since it is evident that we have been most careful to keep new and wicked dogmas from creeping into our churches'.[5] And in the conclusion to its first part the confession even claimed to contain 'nothing that departs either from the Scriptures or from the Catholic Church or from the Roman church, insofar as this is known to us from its writers'.[6] Both these claims were an effort to drive a wedge between Rome and the Catholic tradition, or between the Rome of tradition and the Rome of Eck and Cochlaeus. That effort helps to account for the conservatism of the confession in

[1] Cf. Hugo Lämmer, *Die vortridentinisch-katholische Theologie* (Berlin, 1858), p. 161.
[2] *Ibid.*, p. 58, p. 22, on Donatism; on Anabaptism, cf. pp. 229-230.
[3] Augsburg Confession, VIII, 3, *Bek.* 62 (*BC* 33); see p. 23 and p. 35 above.
[4] Especially in Art. IX, *Bek.* 63 (*BC* 33).
[5] Augsburg Confession, 'Conclusion', 5, *Bek.* 134 (*BC* 95). For an informed and balanced study cf. Peter Fraenkel, *Testimonia Patrum*. The Function of the Patristic Argument in the Theology of Philip Melanchthon (Geneva, 1961).
[6] Augsburg Confession, XXI, 'Conclusion', 1, *Bek.* 83c (*BC* 47).

both form and content. Thus its statement concerning the real presence of the body and blood of Christ in the eucharist almost won the approval of the Roman Catholic opponents, and then was reinforced in the strongest of terms by the Apology.[1] This statement was no isolated concession to Roman traditionalism, but part of the growing realization by both Luther and Melanchthon, each in his own way, that the rise of other Protestant movements compelled Lutheranism to declare its loyalty to the Catholic tradition of the West in as unequivocal a statement as possible.

THE STRUCTURE OF THE CONFESSION

The opening of this second front—actually, there were several fronts on the left—made Luther and Melanchthon introduce their entire argumentation with Rome by articulating their position on the pivotal doctrines of the Trinity, original sin, and the person of Christ in such a way as to include the Roman and the Lutheran viewpoints within the unitive formulas of the Catholic tradition. Following Luther's lead in earlier confessional statements, the Augsburg Confession then sought to articulate its dissent from Rome on the basis of the agreement with tradition stated in the first three articles. Thus Article I stated the Trinitarian faith in traditional, almost austere terminology, none of which is distinctively Lutheran.[2] Some of Luther's statements on the Trinity had been seized by his opponents to prove that he was an Arian, and this article was an affirmation of fidelity to the Trinitarian tradition.

A similar affirmation was expressed in Article II on original sin. Here the confession appropriated a definition of original sin derived from Aguinas, who had based it upon certain formulations of Augustine.[3] Sin consisted negatively of 'a lack of original righteousness' and positively of 'concupiscence'. To this definition the confession added a rather conventional condemnation of 'the

---

[1] Augsburg Confession, X, *Bek.* 64-65, with accompanying notes (*BC* 34); Apology, X, *Bek.* 247-248 (*BC* 179-180).
[2] Even Carl Stange, 'Die Bedeutung des Augsburger Bekenntnisses', *Zeitschrift für systematische Theologie*, VIII (1931), 599-600, cannot make a convincing case for its distinctively Lutheran character.
[3] Thomas Aquinas, *Summa Theologica*, I-II, Q. 82, Art. 3. For a modern restatement of this definition, cf. Paul Tillich, *Systematic Theology*, II, 47; also my comments on Tillich's use of this definition, 'Ein deutscher lutherischer Theologe in Amerika. Paul Tillich und die dogmatische Tradition', *Gott ist am Werk: Festschrift für Landesbischof D. Hanns Lilje* (Hamburg, 1959), pp. 29-31.

Pelagians and others'. As a matter of fact, this definition of original sin did not do justice to the more thoroughgoing interpretation of human corruption that Luther had developed, and in the Apology Melanchthon was compelled to clarify the point. What was condemned about 'the Pelagians and others', moreover, was not what the Pelagians had taught, but what some medieval theologians had been teaching. But taken just as it stands, Article II of the Augsburg Confession avoids the entire cleavage between Rome and the Reformers, contenting itself with a traditional formulation of the doctrine. Even in the form in which Luther's opponents used it—and much more in the form in which Luther understood it—the traditional Augustinian doctrine constituted an adequate basis for the explanation of justification that was to follow. Not Luther's private ideas, but the 'great consensus' of the confessing churches on the basis of the Catholic tradition was the content of Article II.

After affirming its loyalty to the traditional doctrine of the Trinity and to the Augustinian doctrine of man, the confession devoted Article III to the doctrine of Christ. Here its formulation amounts to little more than a paraphrase of the Apostles' Creed, to which its concluding paragraph also makes reference. In this doctrine, especially as regards the work of Christ, Luther had gone beyond the traditional Western interpretation; but except for echoes, there is little of this in Article III, which chose to describe reconciliation in the ancient sacrificial metaphor of Christ as *hostia*, an image that not only had most of the tradition on its side, but was common to both Luther and the scholastics.[1] Thus Articles I, II, and III of the Augsburg Confession sought to provide a basis in the Catholic tradition for the doctrinal conflict between Rome and the Reformers. The conflict with Rome over the doctrine of justification was on this basis. If the Holy Trinity was as holy as the Trinitarian dogma taught; if original sin was as

---

[1] On the early Christian use of *hostia*, cf. Albert Blaise and Henri Chirat, *Dictionnaire latin-francais des auteurs chrétiens* (Strasbourg, 1954), p. 395. On Cyprian's phrase, 'dominicae hostiae veritatem', *The Unity of the Catholic Church*, 17, which is one of the earliest instances of this usage, cf. the note of Maurice Bévenot (ed.), St Cyprian, *The Lapsed* and *The Unity of the Catholic Church*, 'Ancient Christian Writers', 25 (Westminster, Md., 1957; London, n.d.), 119, note 139. See also the fifth stanza of *Verbum supernum prodiens*, hymn of Thomas Aquinas, the 'O salutaris hostia', *The Oxford Book of Medieval Latin Verse*, ed. F. J. E. Raby (Oxford, 1959), p. 403.

virulent as the Augustinian tradition said it was; and if Christ was as necessary as the Christological dogma implied—then the only way to treat justification in a manner faithful to the best of Catholic tradition was to teach justification by faith.

The doctrine of justification by faith thus provided a link between the three great dogmas of the tradition—God, man, and Jesus Christ—and the other points of doctrinal dispute. On some of these points a large part of the tradition opposed the Reformers; sometimes it was Rome, sometimes more radical Protestants, who seemed to have the tradition on their side.[1] But by means of this link in the doctrine of justification, Melanchthon proposed to rescue the tradition from itself, to treat questions like the doctrine of the word, baptism, civil government, and the power of bishops in a way that was faithful to the doctrine of justification and therefore to what was normative in the tradition. Articles VII and VIII supported the tradition in condemning Donatism, but also declared that Christian unity did not demand a uniformity of ceremonies 'instituted by men'.[2] The phrase 'instituted by men' is both an echo of the doctrine of justification and a defence against the charge that the Reformers were eliminating the sacraments from a consideration of what was necessary for the unity of the church. The sacraments—and here Melanchthon was quite willing to accept traditional ways of defining and even of numbering[3] —were necessary by virtue of their institution at the hands of Christ. Human ceremonies were not, and it is these ceremonies that are usually meant by the term *traditio* in the Augsburg Confession and the Apology. It was contrary to the heritage (in this sense, tradition) of the church to call such ceremonies (in this sense, traditions) necessary.

The dual character of the attitude toward tradition that is evident in the Augsburg Confession seems to be made possible and necessary by the continuing ideal of one church and one great

---

[1] The treatise, *Quid de eucharistia veteres tum Graeci tum Latini senserunt,* published by John Oecolampadius in 1530 (a copy of which is in the library of Union Theological Seminary, New York), had seriously troubled Melanchthon, making him wonder whether the weight of the ancient tradition favoured a 'spiritualistic' interpretation of the presence in the Lord's Supper; cf. Otto Ritschl, *Dogmengeschichte des Protestantismus,* I, 279ff.

[2] Augsburg Confession, VII, 3, *Bek.* 61 (*BC* 32).

[3] Cf. Apology, XIII, 'The Number and Use of the Sacraments', *Bek.* 291-296 (*BC* 211-214).

tradition, within which the conflict over particular traditions was going on. During the generation that followed, several developments combined to discredit that ideal and any attitude toward tradition predicated upon it. The political situation, epitomized by the Smalcaldic War, made its peace with the fact of religious pluralism within the empire, if not within individual principalities. Lutheranism saw that other Protestant movements had also come to stay, and that it had to define its view of doctrine and tradition in relation to these, not merely in relation to Rome. And Rome itself took actions at Trent that compelled some reappraisal of a position which had been taken when the Roman tradition was undefined.

A REFORMATION ANSWER TO TRENT

The task of restating the attitude of Luther's Reformation toward tradition in the face of these developments fell to Martin Chemnitz (1522-1586). Three works come particularly into consideration here: above all, his great *Examen* of the Council of Trent, published from 1565 to 1573; his treatise on the two natures in Christ, published in 1571; and his contribution to the Formula of Concord of 1577, especially the 'Catalogue of Testimonies' appended to it. A study of the parallels between these last two would cast considerable doubt upon the validity of Otto Ritschl's thesis that the Formula of Concord was a repudiation of Melanchthonian traditionalism.[1] Though the preface to the Formula may indeed be a statement of the Protestant principle of 'Scripture alone', the actual theological method of the Formula, especially in Article VIII on the person of Christ, would tend to bear out another interpretation. The Formula faced the responsibility of summarizing and defending Luther's teachings, in this case the Christological formulations of his writings against Zwingli. It faced the assignment of refuting the Protestant opposition, in this case the Christology of Calvinism. And it had to resolve conflicts within Lutheranism itself, in this case the debate between Chemnitz and John Brenz. Not merely by the Protestant principle, but by a formidable array of evidence from the substance of the Catholic tradition, Chemnitz' Christology dealt with the challenges of Luther, Calvin, and Brenz—though with each in a different way.

[1] Ritschl, *op. cit.*, pp. 390-403.

But the detailed exposition of the theological method of Chemnitz is not our concern here.[1]

Chemnitz was able to handle tradition this way because of his subtle and scholarly understanding of tradition, which represented a considerable development beyond the view espoused by Melanchthon. He was compelled to clarify his view not primarily by any of the stimuli just described, but by the Council of Trent, against which he wrote his *Examen*. Wilhelm Pauck has said of this book:

> With great thoroughness and an impressive display of learning in historical theology and without any of the passionate hatred and intemperance that had characterized the polemics of the Reformation age, he endeavoured to prove that the Roman Catholic doctrine was against Scripture and the teachings of the ancient Fathers. It was his major purpose to demonstrate that not Protestantism but Roman Catholicism could justly be accused of having fallen away from the teachings and practices of the ancient church. . . . Translated into German and French and frequently republished, even in the nineteenth century, it remained the most useful Protestant criticism of the Council of Trent.[2]

Chemnitz' view of tradition, as defined in the *Examen*, went beyond Melanchthon's by including in the term 'tradition' much of what Melanchthon had said, in the Apology and elsewhere, under other rubrics.

There were, according to Chemnitz, eight different senses in which the word 'tradition' may be used in theology. For each sense he provided an abundance of patristic and sometimes scholastic passages. Maintaining that the Roman Catholic position was based upon a confusion of the various senses of the word, Chemnitz declared that 'this dispute about traditions cannot be more simply explained nor can a reply be more easily put to the quotations from the fathers which the papists set forth at great length in the dispute than by a distinction'.[3] The eight senses of the word *traditio* that Chemnitz distinguished are these:[4]

---

[1] The most recent study known to me is that of Gottfried Noth, *Grundlinien der Theologie des Martin Chemnitz* (Erlangen, 1930), which, unfortunately, prints only the third part of Noth's dissertation, that dealing with the Eucharist and with Christology. See the older work of Reinhard Mumm, *Die Polemik des Martin Chemnitz gegen das Konzil von Trient* (Naumburg, 1905), with a detailed list of writings against Trent.

[2] Pauck, *The Heritage of the Reformation*, p. 161.

[3] Martin Chemnitz, *Examen Concilii Tridentini*, pp. 69-70.

[4] The eight senses are discussed, *ibid.*, pp. 70-99; in the case of each, I have

1. Those things which Christ and the apostles handed down in a living voice and which the evangelists and the apostles subsequently reduced to writing are often called *traditio*.
2. Without any temporal interruption and in a certain connected succession, the books of Sacred Scripture were cared for by the church, faithfully transmitted to subsequent generations, and handed down [*traditi*] to us as though by hand.
3. Irenaeus and Tertullian . . . celebrate the apostolic tradition . . . [and] recite almost verbatim those articles of faith which are today contained in the symbol known as the apostles'.
4. Undoubtedly the primitive church received from the apostles and from apostolic men not only the text of Scripture, but also its legitimate and proper interpretation, which the primitive chuch preserved without corruption.
5. What the fathers sometimes call those dogmas not set down in Scripture in so many words, but drawn from clear passages of Scripture by good, sure, firm, and clear reasoning.
6. The Catholic consensus of the fathers.
7. The ancient rites and customs which, because of their antiquity, were referred to the apostles.
8. The Council of Trent attributes to unwritten traditions pertaining to both faith and morals a right to the same reverence and piety as Sacred Scripture itself.

It was this eighth sense of the word *traditio* that was most directly involved in the controversy with Rome.

THE DOCTRINE OF JUSTIFICATION

The purpose of this distinction was to avoid being caught in the earlier Melanchthonian definition of tradition as ritual and ceremony, and to turn the tradition against Trent. In general, Chemnitz accomplished this latter purpose by interpreting Trent against the background of unresolved contradictions in pre-Reformation theology. With his vast learning in patristic and scholastic literature, he was able to show that in condemning the Reformers Trent was also condemning a considerable portion of the very Catholic tradition it claimed to be exalting. A consideration of how Chemnitz analysed the Tridentine formulation of the doctrine of justification is a good sample of the procedure he employed and the view of tradition underlying it.[1]

Existing side by side in pre-Reformation theology were several

---

selected that definition or statement which seems to me to summarize what Chemnitz says.

[1] The discussion of justification and of justifying faith appears, *ibid.*, pp. 144-199.

ways of interpreting the righteousness of God and the act of justification.[1] They ranged from strongly moralistic views that seemed to equate justification with moral renewal to ultra-forensic views, which saw justification as a 'nude imputation' that seemed possible apart from Christ, by an arbitrary decree of God. Between these extremes were many combinations; and though certain views predominated in late nominalism, it is not possible even there to speak of a single doctrine of justification. The Apology of the Augsburg Confession made the most of this situation. One of the most penetrating discussions in the Apology is its analysis of the several doctrines of justification characteristic of its opponents.[2] Among the various theories present in Western Catholic thought, the Reformers also claimed to find the ancestry of their own view. But instead of selecting this view or at least leaving it open as a possibility, the Council of Trent seemed to Chemnitz to select the extreme opposite, the Pelagian or at least semi-Pelagian doctrine. At the same time, Chemnitz repudiated any doctrine of 'nude imputation' and sought to root justification in the life, death, and resurrection of Christ rather than in the absolute will of God. This stress upon the 'ordered' rather than the 'absolute' will of God set Chemnitz apart from many earlier opponents of moralistic teachings about justification.[3]

By adopting this teaching and by anathematizing Luther's doctrine, Trent seemed to Chemnitz to be condemning not only the Protestant principle of Luther's Reformation, but considerable portions of the Catholic substance it purported to defend. For the weight of the Catholic tradition supported justification by grace alone without human merit, particularly if 'Catholic tradition' included, as it did for Chemnitz, not merely learned theology, but also 'all the prayers of the saints in which they ask to be instructed, illumined, and sanctified by God. By these prayers they acknowledge that they cannot have what they are asking for by their own natural powers.'[4] With the weight of such tradition on

---

[1] Previous discussions of this issue are evaluated and corrected by Oberman, *Harvest of Medieval Theology*, Ch. VI: 'The Process of Justification', pp. 146-184; and by his paper, 'The Tridentine Doctrine of Justification in the Light of Later Medieval Theology', American Society of Church History, December 28, 1963.

[2] Apology, IV, 287-289, *Bek.* 217 (*BC* 151).

[3] *Examen*, p. 160.

[4] Formula of Concord, Solid Declaration, 15, *Bek.* (*BC* 523).

his side, Chemnitz could accuse Trent of setting the unwritten tradition which it itself had invented against the 'true and certain traditions of the apostles'.[1] Thus he demonstrated the truly traditional and Catholic character of the Reformation doctrine, implying that by closing the door to this doctrine Trent was making Rome a sect. Pointing to the antithesis between the Thomistic and the Scotistic views of justification, many Protestant scholars have come to conclusions that support Chemnitz, while recent Roman Catholic scholars tend to see the Tridentine decree on justification as a conciliatory statement.[2]

An undertone accompanying Chemnitz' entire discussion is the restatement of a motif heard already in the Augsburg Confession and the Apology—the note of poignancy over the growing realization that the division may be permanent. Precisely because the Catholic tradition was as multiform as Chemnitz' polemics demonstrated it to be, it was necessary to reconsider any attestation of loyalty to that tradition which moved, as Chemnitz' systematic theology did, in the direction of uniformity. It was one thing to conduct the discussion when 'the usual form of doctrinal expression'[3] was so much a given fact that *traditio* could be used in the narrow and pejorative sense in which the Augsburg Confession and the Apology used it. The broadening of the concept by Chemnitz is itself a testimony to the loss of that given fact. Once it had been lost, what was needed was a new sense of history, in which both Catholic substance and Protestant principle could be interpreted more profoundly. Chapter II has shown that the elements of such a new sense of history were present in Luther's Reformation. Chapter IV will analyse in depth the most sophisticated historical analysis to come from Luther's pen, his treatise on church councils, for here the meaning of 'critical reverence' toward the Catholic tradition was made explicit.

[1] *Examen*, p. 173.
[2] Hanns Rückert, *Die Rechtfertigungslehre auf dem tridentinischen Konzil* (Bonn, 1927), pp. 134-190; Eduard Stakemeier, 'Trienter Lehrentscheidungen und reformatorische Anliegen' in *Das Weltkonzil von Trient*, ed. Georg Schreiber (Freiburg, 1951), I, 97-104; the thorough bibliography in Hubert Jedin, *Geschichte des Konzils von Trient* (Freiburg, 1951ff.), I, 475, note 5; and Hans Küng, *Rechtfertigung* (Einsiedeln, 1957).
[3] Apology, 'Preface', 11, Bek. 143 (*BC* 99).

IV

THE AUTHORITY OF CHURCH COUNCILS

THE general councils of the church can err; and in fact the Council of Constance, the sixteenth of the general councils of the church, had erred when it condemned certain of the teachings of John Hus and Jerome of Prague. As Chapter VII of this study will show, this admission at the Leipzig Debate in 1519 made both Luther and his opponents begin to recognize the extent of the alienation between him and the Roman Church. This admission, more than either the ninety-five theses of two years earlier or even his excommunication of two years later, initiated Luther's Reformation.[1] Just a little more than a quarter of a century later, as Luther lay dying in February 1546, another church council was in session at Trent—the nineteenth of the general councils—to discuss, among other issues, some of the doctrinal and disciplinary questions raised by Luther's Reformation.

Luther's career as a Reformer spanned the interval between Leipzig and Trent. During almost every year of that career he found himself constrained to think and speak about the problem of a church council.[2] Indeed, he had already appealed for a council on November 28, 1518.[3] He was hopeful, at least for a while, that a free ecumenical council could reopen the question of restoring the chalice to the laity.[4] In June 1520 he composed his *Letter to the*

---

[1] Cf. pp. 109-111 below.
[2] Theodor Kolde, *Luthers Stellung zu Konzil und Kirche bis zum Wormser Reichstag* (Gütersloh, 1876), while outdated, is still useful; see also Robert Stupperich, 'Die Reformatoren und das Tridentinum', *Archiv für Reformationsgeschichte*, XLVII (1956), 20-62, especially the section on 'Luthers Stellung zum konzil im Allgemeinen', pp. 23ff.
[3] *Appeal of Brother Martin Luther to a Council, WA* 2, 36-40.
[4] *The Blessed Sacrament of the Holy and True Body of Christ and the Brotherhoods, WA* 2, 742 (*LW* 35, 49).

Christian Nobility, setting forth some of the chief abuses with which such a council would have to deal and outlining the conditions under which it should be convoked.[1] Many of the themes sounded in this treatise dominated Luther's thought about a council to the end, and he reverted to them each time the prospects for a council seemed likely. Repeatedly, however, these prospects were dimmed by imperial politics or by church politics; first one party, then another, found a church council inexpedient when it was proposed. Everyone remained theoretically committed to the idea of a council, but in practice there was strong opposition to the idea both in Rome and elsewhere. During the 1530s, at the urging of Paul III, who had become pope in 1534, the council almost became a reality on two occasions—at Mantua in 1537 and at Vicenza in 1538.[2]

To prepare for these occasions, Luther re-examined his ideas about a council of the church in the light of the changed religious and political alignment. For each of the major forces had been altered radically since the *Letter to the Christian Nobility* of 1520. New light on the conciliar question came from another source as well, a deepened study of church history. Both the decrees of the ancient ecumenical councils and the acts of the more recent councils, especially of the Council of Constance, helped to shape the ideas of Luther about what a council, if one were ever actually to meet, could and should undertake.[3] The influence of this historical study is evident in many writings from the last decade of Luther's life, including some writings, such as those on the Lord's Supper, that were not specifically directed to the conciliar controversy.[4] The preoccupation of modern Luther research with 'the young Luther', or at best with the mature Luther, has relegated this final decade of his career to a position of secondary significance. Yet it was during this decade that Luther was forced, regretfully and

---

[1] *An Open Letter to the Christian Nobility*, WA 6, 404-469 (*WML* 2, 8off.).
[2] The most recent and balanced account of these negotiations is Hubert Jedin, *Geschichte des Konzils von Trient*, I.
[3] Cf. W. Köhler, *Luther und die Kirchengeschichte* (Erlangen, 1900), and Ernst Schäfer, *Luther als Kirchenhistoriker* (Gütersloh, 1897). Luther's historical study had been facilitated by the appearance in 1538 of Peter Crabbe's edition of the acts of the councils, *Concilia omnia* (cf. WA 50, 502). A copy of Crabbe's book is in the Library of Congress; cf. the note by John T. McNeill in his edition of John Calvin, *Institutes of the Christian Religion*, 'Library of Christian Classics', XXI (Philadelphia, 1960; London, 1961), 1128, note 23.
[4] Cf. Schäfer, *op. cit.*, pp. 83ff.

reluctantly, to formulate his personal assessment of a career that had begun with the intention of reforming the Christian church but had ended with the irrevocable division of Catholic Christendom. It was also during this decade, therefore, that the paradox of Catholic substance and Protestant principle in Luther's Reformation became most poignant. No issue better documents that poignancy than Luther's attitude toward the authority of church councils; for in 1539 Luther composed his most important historical book, *On the Councils and the Church*,[1] which is also the most significant single statement of his critical reverence toward the the Catholic substance of tradition. We must turn now to a close reading of this treatise.

THE APPEAL OF A COUNCIL

'We cry out and appeal for a council and beseech all of Christendom for its advice and help.' 'You say that there is no hope for such a council any longer; I suppose I agree with you.'[2] The juxtaposition of these two declarations in the treatise is an indication of Luther's ambivalence toward the prospect of the forthcoming council. He had been appealing for a council and to a council for twenty years, taunting his opponents with the contradiction between their protestations of loyalty to the conciliar ideal and their dilatory tactics. Now a new pontiff, Paul III, was bent on finally convoking the long expected council; and now it was Luther's turn to see his declarations about a council challenged. The strategy and propaganda of the Reformation seemed in danger of losing the advantages they had gained from papal hesitation about a council. Thus Luther had to summarize his position in a way that took account of this shift. He was convinced that there was no hope for genuine reformation in any conclave to which Rome would give its consent; yet the onus of the responsibility for this had to rest not on the Reformers but on Rome. To assure this, Luther coupled his continuing appeal for a council with a threefold attack on the motives of the ecclesiastical authorities who were summoning the assembly.

[1] German original, *WA* 50, 509-653; English translation, *WML* 5, 131-300. Since most of the references in this chapter are to this treatise, I shall simply cite it according to its location in these two editions, without repeating the title each time.
[2] *WA* 50, 620 (*WML* 5, 258); *WA* 50, 623 (*WML* 5, 262).

The very first paragraph of the treatise set forth the first attack: The pope was not sincere in his invitation to the council. He was trifling with the hopes of those who longed for a settlement of the issues dividing Christendom, as one teases a dog by waving a morsel before its snout on a knife and then striking it with the butt of the knife when it snaps at the morsel.[1] In substantiation of this charge, Luther levelled at his opponents his oft-repeated accusation that they actually acknowledged the correctness of his teachings and knew that their own doctrine could not be substantiated from the Scriptures.[2] In spite of this they insisted upon having their own way. Therefore they had no right to plead ignorance, but were acting contrary to Scripture and contrary to their own better knowledge and judgment. The wilfulness of this opposition to the evident truth was proof to Luther that any council was doomed to failure before the first session was ever called to order. 'Thus the council is settled before it even begins: Nothing is to be reformed, but everything is to be retained in accordance with past usage. What a fine council that is!'[3] Long before the Vatican Council of 1870, 'irreformability' was a fundamental point of conflict between the Catholic substance as Rome understood it and the Protestant principle as the Reformers interpreted it. Luther was sure that no council called by the pope could be expected to effect any fundamental changes in the life and teaching of the church.

In 1539 there were still those who held out the sincere hope that a general council of the church could effect some fundamental changes. In support of this hope they cited the precedent of the earlier general councils of the church, maintaining that 'a fine reformation . . . could be achieved on the basis of the fathers and the councils'.[4] The researches of Brian Tierney have illuminated the origins of this Catholic conciliarism.[5] But Luther's own historical studies and his experience in two decades of debate had deepened the Protestant principle of suspicion toward both 'the fathers and the councils' as a basis of genuine reform. Neither the

[1] *WA* 50, 509 (*WML* 5, 131).
[2] *WA* 50, 511 (*WML* 5, 133). See other passages collected in my notes, *LW* 13, 352, notes 2-3.
[3] *WA* 50, 510 (*WML* 5, 131).
[4] *WA* 50, 519 (*WML* 5, 142).
[5] Brian Tierney, *Foundations of the Conciliar Theory*. The Contribution of the Medieval Canonists from Gratian to the Great Schism (Cambridge, 1955).

councils nor the church fathers had achieved true unanimity in their teaching. Therefore it was possible for either party in the controversy of the sixteenth century to select from the fathers and councils whatever seemed to suit and substantiate its own position.[1] But such proof was finally no proof; for the presuppositions of the combatants, not the actual writings of the fathers or the decrees of the councils, determined what was to be accorded the status of normative Catholic substance.

Luther's second charge against the pope's sudden conversion to the conciliar position dealt with the question of his readiness to compromise. Chapter IX of this volume will show that although Luther is not known in the history of theology as an irenic or mediating theologian, he did repeatedly declare his willingness to compromise on any but the essential issues. 'Thank God', he asserted, 'we are not so far gone that we would permit the church to perish rather than compromise, even on weighty issues, so long as they are not against God. No, we ourselves are ready to perish and to be stripped completely ... rather than to let calamity or danger befall the church.'[2] There is no reason to doubt the sincerity of this protestation. The historical studies upon which *The Councils and the Church* was based had shown Luther that conflicts of personality had been prominent in the determination of dogmatic issues at the ancient councils. He urged that in the debates of the fifth and sixth centuries over the subtler problems of the doctrine of the person of Christ not a proud condemnation of the errorist, but 'instruction with gentleness' had been called for.[3] Thus he knew that the recalcitrance of an orthodoxy that refused to compromise even where some compromise was permissible had to share with heresy the responsibility for schism and dissension in Christendom. For such recalcitrance permitted heretics to excuse themselves with the claim that they had been overcome not with truth but with violence, injustice, and a distortion of their views.[4] Both from his study of the history of councils and from his evaluation of the contemporary conflicts Luther knew that some concession on non-essentials was necessary if a council were to have any hope of succeeding.

Did the pope's summons to a council mean that he was prepared

[1] *WA* 50, 542 (*WML* 5, 168).   [2] *WA* 50, 516 (*WML* 5, 139).
[3] *WA* 50, 601 (*WML* 5, 237).   [4] *WA* 50, 594 (*WML* 5, 228).

to make such a concession? Luther put his answer to this question frankly or, as he said, 'in German'. There were two fundamental concessions that the pope had to make. First, he had to abolish the tyranny of the human regulations that he had substituted for divine commandments. Second, he had to grant that even faithful obedience to these divine commandments 'cannot help to achieve righteousness, to atone for sin, to obtain the grace of God, but only faith in Christ, who is the king of righteousness in us, through his precious blood, death, and resurrection, with which he has atoned for sin, rendered satisfaction, reconciled God, and redeemed us from death, wrath, and hell'.[1] From any council that did not grant these two concessions Luther expected no good. And it had to grant both of these concessions; there was to be no giving with one hand and taking away with the other. He thought that his opponents were insincere enough to make the concession that only the grace of Christ saves, but they would immediately add the stipulation that works are necessary for satisfaction or righteousness. Their indifference to the seriousness of true doctrine should have permitted them to compromise even on the issues that were most important to the Reformers; their unwillingness to grant such compromises doomed any council to failure.

The third argument that Luther directed against the pope's council was a criticism of its proposed composition. As matters turned out—although, of course, Luther was not yet aware of this —the delegates to the Council of Trent had one vote each; at Constance, by contrast, they had voted by national delegations. But Luther did foresee that the papacy would try to have priests friendly to its cause chosen as delegates, and he urged that delegates be chosen on the basis of other criteria than their loyalty to the pope: 'from every country those who are thoroughly learned in the Holy Scriptures and who are seriously and sincerely devoted to the glory of God, the Christian faith, the church, the salvation of souls, and the peace of the world.'[2] In addition, for reasons to be expounded later in this chapter, Luther believed that some of the delegates should be chosen from the secular government, since the business of the council concerned them too. Persuaded as he was that the pope would never be willing to accept a council thus defined, Luther laid down an either-or con-

[1] *WA* 50, 621 (*WML* 5, 260).   [2] *WA* 50, 622 (*WML* 5, 261).

dition: If such a council as he envisaged was impossible, there should be none at all. Impossible though this council was, Luther wanted to be sure that he and his followers did not receive the blame for the collapse of the ideal of an ecumenical council. Therefore he continued to call for such a council even when he knew that it could never be.

THE FUNCTIONS OF A COUNCIL

Luther's rejection of the pope's plans for a council was grounded, therefore, not merely in a polemical position, but in a positive definition, based upon church history, of the proper functions of a council. Both Catholic substance and Protestant principle were involved in it. Generalizing from his study of the first four ecumenical councils and from the critical reverence of his own theological assumptions about the nature of the church and the meaning of religious authority, Luther sought to demarcate the rights and duties of church councils in three areas of Christian concern: Christian doctrine; Christian life, including both good works and ecclesiastical ceremonies; and secular government and law. Both his descriptions of what councils had done and his prescriptions of what any true council should do concentrated upon these three areas. In fact, he maintained that the criteria he was laying down in these areas applied to 'all other councils, great or small, even though there were many thousands of them'.[1] For the church had 'miniature councils' going on within it all the time, in its parishes and schools.[2] These 'miniature councils', too, dealt with the three areas.

CHRISTIAN DOCTRINE

First and foremost, a council had 'no authority to establish new articles of faith, even though the Holy Spirit were present in it', but only to suppress and condemn doctrinal innovations.[3] As later discussion will show, even the presence of the Holy Spirit in a council did not, according to Luther's definition, give such a council authority to create new doctrines. Luther went to pains to demonstrate that none of the first four ecumenical councils had arrogated to itself any such authority. Thus the Council of

[1] *WA* 50, 606 (*WML* 5, 262). [2] *WA* 50, 616-617 (*WML* 5, 252-253).
[3] *WA* 50, 607 (*WML* 5, 243).

Nicaea of 325 had not invented a new doctrine, but had 'preserved the old article of faith, that Christ is true and very God, against the innovating cleverness of Arius'.[1] Again, since the Council of Constantinople of 381 had itself acknowledged that its decrees were 'the ancient and true faith, in which we have previously been baptized and instructed, why should we give councils the great authority of establishing new doctrines and of burning as heretics all those who do not believe them?'[2] Nor did the Council of Ephesus of 431 usurp such authority; it merely 'defended the ancient faith against the innovating suppositions of Nestorius'.[3] Finally, the last of the great ecumenical councils, the one held at Chalcedon in 451, provided no support for the contention that councils had a right to establish new doctrines in the church.[4]

Here Luther drew the logical consequences of his stand at Leipzig twenty years earlier. He rejected the formal authority of church councils in matters of faith and doctrine, and asserted that councils merely applied the doctrine of Scripture to the new issues that had arisen. But Chapter I of this volume has pointed out that both the left wing of the Reformation in his century and theological liberalism in our century recognized the paradox that this rejection of formal conciliar authority was accompanied by a loyal submission to the material authority of the dogmas defined by the councils. During most of Christian history the authority of dogmas has depended upon the authority of the church as defined in a council, and indeed upon the capacity of the secular government to enforce dogmatic orthodoxy by police power. In the eyes of Luther's Roman Catholic opponents, the Protestant principle of repudiation of conciliar authority would inevitably lead to apostasy from the Catholic substance of creed and dogma. Luther's reply to this interpretation of his stand was a critical reappraisal both of what in principle councils could do in the church and of what in fact the great ecumenical councils had done. He argued that the dogmas of the Trinity and of the two natures in Christ, as defined by the first four ecumenical councils, did not depend for their validity upon an acceptance of the infallibility of the councils. For the fathers who formulated these dogmas did not intend to state a new doctrine, but only to defend the

[1] *WA* 50, 551 (*WML* 5, 178).   [2] *WA* 50, 581 (*WML* 5, 213).
[3] *WA* 50, 591 (*WML* 5, 225).   [4] *WA* 50, 603 (*WML* 5, 239).

primitive faith of the church as given in the Scriptures. A criticism of the councils in the name of the Scriptures, therefore, was more faithful to their authentic spirit than the misplaced loyalty of an uncritical traditionalism.

As examples of this authentic spirit Luther cited the works of Athanasius and Hilary, who opposed the heretics not with their own ideas or authority, but with the authority of the Scriptures. 'At Nicaea', he insisted, 'the creed was substantiated by the apostolic Scriptures. Otherwise, if it had not been for the Scriptures of the apostles and prophets, the mere words of the council by themselves would have accomplished nothing.'[1] What the Council of Ephesus promulgated 'had been in the church since the beginning; it was not invented by the council, but preserved by the gospel or the Holy Scriptures'.[2] Citing passages from both the Old Testament and the New in opposition to the Eutychian heresy, Luther summarized his interpretation of conciliar authority: 'Even if I do not . . . understand [this council] correctly, I still have these passages and understand them correctly. The council itself is obliged to be guided by this Scripture, and this is more certain to me than all the councils.'[3] In fact, even if most of the New Testament were to disappear and only the Gospel of St John were to remain, this one book would state the doctrines of all four ecumenical councils more amply and powerfully than they did.[4] Luther's rhetoric moved him to exclaim: 'The poor, insignificant pastor of Hippo, St Augustine, taught more than all the councils. . . . I will go even further: More is contained in the children's creed [the Apostles' Creed] than in all the councils. The Our Father and the Decalogue also teach more than all the councils do.'[5] The genuine defenders of the councils and of their Catholic substance, then, were not those who claimed supreme authority for the councils, but those who, like the fathers at the councils themselves, subjected the authority of the councils to the authority of the Scriptures.

When the self-styled defenders of the councils demanded submission to their authority, they demanded the impossible. For anyone who had ever studied the councils and the fathers had

---

[1] *WA* 50, 552 (*WML* 5, 179), quoting the *Historia tripartita*, V, 29.
[2] *WA* 50, 591 (*WML* 5, 225).   [3] *WA* 50, 604 (*WML* 5, 240).
[4] *WA* 50, 605 (*WML* 5, 241).   [5] *WA* 50, 615 (*WML* 5, 252).

learned that they were not only inconsistent, but downright contradictory. Hence no one could obey all of their decrees at the same time. An illustration upon which Luther dwelt at considerable length was the legislation of the Council of Nicaea regarding those who left the military service for the sake of a religious profession and then returned to their old way of life; the council prescribed a long severe period of penance in such cases. Luther cited this example to show that even those who were now clamouring for a submission to conciliar authority refused to obey an ecumenical council when its legislation did not suit them. Although the bishops and popes waged war themselves and thus violated this rule, 'they incessantly shout "Councils, councils! Fathers, fathers!"—except, of course, that they are free to act contrary to this and to choose the things they want us to do.'[1] Luther did not accept this decree of Nicaea, but he was contending that no one could be obedient to all the legislation of all the councils.

A CRITIQUE OF COUNCILS

Sometimes, however, his criticism of conciliar authority went beyond this formal demonstration of inconsistency and contradiction to a material examination of the content of conciliar decrees. There were at least three such material critiques in *The Councils and the Church*: the concentration of the councils upon one article of faith, at the expense of the totality of the faith; the preoccupation of the Council of Ephesus with the heretical Mariology of Nestorius rather than with the other dangerous implications of his teaching; and the endorsement of celibacy and monasticism by the very councils that condemned the heretics.[2]

As he developed the first of these critiques, Luther found himself contrasting the councils with Peter Lombard, on whose *Sentences* he had lectured many years before. The contrast came out much to the advantage of the Lombard, whose study of St Augustine led him to summarize all the main doctrines of the Christian faith—almost all, at any rate, for he was weak on the doctrines of justification and of faith. But the councils had often permitted the heretics to force upon them a preoccupation with one doctrine and consequent distortion of focus. Ultimately, of

[1] *WA* 50, 534 (*WML* 5, 158).
[2] *WA* 50, 546 (*WML* 5, 172); *WA* 50, 591 (*WML* 5, 224); *WA* 50, 609 (*WML* 5, 246).

course, neither the councils nor Augustine nor Peter Lombard, but only the Scriptures contained the whole of Christian doctrine.[1]

Not only had the councils paid attention to one doctrine at the cost of the totality of Christian teaching, but they had sometimes concentrated upon a less important doctrine and missed the main issue. For example, Luther's own controversies with 'the Nestorians I myself have had',[2] that is, with Zwingli and with others who denied the real presence of the body and blood of Christ in the eucharist, had made him conscious of the far-reaching implications of Nestorian Christology. The passion of his attacks upon Zwingli's principle of distinguishing between those New Testament statements that applied to the human nature of Christ and those that applied to the divine nature shows how much he believed to be at stake in any separation of the two natures in Christ. Nothing less than the very meaning and efficacy of the saving work of Christ came under threat from such separation. Although he acknowledged that personal factors had played a role in the controversy and that the opponents of Nestorius had not understood him because they had not wanted to understand him, this did not obscure the threat to faith posed by the Nestorian doctrine. Apparently the Council of Ephesus had not grasped the real threat. Therefore 'this council condemned far too little in [the teaching of] Nestorius. For it dealt only with one property [of Christ], namely, that God was born of Mary. Hence the histories record that in this council it was decided, in opposition to Nestorius, that Mary was to be called Theotokos, that is, God-bearer. Yet Nestorius denied all the properties of human nature to God in Christ, such as dying, being crucified, suffering, and whatever is inconsistent with deity'[3].

The third of Luther's material critiques of the councils, and one to which he reverted several times in this treatise, was aimed at their failure to condemn monasticism and celibacy, which were, in Luther's judgment, logically connected with heresy. In fact, he was even ready—without historical grounds—to blame the endorsement of celibacy at the Council of Nicaea upon the presence of

[1] *WA* 50, 543-546 (*WML* 5, 169-173).
[2] *WA* 50, 591 (*WML* 5, 224). On this parallel cf. Hermann Sasse, *This Is My Body*. Luther's Contention for the Real Presence in the Sacrament of the Altar (Minneapolis, 1959), pp. 148-155.
[3] *WA* 50, 580 (*VML* 5, 224).

bishops who were inclined to Arian doctrine.[1] An extended excursus in his definition of what a council may legislate about good works criticized the ecumenical councils for not having condemned the dangerous novelty of the monastic life even as they were condemning the dangerous novelty of the heretical doctrines.[2] Thus Luther claimed that the false teachings of Arius, Nestorius, and Eutyches regarding the Trinity and the person of Christ were consistent with the false teachings of those who demanded clerical celibacy and who praised the monastic estate as a purer form of Christian obedience. The councils did not recognize this consistency; if they had, 'they would have condemned the archimandrite Eutyches not only on the grounds of faith (as they earnestly did), but also on the grounds of his monasticism (as they did not do, endorsing it instead)'.[3]

From these three material critiques and from his other statements about the ecumenical councils it is evident that Luther did not shrink from applying to the councils the canons of both theological and historical evaluation. As he never tired of saying, the fathers were human beings, who had never 'transcended the seventh chapter of Romans'[4]; they were fallible as individuals, and even when gathered together in councils they could and did err. Therefore their authority was not to be put on an equal plane with that of the Scriptures, to which they themselves wanted to be subjected. Nevertheless, the statement of this Protestant principle must not be permitted to obscure Luther's thoroughgoing dogmatic orthodoxy: he pitted the authority of the Scriptures against the authority of the councils, but what he found in the Scriptures was the Catholic substance that the councils had formulated on the basis of the Scriptures. Historically speaking, Luther could not have been the theologian he was without the help of the very councils whose infallibility he denied. Sometimes he even contended that not by assigning to the councils an infallibility they neither possessed nor claimed, but only by acknowledging their fallibility with critical gratitude, could one preserve the dogmas of the councils against their enemies.

---

[1] *WA* 50, 539 (*WML* 5, 165). [2] *WA* 50, 607 (*WML* 5, 244).
[3] *WA* 50, 618 (*WML* 5, 256).
[4] *WA* 50, 525 (*WML* 5, 149); on the significance of this, see p. 36, note 1 above.

CHRISTIAN LIFE AND WORSHIP

As a council was not permitted to create new articles of faith, so it had 'no authority to command new good works . . . for all good works are already amply commanded in the Sacred Scriptures'; similarly, 'a council does not have the authority to prescribe new ceremonies for Christians and to require their observance as a matter of conscience or under pain of mortal sin'.[1] Rather, its task was to guard against the introduction of any such new rules into Christian life and worship and to condemn them when they arose. A council was to condemn not only the obviously wicked works such as murder and adultery, but also the glittering new works invented by the devil as a cover for idolatry; for these new works, of which monasticism was the outstanding instance, were 'a menace to Christian faith and an offence to Christian life'.[2]

This did not mean, of course, that a council had no right at all to consider problems of administration and discipline for which there were no explicit commands or prohibitions in the Scriptures, or matters of liturgical usage that were neither forbidden nor prescribed there; as the next two chapters of this book will make clear, Luther was aware of the complex problem of defining what makes a particular liturgical form 'scriptural'. But his principle did mean that such administrative and liturgical regulations were not the reason for which a council should be summoned. When the bishops at Nicaea had attempted to introduce jurisdictional disputes into the proceedings, Constantine had wisely refused to be party to their 'clerical squabbles'.[3] Liturgical details were also too trivial a matter for councils to waste their time debating. It was better left to schoolmasters, who could train the children to genuflect at the *Et homo factus est* of the Nicene Creed or to remove their hats and genuflect at the mention of the name of Jesus.[4] Such ceremonies were a good thing and useful in the life of the church, so long as they were not made obligatory and tyrannical. When the externals of ecclesiastical discipline or of ceremonial usage became tyrannical, it was the task of a council to speak out against them.

Nevertheless, just such externals of ecclesiastical discipline and ceremonial usage had been responsible for the first 'church council', described in the fifteenth chapter of the Book of Acts.

[1] *WA* 50, 613 (*WML* 5, 250).   [2] *WA* 50, 607-608 (*WML* 5, 244).
[3] *WA* 50, 552 (*WML* 5, 180).   [4] *WA* 50, 619 (*WML* 5, 257).

This meeting had established many precedents for subsequent councils. To determine what a council had the right to do, therefore, it was necessary to go behind the four ecumenical councils to 'the very first council, that of the apostles, held in Jerusalem, about which St Luke writes in Acts 15 and 16'.[1] The terms of its fourfold prohibition—'that you abstain from what has been sacrificed to idols and from blood and from what is strangled and from unchastity' (Acts 15. 29)—had figured prominently in the debates of the Reformation. The first three prohibitions were suspended in the course of later church history. This suspension was interpreted as proof for the claim that other commands and prohibitions of the New Testament were also subject to revision or suspension by the church. It was cited to show that the church did have the right, despite the words of institution, to withhold the chalice from the laity and to administer the Lord's Supper under only one kind.[2] Fifteen years before he wrote *The Councils and the Church*, in June 1524, Luther took up this claim in a series of sermons on Acts 15 and 16.[3] When he dealt with the interpretation of these chapters in the present treatise, therefore, he brought to it a long period of reflection and study. This much was clear to all: the apostolic council had indeed forbidden these four items, but after centuries of Christian history only the prohibition of unchastity still belonged to the Christian ethic. The council in Acts 15 was therefore a crucial case in any determination of the rights and the authority of church councils. Luther dealt with the case by examining various possible explanations for the suspension of these rules and then by suggesting his own, which he applied to all councils.

The simplest explanation for the suspension was to say that 'it is impossible to carry out [the requirements of] this council, because the contrary course of action has established itself too securely'.[4] Luther saw that this way out of the dilemma was too facile. For one thing, if the awesome formula of Acts 15. 28, 'It has seemed good to the Holy Spirit and to us', meant what it said, it was illegitimate to plead that observance of the council's require-

---

[1] *WA* 50, 526 (*WML* 5, 150).
[2] Cf. Luther's *Theses in Opposition to the Council of Constance*, *WA* 39, 22, on this argument.
[3] The sermons appear in *WA* 15, 571-602.
[4] *WA* 50, 527 (*WML* 5, 151).

ments was impossible. In his lectures at this very time upon the
patriarchal narratives in the Book of Genesis, Luther developed
his theory that man had originally been a vegetarian.[1] Hence it was
possible, by avoiding meat altogether, to obey all three of the
dietary prohibitions promulgated by the apostolic council. Thus
the argument from 'impossibility gives us no help in comforting
our conscience against the Holy Spirit'.[2]

Another explanation given for the suspension of this decree was
to argue that the church had the authority to change even the
mode of administering the eucharist, just as it had eventually
amended these decrees of an apostolic council, which had been
issued by the authority of the Holy Spirit. To this explanation
Luther replied, first, that the church had no such prerogative to
amend a divine decree. In addition, he pointed out a fundamental
inconsistency: Although the church claimed the right to interpose
its authority into the administration of a divine institution like the
Lord's Supper, it demanded that its own disciplinary and liturgical
decrees be obeyed and enforced as though they had been promulgated by divine right.[3] The institution of Christ and the
decrees of the Holy Spirit could be suspended, but the institutions
of the church and the decrees of the pope had to be obeyed at any
cost! This was, in Luther's eyes, a basic distortion of the function
of a church council.

Yet if the church did not have the right to amend a rule laid
down with divine authorization, this did not mean that the
enforcement of the prohibitions of the apostolic council had
simply withered away in the course of time without any explicit
action by the church at all. A jurist would point out the specious-
ness of such reasoning. The non-enforcement of a law at a particular place and time did not mean that the law had been repealed. By
the same argument an immoral person could argue from the
prevalence of immorality that the moral law was invalid. 'In fact,
we children of Adam would hold a council together with the devils
and conclude: "Are you listening, God? Among us men and
devils all your commandments have fallen into disuse. Therefore

---

[1] *Lectures on Genesis, WA* 42, 54-55 (*LW* 1, 71-72); on this notion in the context
of Luther's picture of the state of innocence, cf. Jaroslav Pelikan, 'Cosmos and
Creation: Science and Theology in Reformation Thought', *Proceedings of the
American Philosophical Society*, 105 (1961), 465-466.
[2] *WA* 50, 528 (*WML* 5, 152).   [3] *WA* 50, 528 (*WML* 5, 152-153).

we should no longer observe them".'[1] Despite his rejection of this argument, Luther was willing at times to reason *a posteriori* that the prohibitions of the apostolic councils could not have been intended to be permanently binding because they had in fact lapsed. Thus he could speak of 'certain incidental and external articles' that were decreed by the council, 'but not with the intention that an eternal rule should remain in the church as an article of faith; for it has lapsed'.[2] He could maintain that 'now that [*weil*] it has lapsed', it was permissible to ignore this decree.[3] It seems evident, however, that Luther was not contradicting his fundamental argument here, but only using this *a posteriori* reasoning to corroborate a repeal that he justified on other grounds.

In short, Luther rejected the idea that on its own authority the church had amended the apostolic council; and though it was true to say that the decrees of the council had lapsed, this was not a satisfactory explanation. Rhetorically Luther suggested that perhaps the way out of the difficulty was to erase the word 'Holy Spirit' from the record and to interpret the decree as the opinion merely of the apostles, not of the Holy Spirit. It was obvious that this evasion would not do either: 'This is ridiculous! You will have to think up something better.'[4] Another evasion that did not provide a workable solution was to declare that the council was speaking not of the entire law of Moses, but only of portions of it, some of which could be imposed upon the Gentiles and others of which could not be imposed.[5] This would have been a new patch on an old garment, and a violation of St Paul's dictum that anyone who obeyed the law in one point would have to obey it in all points (Gal. 5. 3). None of these explanations, some of them suggested facetiously by Luther and others advanced seriously by his opponents, could account for the eventual suspension or repeal of decrees that had been promulgated not by mere bishops, but by the very apostles, not on their own authority but with the supporting authority of the Holy Spirit. Did this imply that the decrees were eternally binding, or was there another

---

[1] *WA* 50, 529 (*WML* 5, 153).   [2] *WA* 50, 560 (*WML* 5, 188).
[3] *WM* 50, 564 (*WML* 5, 194). It is interesting that the modern German editions of Luther (e.g., *StL* 16, 2203) keep *weil* here, as though it meant 'because', as it does in modern German, rather than 'while', as it does in modern English.
[4] *WA* 50, 529 (*WML* 5, 154).   [5] *WA* 50, 563 (*WML* 5, 191).

interpretative device by which to show that they were not?

The interpretative device that Luther employed was to contrast the fourfold decree of the apostolic council in Acts 15. 29, which was based upon the recommendation of the apostle James in Acts 15. 20, with the main address of the apostle Peter in Acts 15. 7-11, and particularly with the question of v. 10: 'Why do you make trial of God by putting a yoke upon the neck of the disciples which neither our fathers nor we have been able to bear?' This contrast, which contained many echoes of Luther's more familiar contrast between James and Paul, noted that while Peter sought to excuse the Gentile converts to Christianity from the entire Mosaic law, James still wanted to require of them that they obey some of its prohibitions. Luther accused his Roman Catholic opponents, who claimed that the pope was the successor of St Peter, of ignoring St Peter and concentrating only upon St James and his four points. Yet the main issue of the council was the one stated by St Peter: that Gentile converts should know that they were saved by grace. If there was a contradiction between this main issue and the four points of James, Luther was willing to say: 'If we cannot harmonize them, we shall have to let St James go with his article and keep St Peter with his chief article, on account of which the council was held; for without St Peter's article no one can be saved.'[1] This distinction between the 'chief article' and the 'peripheral matters', the full implications of which were to become a key to the entire conciliar question, enabled Luther to dismiss the fourfold prohibition of the apostolic council as a temporary regulation. St Peter's article had to do with faith, St James's with love. The basis of faith was permanent; therefore St Peter's article was intended to be binding on the church in every age. The basis of love changed from one age to another; therefore St James's article was relevant to the problem of Gentiles who did not want to offend their Jewish fellow-Christians, but it no longer applied when the reason for this restraint was gone.[2] By means of this contrast and distinction Luther was able to take his opponents' arguments, based upon the apostolic council in Acts 15, and to use them in support of his contention that a council had

[1] *WA* 50, 564 (*WML* 5, 193).
[2] *WA* 50, 567 (*WML* 5, 197).

no authority to command new good works or to prescribe new ceremonies.

THE ROLE OF GOVERNMENT

After laying down the principles that a council had no right to promulgate new doctrines or to command new good works and ceremonies, Luther continued: 'A council has no right to meddle in secular law and government.'[1] The full implications of this principle, however, do not come into view until one sets it into the context of Luther's interpretation of the role of secular government in a council. For although he expressly forbade interference by a council in the business of government, he did not forbid interference by government in the business of a council. In fact he maintained, both from history and from an analysis of the contemporary scene, that the convoking of a church council was the business of government. As the government was obliged to come to the rescue in the case of a fire in a private dwelling, so it could spring to the aid of the church in an emergency by calling a council.[2] On the other hand, he interpreted the efforts of the pope to convoke a council as proof that the pope had designs on secular authority and monarchy.[3]

In support of this interpretation Luther cited historical precedents. The outbreak of the Arian heresy had proved too much for the clergy of Alexandria and even for other clergy. Therefore 'the pious emperor Constantine' added his authority to theirs and convoked the Council of Nicaea.[4] Luther's narrative of the circumstances leading up to the Council of Nicaea described the disappointment of the emperor when the church to which he had just granted peace was torn by strife over Arianism. Luther admired the patience and humility of Constantine and half-humorously contrasted it with his own polemical style, confessing that he could never have written as gentle a letter as Constantine did to Arius and Bishop Alexander—especially if he had been emperor![5] Hence it was thanks to the emperor, not to the pope, that the church had obtained the benefits of Nicaea. Whether Luther's opponents liked it or not, 'history proves that if it had

[1] *WA* 50, 613 (*WML* 5, 250-251).   [2] *WA* 50, 616 (*WML* 5, 254).
[3] *WA* 50, 523 (*WML* 5, 147).   [4] *WA* 50, 616 (*WML* 5, 254).
[5] *WA* 50, 548 (*WML* 5, 176).

not been for the emperor Constantine and if it had been up to Sylvester, the bishop of Rome, the first Council of Nicaea would never have been convoked'.[1] The same was true of all four great ecumenical councils. Bishops did call local synods on their own; but when an ecumenical council became necessary, the emperors had done the summoning.[2] The council after Nicaea, that of Constantinople, was summoned by Theodosius, also a 'pious emperor'.[3] When Damasus, the bishop of Rome, attempted to summon a council without imperial authority a year later, the other bishops had refused to come.[4] As for the Council of Ephesus, 'Latin writers would like to give the impression that the pope had a part in calling it, but the truth is that not the pope but the emperor had to summon this council'.[5] The same was true of the Council of Chalcedon.[6]

On the the basis of these historical precedents Luther had maintained all along that summoning a council to meet the challenges of the sixteenth century was a responsibility also of the secular rulers. During the early years of the Reformation it had been his hope that Emperor Charles V could be prevailed upon to live up to this responsibility. He was persuaded that the pope would never consent to a council unless he were sure that he had the emperor, the kings, and the princes firmly in hand before the council was even assembled.[7] In the course of the years—the Diet of Augsburg in 1530 seems to have been the dividing line—Luther had reluctantly come to the conclusion that the emperor could probably not be relied upon to meet this responsibility. Even in this treatise he could say: 'The emperor and the kings should take hold here. And if the pope is unwilling, they should force him, as the emperors did in the case of the four chief councils.'[8] But the facts of life in both the spiritual and the secular realm had made it clear by the end of the 1530s that the emperor would not take the lead in summoning the 'free Christian council' for which the Reformers had been appealing. In part at least, the disappointment of his hopes about the emperor accounted for Luther's

[1] *WA* 50, 522 (*WML* 5, 146).   [2] *WA* 50, 592 (*WML* 5, 226).
[3] *WA* 50, 576 (*WML* 5, 207).   [4] *WA* 50, 576 (*WML* 5, 207).
[5] *WA* 50, 581 (*WML* 5, 213).
[6] *WA* 50, 592 (*WML* 5, 226). Luther gives the date of the Council of Chalcedon as 455 rather than 451.
[7] *WA* 50, 510 (*WML* 5, 132).
[8] *WA* 50, 622 (*WML* 5, 260).

pessimism about the prospects for a council, about which we spoke at the beginning of this chapter.

Yet if there could not be an ecumenical council under the auspices of the emperor, perhaps it would be possible for the emperor and the German princes to convoke a provincial synod, one confined to the German lands.[1] More timid souls than Luther were afraid that such a council could cause a schism, although this is difficult to understand in view of the schism that had already become obvious by this time. Luther was not put off by such fear. On the contrary, he suggested the possibility that exactly the opposite could be the result of such a provincial council. If other rulers saw the accomplishments of the provincial synod, they might be persuaded to accept its decisions even though they had not been participants in it. Perhaps a council, with its 'strong voice that can be heard from afar', could accomplish what an individual theologian or preacher had been unable to accomplish. At least it was worth trying.[2] And even if this stratagem proved to be unrealistic and the emperor were unwilling to convoke a German council, Luther was already considering the possibility of a still narrower constituency. Perhaps the Reformation party could hold its own council, without the pope and his supporters.[3] Even by 1539 there were already enough problems within Protestantism itself to suggest to leaders in both the secular and spiritual realm the idea of a purely Protestant assembly. This, too, would be a council summoned and assembled under the aegis of the government. For secular rulers, 'because they are Christians, have the obligation to convoke a council'.[4]

THE PRIMARY CONCERN OF A COUNCIL

From this detailed interpretation of the authority of church councils it is clear that by 1539 Luther had developed a key to the interpretation of councils past and present that was faithful to both Catholic substance and Protestant principle. With its help he was able to make sense of the four great ecumenical councils, as well as of the 'apostolic council' spoken of in the Book of Acts; at the same time he was able both to describe and to circumscribe his

---

[1] *WA* 50, 623 (*WML* 5, 262).   [2] *WA* 50, 623 (*WML* 5, 262).
[3] *WA* 50, 514 (*WML* 5, 136); the suggestion had come from John Frederick of Saxony.
[4] *WA* 50, 623 (*WML* 5, 262).

expectations of a future ecumenical council, if indeed there was to be one.

The key was this: Every council had one primary concern, one principal doctrine, one chief issue, for the sake of which it was convoked. The decisions of the apostolic council and of the ecumenical councils on the primary concern facing them were permanently binding. Other decisions, having to do with secondary and temporary concerns, were binding only so long as the conditions that called them forth still obtained. In opposition to the exaltation of conciliar authority by his opponents, therefore, Luther claimed to be reading the councils and fathers as they had wanted to be read, namely, as interpretations of Scripture, and to be concentrating upon the doctrinal questions that constituted the primary concern and the continuing importance of the councils. Using to good advantage his new-found historical knowledge about the councils, Luther analysed the source material before him in order to identify the primary concern of each council and hence to label as peripheral all those features of conciliar legislation which, on the strength of their being incorporated into the canon law, continued to claim authority in the church.

As we have seen, Luther founded this distinction between the primary concern of a council and its peripheral legislation upon the precedent of the apostolic council. Its primary concern was expressed by Peter's insistence that no unnecessary burden be laid as a yoke upon the necks of Gentile converts to Christianity. At stake in this primary concern was the gospel itself. The other actions of the council, i.e. its fourfold prohibition, had to be seen only in the light of this primary concern. Failure to read the acts of the apostolic council in such a light could lead one to repudiate its primary concern and to canonize its temporary and external legislation. It could lead also to a distorted conception of the business of a council, the notion that a council could and should promulgate new dogmas, prescribe new good works, invent new ceremonies that were binding upon consciences, and pass new laws for the secular government. Even the apostles in council assembled had refused to be innovators, but had grounded their decision about the primary concern of the council in the precedents of the Old Testament.[1] How much less right did any subsequent

[1] WA 50, 562 (*WML* 5, 192).

council have to demand eternal obedience for its temporary legislation! The great councils of the church had been great for the very reason that each of them had paid attention to its primary concern, disposing of other issues as the peripheral problems that they were.

This, then, was Luther's basic thesis about the authority of the ecumenical councils: 'The decrees of the genuine councils must remain in force permanently, just as they have always been in force, especially the primary concerns for whose sake they are councils and are called such.'[1] The Council of Nicaea 'dealt primarily with the doctrine that Christ is true God. It was convoked for the sake of this, and for the sake of this it is a council and is called such. Besides this they also dealt with certain accidental, temporal, external, and temporary matters, which are to be regarded as purely secular, not to be put on a par with the articles of faith and not be observed as permanent law.'[2] Hence fidelity to Nicaea meant the affirmation of its primary concern, not the observance of its temporary regulations about the defection of soldiers.[3] Similarly, the doctrine of the deity of the Holy Spirit was the primary concern of the Council of Constantinople, 'the sole reason why it was held, on the basis of which the intention of the council can be understood'. Other decisions of this second council, such as those regarding the elevation of the bishop of Constantinople to the rank of patriarch, were 'not an article of faith, but an external and empirical work, which even reason can and should perform'.[4] The Council of Ephesus condemned the Nestorian heresy; its other decrees 'have to do with temporal matters. . . . These we ignore'.[5] When he came to consider the Council of Chalcedon, Luther's sources of historical information were unclear. He confessed: 'What the reason for this council was, I myself would like to learn from someone else.'[6] But his subsequent discussion of Eutyches showed that he was still operating with his key distinction between the primary concern of a council and its secondary, peripheral decrees.

Just as 'Luther's discovery and appropriation of the history of the Council of Nicaea presents the most significant single example

---

[1] *WA* 50, 563 (*WML* 5, 192-193). [2] *WA* 50, 559 (*WML* 5, 188).
[3] *WA* 50, 534 (*WML* 5, 158). [4] *WA* 50, 579 (*WML* 5, 211-212).
[5] *WA* 50, 582 (*WML* 5, 216). [6] *WA* 50, 592 (*WML* 5, 226).

of the exploitation of the historical argument and its effective use as a tentative norm',[1] it also represents the most striking instance of the juxtaposition of Catholic substance and Protestant principle in his critical reverence toward Christian tradition. As a Protestant, he subjected the authority of church councils to the authority of the word of God; as a Catholic he interpreted the word of God in conformity with the dogmas of the councils and in this sense made the councils normative. This attitude was an inconsistency according to both the traditionalists and the iconoclasts; for neither of them could see that Catholic substance and Protestant principle belong together, not only in Luther's Reformation, but in the life of the church and indeed in the very message of the New Testament.

[1] Headley, *Luther's View of Church History*, p. 164.

V

THE PRESERVATION OF CATHOLIC
LITURGICAL SUBSTANCE

O UR discussion of the critical reverence of Luther's Reformation toward tradition has concentrated so far upon the theological teachings of Luther and of the confessions that were based
upon his work. This is as it should be, both because of the prominence of theology in the debates of the Reformation and because
of the central place of doctrine in Luther's own interpretation of
the life of the church. But 'the liturgical formula . . . is almost
immortal'[1]; therefore not only doctrinal language but also liturgical
observance must be examined for its evidence about the critical
reverence of the Reformation toward the Catholic substance of its
past. In the next two chapters we shall investigate Luther's liturgical views for their bearing on this question, paying attention first
to his preservation of Catholic liturgical substance and then to his
application of the Protestant principle to the forms and practices of
liturgical worship.

THE INEVITABILITY OF FORMS

According to Luther, worship was not exclusively a matter of
forms. The literature of the past generation on Luther's view of
worship, from the splendid study by Allwohn to the excellent book
of Vilmos Vajta, has demonstrated the preponderance of theological over liturgical considerations in Luther's thought. Worship did
not mean chiefly ceremonies for Luther—on this all agree. But
that is not the same as saying that worship did not mean ceremonies
at all, which is the conclusion that many have drawn. Luther regarded ceremonies as matters of indifference theologically, as we
shall see. But he was not indifferent to ceremonies.

[1] Friedrich Heiler, *Prayer*, tr. Samuel McComb (Oxford and New York,
1932), p. 310.

Both observation and the study of Scripture had taught Luther that there was no public worship without forms. In an extended discourse on ceremonies attached to his commentary of 1520 on the fourteenth Psalm he pointed out the necessity of ceremonies in the courts of kings and in the worship of God.[1] Wherever there were relations among men, certain forms and rituals arose by means of which men sought to represent and symbolize these bonds between them. Ritual was part of the nature of man. Commenting upon Isaac's blessing of Jacob, Luther remarked: 'Ceremonies are added here, for external spiritual matters cannot be administered without external ceremonies. The five senses and the whole body have their gestures and their rituals, under which the body must live as though under some sort of mask.'[2] Luther saw that forms and rituals provided both meaning and stability in human life, and that any life beyond the most shallow had to have them.

As ritual was characteristic of life in general, so it was particularly an attribute of man's religious life. The history of Israel was a documentation of the fact that all worship, whether false or true, must take on forms in order to function. Within these set forms it operated, and it was self-deception to imagine that one could evade forms. Already in the two sacrifices of Cain and Abel, indeed, even in the prohibition of the tree of the knowledge of good and evil, 'outward worship was established'.[3] Although the only non-Christian religions about which Luther knew very much were Judaism and Islam, both of which were 'book monotheisms', he used what knowledge he did have about the history of religions to emphasize the inescapable nature of form in worship.

What is more, the revelation of God itself had to assume external, visible form to be apprehended. Since it was natural for man to require forms and signs, God had accommodated himself to that nature when he wanted to disclose himself to man. As Luther put it in his comments on Psalm 45, 'God has always made a practice of giving signs or adding miracles along with the word. And a new word is never revealed without accompanying signs.'[4] He was re-

---

[1] Adolf Allwohn, *Gottesdienst und Rechtfertigungsglaube*. Luthers Grundlegung evangelischer Liturgik bis zum Jahre 1523 (Göttingen, 1926); Vilmos Vajta, *Luther on Worship, An Interpretation*, tr. U. S. Leupold (Philadelphia, 1958). *Commentary on Psalm 14, WA* 5, 401-408.
[2] *Lectures on Genesis, WA* 43, 521.
[3] *Ibid. WA* 42, 105 (*LW* 1, 140).
[4] *Commentary on Psalm 45, WA* 40-II, 569 (*LW* 12,269).

ferring here primarily to the sacraments of the New Testament church, but the context shows that the principle of 'word plus sign' was axiomatic for him. Indeed, there are passages in Luther's writings which sound as though the incarnation itself were merely a specific instance of this general axiom that God assumes external, visible form when he wants to reveal himself. Luther's actual position would appear to the converse of this: from the disclosure of God in the incarnate Christ we must conclude that this is his manner of disclosing himself generally. In any case, however, Luther insisted that it was the way of God to use concrete forms when he wanted to speak or act.

Luther's sensitivity to the psychological importance of form and ritual also helps to explain his hostility to innovation and improvisation in the forms of worship. Although we have Christian liberty even and especially in liturgical matters, we must exercise this liberty in love. And in the *German Mass*[1] Luther warned against those liturgical stylists who felt obliged to come out with a new form just when people had grown accustomed to the old one. The purpose of form in worship was to provide the order and stability within which worship and instruction were possible. And form there would inevitably be, because that was how man was constituted, whether by the creation or by the fall or by both.

LITURGY AS ACCOMMODATION

As the history of Israel proved the necessity of forms in the worship of God, so it also provided a case study of how easily even the worship of God could be perverted and of how rare such worship really was. Luther's religious sense and his imagination combined to make him a discerning student of Old Testament history. Heinrich Bornkamm has made the telling observation that if Luther belonged to a present-day theological faculty, he would be professor of Old Testament.[2] This saturation in the Old Testament explains many things in Luther's thought that would otherwise seem enigmatic—his sacramental realism, his concrete doctrine of God, and his scepticism about the idea of an empirically pure

---

[1] *German Mass. WA* 19, 97 (*WML* 6, 182).
[2] Heinrich Bornkamm, *Luther und das Alte Testament* (Tübingen, 1948), p. 6; cf. Pelikan, *Luther the Expositor*, pp. 89-108.

church. The way God had dealt with his ancient people and the way they had responded to his dealing with them prepared Luther for the traumatic experience of watching the impact of the gospel upon Germany.

But Chapter II has shown that, unlike many others who have discovered that the company of those who name the name of Christ is not made up of pure saints, Luther was not moved by this discovery to either cynicism or sectarianism. It caused him instead to ponder the pedagogical function of such casual church membership. The broad mass of people connected with the churches were not very serious about their Christian profession. In the early years of his reforming activity Luther believed that such people had been the victims of poor preaching in the medieval church and that they, together with the Jews, would come to the knowledge of the truth now that the gospel once more had free course.[1] Experience showed that this expectation was false. In the *German Mass* Luther complains that people have become as lackadaisical about services in the vernacular as they used to be about Latin services.[2] He therefore sought to use liturgical forms and other pedagogical devices as means for meeting people where they were and for bringing them to a deeper awareness of the meaning of Christian profession. The state church, as one observer has put it, provided Luther with a mission field;[3] and the liturgy provided him with a framework for his missionary preaching.

These were the people, as Luther says in the *German Mass*, who 'stand around and gape in the hope of seeing something novel'.[4] It was for the sake of such people that what he calls the 'child's play'[5] of the Passover lamb had been instituted in the Old Testament. The sacrifices were 'a sort of pedagogical exercise' for the people of the Old Testament.[6] God had ordained them for a while 'so that this uneducated nation must be drawn by some sort of show to the true worship and knowledge of God'.[7] But through

---

[1] Cf. Armas K. E. Holmio, *The Lutheran Reformation and the Jews* (Hancock, 1949), pp. 89-119.
[2] *German Mass*, *WA* 19, 112 (*WML* 6, 185).
[3] Gerhard Hilbert, *Ecclesiola in ecclesia*. Luthers Anschauungen von Volkskirche und Freiwilligkeitskirche in ihrer Bedeutung für die Gegenwart (Leipzig, 1920), p. 11.
[4] *German Mass*, *WA* 19, 74 (*WML* 6, 172).
[5] *Sermons on the Gospel of St John*, *WA* 46, 676 (*LW* 22, 162).
[6] *Lectures on Genesis*, *WA* 43, 368.
[7] *Ibid. WA* 44, 173.

such ceremonies, as preserved for example in the household of Ishmael after his expulsion, 'some members of his household and his children came to a knowledge of true piety'.[1] And therefore 'it is not right to minimize the ceremonial things of the Old Testament . . . . In addition to serving as the means by which God distinguished his people from the other nations and by which the people testified to their obedience, these services were also symbols of the future sacrifice of Christ, by which the people were to be reminded of their future redemption.'[2] The external liturgical order of the Old Testament cultus, therefore, was the training ground on which God met the people of Israel at their level and on which the true believers among the Israelites learned the devotion and spiritual hope through which they were saved.

Now all of that belonged to the Old Testament, and with the coming of Christ there were no more compulsory forms of worship, as we shall see in Chapter VI. But a persistent theme of Luther's exegesis of the Old Testament is not only the parallel between the true Israel and the true believer in every age, but also the parallel between the physical Israel and Protestant Germany. What Ferdinand Kattenbusch calls the ambiguity in Luther's view of the church[3] expresses itself liturgically in Luther's reluctance, voiced in the *Formula of the Mass*,[4] to throw the communion open to all comers who belonged to the external fellowship of the church, and in his suggestion immediately thereafter that the communicants gather in a special place in the church building, to be seen by both those who were communing and those who were not, since participation in the sacrament was a 'part of the confession by which they confess in the sight of God and angels and men that they are Christians'.[5] In this way the exclusive-devotional and inclusive-pedagogical functions of the liturgy would both be preserved. And the forms of worship would be accommodated to the present stage of religious development among the people.

[1] *Lectures on Genesis, WA* 43, 372. On the liturgical ideas of Luther's *Lectures on Genesis,* cf. Pelikan, *Luther the Expositor,* pp. 99-100.
[2] *Commentary on Psalm* 51, *WA* 40-11, 454-455 (*LW* 12, 398-399).
[3] Ferdinand Kattenbusch, *Die Doppelschichtigkeit in Luthers Kirchenbegriff* (Gotha, 1928).
[4] *Formula of the Mass, WA* 12, 215 (*WML* 6, 94). Cf. also his Large Catechism, Part V, par. 55-74, *Bek.* 719-722 (*BC* 453-455).
[5] *Formula of the Mass, WA* 12, 216 (*WML* 6, 95).

WHAT IS BIBLICAL IN WORSHIP?

One of the interpretations of the Reformation enumerated in Chapter I is the idea that it replaced the authority of the church and of tradition with the authority of the Bible. In liturgy this meant sweeping out all the accretions of later centuries and restoring the simple and unliturgical worship of the New Testament.[1] This stereotype has just enough truth in it to make it plausible. But, as Chapter III has pointed out, even in matters of doctrine it is an oversimplification to say that Luther's Reformation replaced the authority of the church and of tradition with the authority of the Bible. And in liturgical matters this theory does not apply at all.

For in liturgical matters, as Luther insisted in his *Formula of the Mass*, Scripture had not defined the forms to be used.[2] It had left these matters open and permitted the church to adapt them to the changing conditions and needs of men. In other words, not some pristine deposit of primitive Christian customs, but the historical adaptation and development of Christian usage through the centuries were to shape liturgical practice. This did not mean that New Testament worship had been without forms, so that subsequent liturgical development was an addition to it; it meant that the forms used in New Testament worship were not binding. 'We maintain', wrote Luther against the heavenly prophets in 1525, 'that it is not necessary to do everything that Christ did or to omit everything that he omitted. . . . Therefore we will not be bound by any example, even by that of Christ, much less by that of other saints, unless there is a word of God present that commands us to do so.' He did not want, as he put it, 'to follow the example of Christ so rigidly'.[3] Some of his opponents naïvely equated Scripture and the word of God, and then proceeded on the assumption that the substitution of Scriptural for traditional materials in the liturgy was the proper approach to the problem of liturgical form.

How completely Luther rejected this naïve assumption becomes especially evident in his own liturgical reforms—in his conservative *Formula of the Mass*, but also in his less traditional *German Mass*. In fact, it is in the *German Mass* that he not only reversed the order of words of institution and Lord's Prayer, but also em-

---

[1] See pp. 21-22 above.
[2] *Formula of the Mass*, WA 12, 219 (WA 6, 99).
[3] *Against the Heavenly Prophets*, WA 18, 114-115 (LW 40, 131-132).

ployed a paraphrase of the Lord's Prayer in the form of an exhortation.[1] This paraphrase may be evaluated in various ways.
Liturgically it does seem to leave a great deal to be desired, and it
is fortunate that it was dropped. But it is illustrative of Luther's
attitude toward the question of Scriptural forms in the liturgy, in
contrast to the ideas of his opponents. Even so precious and central a piece of Scripture as the Our Father did not have to be re-
cited in the form in which Scripture contains it, but could be
paraphrased. Similarly, it was permissible to retain in the liturgy
those elements, as, for example, the *Gloria Patri*, which were not
indeed Scriptural in their exact words, but which were in harmony
with the message of Scripture. Loyalty to Scripture did not, therefore, produce liturgical radicalism in Luther's case. The attitude
it did produce is well summarized by Theodor Knolle: 'The worship which God has instituted is the basis of external usage. The
development of forms connected with that worship, wrought by
the Holy Spirit, is a given element granted by God, which dare not
be frivolously or arbitrarily set aside.'[2]

WORSHIP AS SYMBOLIC ACTION

Into the myriad forms and symbols of the Catholic substance,
Luther's Reformation sought to put the centrality of the Christian
proclamation, of what in modern theology has come to be called
the *kerygma*. With this stress upon the means of grace Luther com-
batted the various perversions and dangers to which Christian
piety, Christian theology, but also Christian liturgy were subject.
Anyone who worried about predestination was counselled to take
refuge in the means of grace, and anyone who became proud of his
own ideas needed to be reminded of his baptism, through which
his new birth had come.[3] Not on the general symbolic nature of the
world, but on those specific actions to which God had bound the
church and on the promise of his grace was the Christian faith based
and the Christian message proclaimed.

But true to his genius, Luther refused to let this fundamental

---

[1] *German Mass, WA* 19, 95-96 (*WML* 6, 180-181).

[2] Theodor Knolle, 'Luthers Deutsche Messe und die Rechtfertigungslehre',
Luther-Jahrbuch, X (1928), 185. Cf. Arthur Carl Piepkorn, *The Survival of the
Historic Vestments in the Lutheran Church After* 1555 (2nd ed.; Saint Louis,
1958), on the subsequent history.

[3] See the passages collected in Elert, *The Structure of Lutheranism*, pp. 117-
126.

insight into the priority of the means of grace blind him to the possible significance and value of symbolic actions in the life and worship of the church. The most obvious example in his reform of the mass is probably the elevation of the body and blood of Christ. Whatever may have been its original significance, the elevation had come to be associated in the popular mind and in some parts of medieval theology with the idea of the mass as a propitiatory sacrifice which the church offered to God. That idea was, of course, repugnant to Luther and is one of the principal targets of his polemics against the Roman mass. Nevertheless, he was able to distinguish between the act of elevation itself and the interpretation that had been placed upon it. In the *Formula of the Mass*, therefore, he advocated the retention of the act of elevation for the sake of the weak, adding the hope that vernacular sermons would teach them what it meant.[1] By the time of the *German Mass* he was ready to go more deeply into the possible symbolism of the elevation, interpreting it to mean that the proclamation of the word was a way of remembering and elevating Christ and that the reception of the sacrament was a way of confessing and adoring him.[2] It was fitting, then, that this symbolic act be retained; a few years later it also served as a testimony against those who denied the real presence.[3] Near the end of Luther's life the practice was dropped from the liturgy of the congregation in Wittenberg, apparently with his approval.[4] But the principle of symbolic actions as representations of what the church believed and stood for was a consistent part of his liturgical teaching.

There is an amusing and instructive illustration of this in Luther's sermons of 1537 on St John.[5] It is an anecdote which Luther seems to have read in the *Lives of the Fathers*. There was once a man, Luther says, who refused to bend his knee with the congregation when the phrase *Et homo factus est* was chanted in the Nicene Creed. Thereupon the devil appeared and knocked him

[1] *Formula of the Mass*, WA 12, 212-213 (*WML* 6, 90); cf. also the quotation cited, *WML* 6, 108, note 92.

[2] *German Mass*, WA 19, 99-100 (*WML* 6, 183). From his journey through Italy in 1510 Luther remembered that the Ambrosian Liturgy of Milan did not include the elevation; cf. his *Brief Confession on the Blessed Sacrement*, WA 54, 166.

[3] Cf. the comments, *WML* 6, 188, note 39.

[4] Cf. Luther to George Buchholzer, December 4, 1539, *WA Br* 8, 626 and note 10.

[5] *Sermons on the Gospel of St John*, WA 46, 627 (*LW* 22, 105-106).

off his feet, saying that he should realize that he belongs to a race which has been more highly honoured than any other creature by the incarnation and that kneeling is the least he can do to express his gratitude for such an honour.[1] It was proper, Luther said, that this phrase be sung with special long notes and that Protestant congregations also kneel during its singing, to symbolize their gratitude at the honour paid to humanity when the word was made flesh.[2] Thus also in commenting upon kneeling in the Old Testament, Luther pointed out the propriety of kneeling at the Lord's Supper.[3]

Luther was quite aware of the abuses to which such acts were subject, as Chapter VI will document. He realized, as he once put it at table, that 'the ornamentation, decoration, and vestments which are used at the mass together with other ceremonies in the papacy were taken partly from Moses and partly from paganism. When the clergy saw that the people were being drawn by public shows to the market or the theatre and enjoyed this while the churches stood barren and empty, they were prompted to set up such shows and spectacles in the churches, too.'[4] But he added significantly: 'This would be fine if the superstition had not been added to it.' For in themselves such symbolic gestures were an excellent expression of the church's meaning and message.

THE CONTINUITY OF WORSHIP

Luther's Reformation was intended to meet certain problems in the life of the church, but in so doing it also managed to raise other problems. Among the problems which it raised, one has become very prominent in present-day discussion among the churches: the problem of the continuity of the church through the centuries. In any such discussion, however, it is important to distinguish that which effects or guarantees the continuity of the church from that which merely represents or symbolizes that continuity. As Chapter II has indicated, Luther's Reformation took the

---

[1] On the history of this custom, cf. Josef Andreas Jungmann, *Missarum Sollemnia. Eine genetische Erklärung der römischen Messe* (3rd ed.; Vienna, 1952), I, 477, note 63, and 596, note 17.
[2] *Sermons on the Gospel of St John, WA* 46, 624-625 (*LW* 22, 103).
[3] *Lectures on Genesis, WA* 44, 685; cf. Yngve Brilioth, *Eucharistic Faith and Practice Evangelical and Catholic*, tr. A. G. Hebert (London, 1953), p. 141, pp. 146-147.
[4] *WA Ti* 4, 14-15 (No. 3926).

position that the apostolic succession of ordaining bishops may symbolize the continuity and the apostolic character of the church, but that it did not guarantee it; and for Luther's Reformation the same was true of liturgy.

Nevertheless, given the factors that did guarantee continuity, the liturgy was one of the ways by which the church could symbolize and bear witness to that continuity. It was not his purpose, Luther explained at the beginning of his *Formula of the Mass*, to do away with the liturgy altogether, but to purge the existing liturgy of the abominations that had been added to it.[1] But immediately thereafter he hastened to point out that the 'additions of the early fathers' did not belong to this category, but were commendable and should be retained; such was, for example, the Kyrie.[2] These 'additions' he kept, and thereby he pointed to the continuity between the church of the Reformation and the people of God in previous centuries. The most conspicuous expression of that continuity with the past—and an expression in a class by itself —was the liturgical use of the Old Testament. Luther expressly provided for the use of Old Testament readings in the vesper service,[3] and his own use of it for preaching at various services was part of his desire to declare the oneness of the faith of the people of God throughout the generations. The Psalter, especially, was to be prominent in the service; in the *Formula of the Mass* Luther suggested a return to the usage of earlier centuries, when an entire Psalm was used rather than the few sentences of the introit.[4] That suggestion illustrates both ways in which liturgy could manifest the continuity of the church: the use of ancient forms and the use of the Old Testament.

THE CHURCH YEAR

Both the *Formula of the Mass* and the *German Mass* retained the church year with its festivals. In the *Formula of the Mass*[5] Luther explained that the congregation in Wittenberg had made the festivals of the Virgin Mary festivals of Christ, as they had originally been. Luther's own activity in the pulpit suggests that despite his

---

[1] *Formula of the Mass, WA* 12, 206 (*WML* 6, 84-85).
[2] *Ibid. WA* 12, 206-207 (*WML* 6, 85).
[3] *German Mass, WA* 19, 80 (*WML* 6, 178).
[4] *Formula of the Mass, WA* 12, 208-209 (*WML* 6, 86).
[5] *Ibid. WA* 12, 209 (*WML* 6, 86-87).

strictures upon saints' days, he actually continued the custom of commemorating the lives of the saints and of other men of God, especially men spoken of in the Bible. Here Luther described the careers of such men of God in order to give his hearers an awareness of the grace of God, by which these men had been constituted as saints and by which the experiences of these hearers could participate in the communion of saints.[1] But the sequence of the traditional festivals of Christ was retained so that the saving events in his life, death, and resurrection might be the framework for the church's life of worship. Luther went so far in the *German Mass* as to advocate not only the fixed festivals of the church year and the fixed lessons, but even the use of a fixed postil.[2] Recognizing that not every minister could be trusted to expound the lesson for the day properly, much less to select and to explain a free text or an entire book in a series of sermons, Luther preferred plagiarism to irresponsible ranting.

The rationale behind this retention of the church year became explicit in Luther's Torgau sermon of 1533 on the second article of the Apostles' Creed. When it comes to being a Christian, says Luther, 'we do not want to discuss ourselves at all, what we have or have not done, or what we should still do or refrain from doing. But we want to discuss the ground of our faith. We want to come out of ourselves and to go into this article, in order to learn what this Man has done for us. We want to look at that in sequence. For these words [of the creed] are set down in a fine and orderly way, almost like a calendar through the entire year, in which we celebrate all the feasts of Christ the Lord. . . . It is also proper and necessary that the people be held outwardly to special days in the year, set aside for the exposition and proclamation of these items in their sequence.'[3] In other words, Christians at worship were to get out of themselves and their own subjective feelings, and they were to be grounded in those objective events of the life of Christ which the creed confessed and which the church year celebrated. For true Christian subjectivity, as Luther stressed con-

---

[1] An excellent illustration is Luther's *Commentary on the Magnificat*, *WA* 7, 538-604 (*LW* 21, 297-358).
[2] *German Mass*, *WA* 19, 95 (*WML* 6, 180). Otherwise, Luther said, 'everyone preaches his own whims and instead of the gospel and its exposition we shall again have sermons on blue ducks'.
[3] *On Jesus Christ. A Sermon*, *WA* 37, 48-49.

tinually, was created and sustained by the proclamation and the remembrance of those objective events. And such proclamation was the chief reason, according to Luther, why the church fathers had established the observance of Sunday, Easter, Pentecost, and other festivals.

LITURGY AND NATURE

The primary purpose of the liturgy was to express the inner life of the church, to celebrate the grace of God as it had come in the person and work of Christ, and to communicate that grace to the believers through word and sacrament: this Luther recognized with clarity and consistency. He would not let considerations of tradition or of aesthetics deflect him from his recognition, and this has made him the despair of all aestheticists ever since. Yet he had a highly developed aesthetic sense, though one may not be willing to go as far as Hans Preuss has done and call Luther an 'artist'.[1] Nevertheless, he had deep sensitivities which come to expression in his liturgical theories.

Liturgy was to be related to the world of culture. Luther had occasion to reflect on this view when he was under pressure to compose a mass in the vernacular. That pressure was increased through the composition of German masses by several others. One of the most interesting and most impressive of these is the German mass of Luther's *bête noire*, Thomas Münzer. It is in many ways a beautiful piece of work, liturgically superior to Luther's *German Mass*; and it may well have provided a provocation for the composition of Luther's.[2] But in response to the pressure Luther replied in 1525: 'I should like to have a German mass today, and I am in the process of making one. But I should like it to have a genuinely German style. It is very well to have the Latin text translated and the Latin tone or notes retained, but the result does not sound authentic or proper. Both the text and the notes, the accent, the manner, and the gestures must proceed from the real mother tongue and voice. Otherwise it is all an imitation, like the behavior of the apes.'[3] As he wrote to his friend Hausmann in the

---

[1] Hans Preuss, *Martin Luther der Künstler* (Gütersloh, 1931).

[2] Cf. Karl Schulz, *Thomas Müntzers liturgische Bestrebungen* (Gotha, n.d.), p. 30: 'One must say that Münzer is more conservative than any other liturgist of the Reformation period'.

[3] *Against the Heavenly Prophets*, WA 18, 123 (LW 40, 141).

same year, he was not satisfied to superimpose German words on Latin tones.[1] He recognized, with the profound intuition for language that was one of his greatest gifts, that the cadences of German and the structure of its sentences did not suit a style of music that had been developed for the Latin of the Vulgate.[2] He wanted liturgy to be truly expressive of the best that the German language had to offer, rather than a mere imitation of the Latin liturgy.

Liturgy was also related to the world of nature. Luther had less occasion to contemplate what Peter Brunner has called 'the cosmological setting' of Christian liturgy,[3] but as a student and observer of nature he did consider the relation between man's praise of God and the praises offered by the other creatures in the world of nature. That relation is the theme of Psalm 148. And in a striking passage in his *Commentary on Genesis* Luther applied that psalm to the story of the tree of the knowledge of good and evil. This tree 'was a church, to which Adam and his posterity were to come. After eating from the tree of life, he was to preach God and to praise him for entrusting him with the rule of all the creatures on earth. Thus Psalm 148 and 149 set forth a sort of liturgy of this thanksgiving, where the sun, the moon, the stars, the fish, and the dragons are all commanded to praise the Lord.'[4] Here Luther caught the vision of man at worship surrounded not only by the saints and the angels, but by all his fellow creatures. They shared his divine origin, now they shared his corruption, and some day they would share his glory.

That vision is part of the general outlook on worship and liturgy which belongs to 'Catholic substance'. Here Luther showed himself to be the heir of the broad heritage of Christian culture and churchmanship. All that was noble and good about the word 'Catholic' found an echo in him. Despite his estrangement from Rome, Luther remained a Catholic all his life, and his liturgical views and productions are evidence of this continuing Catholicity.

[1] Luther to Nicholas Hausmann, March 26, 1525, *WA Br* 3, 462.
[2] Cf. William Beare, *Latin Verse and European Song*. A study in Accent and Rhythm (London, 1957), pp. 32-42, 103-109.
[3] Peter Brunner, 'Zur Lehre vom Gottesdienst der im Namen Jesu . . . versammelten Gemeinden', *Leiturgia*, ed. Karl Ferdinand Muller and Walter Blankenburg (Kassel, 1954), III, 168-180.
[4] *Lectures on Genesis*, *WA* 42, 80 (*LW* 1, 105).

VI

THE PROTESTANT PRINCIPLE
IN WORSHIP

THE critical reverence of Luther's Reformation toward tradition led it to affirm both Catholic substance and Protestant principle in its philosophy of worship. As Chapter V has shown, there was much in the tradition of Catholic liturgy that Luther's Reformation felt obliged to retain and defend. Yet a picture of Luther's liturgical views based solely upon his retention of Catholic substance would be a Lutheran counterpart to the Anglo-Catholic reinterpretation of the English Reformation and would be an even greater distortion.[1] For Luther was truly Protestant in his theories of worship. Nor was he a Catholic on some questions and a Protestant on others; in fact, he was both a Catholic and a Protestant in his interpretation of the very same issues. To describe this juxtaposition in Luther's liturgical thought, this chapter will discuss the same issues analysed in the preceding chapter, summarizing the Protestant side of Luther's liturgical thought.

FORMS OF WORSHIP INDIFFERENT

Although Luther consistently recognized the need of forms in the public worship of the church, his work as a reformer led him to stress the change which the coming of the gospel had effected in liturgical forms. The Old Testament might indeed be proof of the principle that forms were inevitable, but it would not do to argue from this that Old Testament legislation regarding the forms of worship was still valid. For the coming of the gospel had repealed that legislation; and as Luther read the Old Testament, it itself had foreseen such a repeal. From the twenty-fifth chapter of

[1] Cf. Yngve Brilioth, *The Anglican Revival*. Studies in the Oxford Movement (London, 1933), pp. 180ff.

Isaiah the true worship of the New Testament was evident: 'not sacrifices, not the building of temples, not masses, etc., but the praise of God and the fear of God. . . . For that fear of God is a worship located not in vestments or other outward pomp, but in the heart.'[1] And Psalm 110 taught him that 'the old form of worship stopped of itself when Christ came to create a new form of service and new servants of God through the gospel'.[2] One of the chief differences between Old and New Testament lay in this very principle, that in the New Testament church the forms of public worship had become a matter of indifference.

Luther found it necessary to emphasize this vigorously because his Roman Catholic opponents sought to enforce their liturgical regulations in the church and were using the Old Testament in substantiation of their position. Against them he set the declaration of his beloved epistle to the Galatians that Christians were free from the whole Mosaic law, especially from the ceremonial law.[3] Therefore Christians had the right to revise and to change liturgical forms, and it was wrong to legislate for them in this area. As he defended against his left wing opponents the freedom to use such forms, so he defended against his Roman Catholic opponents the freedom to dispense with such forms. He claimed to discern that in spite of completely different external appearances, these two groups were very much alike; that was why he called the Anabaptists 'the new monks'.[4] The ancient fathers, who had invented many of these forms, had not intended to bind men's consciences with them. But now men were being required to conform to particular rites and ceremonies, not prescribed by God. This was legalism, and throughout his writings Luther never tired of asserting his Protestant principle that New Testament believers had freedom in liturgical matters.

So pervasive was the influence of that legalism that Luther was constrained to warn against the legalistic adoption of his own liturgical forms. At the very beginning of his *German Mass* he made it clear that the work was not to be used as liturgical legislation or as a snare for consciences. The circumstances and conditions of Christian congregations were so varied that it was not possible,

[1] *Commentary on Isaiah, WA* 25, 168.
[2] *Commentary on Psalm* 110, *WA* 41, 152 (*LW* 13, 293).
[3] *Formula of the Mass, WA* 12, 214 (*WML* 6, 92).
[4] See my note, *LW* 24, 13, note 3, and the cross references given there.

even if it were permissible, to legislate any sort of liturgical uniformity. And at the end of the *German Mass* he reiterated the warning.[1] When any liturgical form, including this one, had outlived its
usefulness, it should be discarded. In and of itself it had no value,
and it was wrong to ascribe to human forms a value and binding
power which properly belonged only to the institution of Christ.
The unity of the church was not to be found in a uniformity of
rites instituted by men: this declaration of the Augsburg Confession, discussed at some length earlier,[2] summarizes Luther's
Protestant principle, in opposition to the attempt to absolutize a
form—any form, whether ancient or modern, Roman Catholic or
Lutheran.

COMMITTED AND FREE

Luther's churchmanship, of which we spoke briefly in Chapter
V, was an effort to come to terms with the realities of church life
and to interpret those realities in the light of the word of God. One
of the realities with which he had to come to terms was the evident
fact of various degrees or levels of seriousness in the Christian profession of church members. Recognition of that fact impelled him,
as we have seen, to relate liturgical forms to a low level of Christianity among some who claimed to be Christian. But he was also
concerned about the significance of liturgical forms for those who
did take their Christian profession seriously. There are some
passages in Luther's writings, especially in those directed against
the papacy, that speak as though the churches of the Reformation
had replaced the casual church membership of Roman Catholicism with the deep spirituality of evangelical faith. Thus Luther
could speak of 'two classes of Christians' and mean thereby the
two parties in Western Christendom.[3]

But in his more thoughtful and candid expressions on the subject Luther was a man of very few illusions about the depth of
evangelical spirituality among the general Lutheran public.[4]
Where such spirituality did appear, however, as a result of the
purified proclamation of the gospel, he wanted to be ready for it—

---

[1] *German Mass, WA* 19, 72 (*WML* 6, 170); *WA* 19, 113 (*WML* 6, 185-186).
[2] See pp. 30-31 above.
[3] *Sermons on the Gospel of St John, WA* 46, 707-708 (*LW* 22, 197).
[4] See the materials collected in the book of Hilbert referred to, p. 80, note 3
above.

ready also liturgically. Although he stood within the form of church-state relations that had begun to emerge between the Diet of Worms in 1521 and the Diet of Augsburg in 1530 and although he was willing to operate within that form, Luther was well aware of the cleavage between this and the ideal of Christian congregational life. What he sought was a form of Christian profession and Christian worship that could, within the structure of the state church, provide for that more intimate and more intense assumption of mutual responsibility which belonged to the New Testament ideal of the church. Most of Luther's statements on this subject are extremely guarded; some of them are certainly ironic, since he consistently refused to classify himself among those who are 'the real Christians'.[1] From his days in the monastery he knew only too well the dangers of a sect that set itself apart from the common herd, and his experience with the left wing Protestants corroborated this.[2]

Nevertheless, when one has laid down all these strictures and qualifications—as one must to be fair to the evidence—one is still forced to recognize that he drew a distinction between the casual and the earnest worshiper. In the *German Mass* he envisages a time when such earnest worshippers will be able to organize themselves for the practice of their sacramental life, for instruction, discipline, and mutual aid.[3] The important feature of this ideal for the question of liturgical form is that, according to Luther, the need for ritual was in inverse ratio to the earnestness of Christian faith. The more serious a group of people became about their Christian profession, the less liturgy they needed. For elaborate liturgical forms were a concession to those who were unable to be content with the simple minimum that Christ had prescribed. That simple minimum was a restoration of the true worship of God as it was practiced by the patriarchs. Luther's *Commentary on Genesis* describes the 'very bare, pure, and simple worship and religion which God gave to Adam, in which there was nothing tedious or elaborate'. It also extols the simple worship of Abraham, which was devoid of decorations and which concentrated on the word of

---

[1] *German Mass, WA* 19, 73 (*WML* 6, 171); on the significance of such statements, cf. Holl, *Luther*, pp. 418-419.
[2] See, for example, *Lectures on Galatians, WA* 40, 603-604 (*LW* 26, 396-397).
[3] *German Mass, WA* 19, 75 (*WML* 6, 173).

God and sound preaching.[1] For such a simplified liturgy Luther suggested that the celebrant in the mass should face the people during the consecration, a suggestion that has also come from spokesmen for the liturgical movement in Roman Catholicism.[2]

When and if it became possible for such a group of earnest Christians to be formed, the traditional ritual of the church was not to be permitted to interfere with their free worship. Meanwhile, people were to be content with the ritual, purged as it had been of the accretions of the late Middle Ages. Recent studies of American denominationalism would raise questions about the relevance of Luther's views for a church system which professes to be based upon the voluntary association of Christian believers (as Luther's ideal church of the future was to be), but which nevertheless produces a casual piety in the majority of its members (as Luther accused the Roman Catholic Church of doing and as he admitted that his own church was also doing).[3] Especially because of the struggles of the church against totalitarian governments, churchmen on the Continent have had occasion in recent decades to reflect on this problem in Reformation theology.[4] But in neither Europe nor America have the liturgical implications of the issue received much attention.

CENTRALITY OF SCRIPTURE

If one had to name Luther's greatest single contribution to liturgy and worship, it would be neither his *Formula of the Mass*, nor his *German Mass*, nor even his hymns for congregational singing. It would be his recovery of the role of the sermon in the service.[5] Liturgically, Luther was not of one mind about where he should put the sermon in the order of the communion service. Tradition was on the side of placing it after the creed, but Luther toyed with the idea of assigning it more prominence by placing it

[1] *Lectures on Genesis*, *WA* 42, 80-81 (*LW* 1, 106); *WA* 42, 500 (*LW* 2, 333-334).
[2] *German Mass*, *WA* 19, 80 (*WML* 6, 178); cf. Ernest Koenker, *The Liturgical Renaissance in the Roman Catholic Church*, pp. 65-67.
[3] Cf. Sidney E. Mead, *The Lively Experiment. The Shaping of Christianity in America* (New York, 1963), pp. 113ff.
[4] See, for example, Wilhelm Maurer, *Pfarrerrecht und Bekenntnis*. Ueber die bekenntnismäszige Grundlage eines Pfarrerrechts in der evangelisch-lutherischen Kirche (Berlin, 1957).
[5] See Bo Giertz, 'The Meaning and Task of the Sermon in the Framework of the Liturgy', *The Unity of the Church* (Rock Island, 1957), pp. 133-141.

before the mass as an invitation issued to the unbelievers in the wilderness.[1] But whatever place it was to occupy in the order of service, Luther wanted to restore the proclamation to the mass. So central was the proclamation in his thinking that he could go so far as to say in the *German Mass* that 'the principal purpose of any service of worship is the teaching and preaching of the word of God.'[2] There are many other passages in Luther's works which would exonerate him of the charge that he looked upon worship as primarily didactic and therefore turned the Christian liturgy into a 'dry mass'.[3] But he did maintain the decisive importance of biblical preaching and teaching within Christian worship.

Therefore he criticized the liturgies developed during the history of the church on the ground that they had frequently made Scripture peripheral in worship. For one thing, they had separated word and sacrament, assigning the weight to the Lord's Supper. Sometimes Luther based his criticism of this on the grounds that 'more importance attaches to the proclamation than to the mass, since the prophet [in Psalm 68] instructs us to proclaim the glory of the Lord but makes no mention of the mass. . . . For all the masses stacked together are worthless without the word of God. However, today this order has been reversed miserably.'[4] But even when he took a more balanced view of the relative importance of word and sacrament, Luther objected to the elimination of preaching from the liturgy. The liturgy had assigned so much prominence to other features that preaching has no opportunity to receive the attention it deserved. Many of these features were innocuous in themselves—chants, commemorations, and the like. Some, like the Lord's Supper, were even divinely commanded. But all of them depended upon Scriptural warrant for their validity. In fact, the retention of the elevation, discussed in Chapter V, depended upon Scriptural preaching, which was to explain what the elevation symbolized.[5]

In addition to these permissible or even required parts of the service that had to be related to Scripture, Luther also gave atten-

---

[1] *Formula of the Mass, WA* 12, 211 (*WML* 6, 88).
[2] *German Mass, WA* 19, 78 (*WML* 6, 176).
[3] Cf. Albrecht Ritschl, 'Die Entstehung der lutherischen Kirche', *Gesammelte Aufsätze* (Freiburg and Leipzig, 1893), pp. 201ff.
[4] *Commentary on Psalm 68, WA* 8, 26-27 (*LW* 13, 27).
[5] See p. 84 above and the accompanying notes.

tion to other additions that had to be eliminated in the name of Scripture. It was on the basis of Scriptural warrant and command that Luther's *Formula of the Mass* finally decided to defy the tradition of administering only one element in the Lord's Supper.[1] Insisting upon this tradition, he said, was tantamount to insisting upon the word of man instead of the word of God.[2] The main liturgical reform necessitated by this loyalty to Scripture was the elimination of the canon of the mass. In the *Formula of the Mass* he called it a 'mutilated' and an 'abominable' thing,[3] and two years later he published a treatise *On the Abomination of the Silent Mass*, which was aimed directly at the canon.[4] The reason for his violence in denouncing it was the prominence it seemed to assign to the idea of propitiatory sacrifice. Although Luther did have a doctrine of sacrifice in the eucharist, it was radically different from that which he saw in some medieval theologians.[5] Instead of teaching from the Scriptures that the death of Christ was the only sacrifice on which to rely, they obscured the message of Scripture by their view of sacrifice. Therefore the canon of the mass had to be eliminated, and a new liturgy had to be devised that would assure the centrality of Scripture and of its message.

POMP AND SUPERSTITION

The liturgical tradition which Luther was attempting to reform by the use of the Protestant principle had concentrated much of its attention upon the details of liturgical correctness and their supposed symbolism. Books had been prepared for the clergy to prescribe the gyrations and manipulations of the various men in the chancel and to explain what was thought to be meant by all this.[6] That a great deal of the symbolism was invented only after the fact and had nothing to do with the origin of the action is obvious. Equally obvious is the concentration of many, among both clergy and laity, upon this sanctified spectacle at the expense of everything else.

[1] Cf. the material collected in p. 112, note 1 below.
[2] *Formula of the Mass*, *WA* 12, 217-218 (*WML* 6, 96).
[3] *Ibid. WA* 12, 207 (*WML* 6, 85).
[4] *WA* 18, 22-36.
[5] Cf. Pelikan, *Luther the Expositor*, pp. 237-254.
[6] See the brief but authoritative discussion of the late medieval development in Jungmann, *op. cit.*, I, 168-186.

Luther's scorn for such 'chancel prancers' was exquisite. 'Everything they do is animated by a concern not for teaching or exhorting, but for performing. This is what they are after, and this they call worship. For them it is enough to have read or chanted or roared in a certain way. It does not even enter their mind to ask what had been read and chanted, or why it had been read and chanted.'[1] Then he went on to describe the minute attention which the monks gave to pauses, accents, and modulations in their chanting. For them 'this is the ultimate purpose of divine worship'. Thus the clergy had been so beguiled by the prescriptions of liturgical minutiae that they paid no attention to their primary task. This shift of importance among the clergy had its counterpart among the people. People very easily came to believe that all of this was more important than the word and preaching. Once more Luther drew upon his knowledge of the Old Testament, especially upon the prophetic tradition, to point out the abuses to which ritual was suceptible in folk piety. Not only did the example of pagans produce pagan ritual among the Israelites, as in the case of the golden calf, but even forms of worship which had originally been prescribed by God became idolatrous when the Israelites stressed the sign at the expense of the thing signified, the picture at the expense of the reality. Luther's exposition of the third chapter of John described the way a divine blessing like the serpent in the wilderness could become demonic when it lost its 'transparency' and men looked at it rather than through it.[2]

In the *Formula of the Mass*, therefore, Luther attacked the superstitious attitude that acted as though the validity and efficacy of the sacrament were dependent upon the vestments of the celebrant.[3] What difference did it make in preaching if the preacher was not wearing the proper vestments?[4] Although the symbolism of vestments, like that of kneeling or the sign of the cross, was true and noble, the ever-present danger was that people would begin to ascribe to the symbol an efficacy it did not possess. One of the chief elements in what Vossberg has called 'Luther's criticism of all religion'[5] was this insight into what we today should call 'fetish-

---

[1] *On Monastic Vows*, WA 8, 621.
[2] *Sermons on the Gospel of St John*, WA 47, 72-74 (*LW* 22, 346-347).
[3] *Formula of the Mass*, WA 12, 214-215 (*WML* 6, 93).
[4] *Sermons on Deuteronomy*, WA 28, 602-603.
[5] Herbert Vossberg, *Luthers Kritik aller Religion* (Leipzig, 1922).

ism', which invested certain objects with the power of that for which they stood; the relics of the saints were the principal such objects in his day. It seems to have been Luther's judgment that fetishism was inevitable, as inevitable as the symbolic forms to which it attached itself. But as a Protestant in the line of the prophets, Luther spoke out against the superstitious and idolatrous devotion of the people to the symbols of Christian worship as though they contained little pieces of God.

Luther objected on another score as well. He saw that people not only ascribed magical powers to symbolic actions, but that they were also tempted to heap ceremony upon ceremony. As William of Occam, in his famous 'razor', declared that abstract ideas were not to be multiplied beyond necessity, so Luther denounced the pomp and show to which Christian ritual could so easily degenerate unless it was carefully guarded; this he did in the name of the simplicity of Christianity, of its message and its worship. This accent may have become less prominent after his controversy of the 1520s,[1] but Luther was devoted throughout his life to the emphasis upon the simple worship of primitive Christianity in both word and sacrament. Here, too, the Protestant principle in his thought is evident. Although he retained many later forms of worship and recognized the value of their symbolism, he was fundamentally suspicious of form for form's sake and of the pomp which it produced. And when as in the papacy, this liturgical pomp was combined with a glorification of man and of a human office, Luther the Protestant struck and he struck hard.

THE SUCCESSION OF THE FAITHFUL

As Chapter V has pointed out, Luther was not devoid of feeling for the historical continuity of Christian worship. He traced certain forms to their sources in the fathers, though not always the right fathers,[2] and he valued the symbol of continuity which he had in the liturgy. The primary stress in his thought about this subject, however, was on the other side of the problem, the insistence that neither liturgy nor polity could guarantee the true continuity of the

---

[1] See p. 82 above.
[2] Thus also, in 1532, Luther wrote a preface to an edition of Athanasius by John Bugenhagen; most of the writings in the edition were ascribed to Athanasius falsely (*WA* 30-III, 530-532).

people of God. The abolition of the historic episcopate in many, though not all, of the Lutheran hands—effected in Denmark, for example, with surprising ease[1]—voiced the reformer's conviction that the apostolic succession of bishops did not make the church nor assure its continuity. The church could be present where it was absent, as Chapter I has shown, and the church could be in hiding even though the external succession might be incontestable.

If the forms of the church's polity could not be counted upon to assure that the church continued from age to age, still less could this continuity be sought in a uniformity of the church's liturgy. For one thing, as Chapter III has indicated, there was no such uniformity. Luther remembered from his monastic experience that the forms of service varied from monastic order to monastic order, even from monastery to monastery.[2] His experience in the visitation of parishes showed him the astonishing heterogeneity of local customs and rituals.[3] He knew from history the differences between East and West regarding the date of Easter and other liturgical matters, although he does not seem to have been acquainted with Eastern liturgies as such.[4] All this empirical evidence proved to him that if there was continuity in the history of the church, that continuity could not be liturgical. What was more, the liturgical forms of past ages were often inaccessible. Against those who insisted that liturgy follow the example of the fathers Luther declared in the *Formula of the Mass* that this was impossible because in so many cases one could not know what the example of the fathers actually was.[5] Many of the liturgical sources available to us today were unknown to the Reformers, and there are many parts of liturgical history about which we are still as ignorant as they were. Liturgical uniformity was therefore impossible, and it had never existed anyway.

But even if this were not so, Luther was prepared to argue that liturgy was not the locus of the church's continuity. As Chapter I has pointed out, he claimed to stand in 'the succession of the faith-

---

[1] Cf. Kurd Schulz, 'Bugenhagen als Schöpfer der Kirchenordnung', *Johann Bugenhagen*. Beiträge zu seinem 400. Todestag, ed. Werner Rautenberg (Berlin, 1958), pp. 51-63.
[2] Sermon on Luke 11: 14ff., *WA* 29, 73.
[3] Cf. the preface to the Small Catechism, *Bek.* 501-507 (*BC* 338-341).
[4] On the Councils and the Church, *WA* 50, 553ff. (*WML* 5, 181ff.).
[5] *Formula of the Mass*, *WA* 12, 219 (*WML* 6, 99).

ful',[1] for he proclaimed the apostolic faith of the church; and the true continuity of the church with the apostles lay here. It was in the church's proclamation and confession of faith, rather than in the forms of its liturgical life, that Luther found the continuity of the people of God, a continuity older than Christianity, because the faith of the patriarchs and the faith of the church were essentially the same.[2] That faith was nurtured by the preaching of the word and the administration of the sacraments. Although the word was preached in a variety of ways and although the forms for the administration of baptism and the Lord's Supper were different in different places at different times, this did not invalidate the continuity of the church. The marks of the church's presence were also the warrant of its continuity, and in the confession of faith the church bore witness to this continuity.

Luther's specific liturgical work substantiates this interpretation of his theory. Liturgical scholars who stand in the tradition of Luther's Reformation admit that 'we must clearly recognize Luther's limitations in the field of liturgics'.[3] Above all, they regret that the only rites available to him were those of the late Middle Ages, in many ways the nadir of Western liturgical development.[4] But even these rites had an inner integrity and structure which Luther did not recognize, to judge by what he did to them in his *Formula of the Mass* and particularly in his *German Mass*. By reversing the order of the words of institution and the Lord's Prayer and by substituting an exhortation for the preface he broke up the logical connection between those elements which he did keep.[5] Whether or not one agrees with this estimate of the changes Luther made, however, it is clear that he was completely untrammelled in his willingness to dispense with historic forms, however old; for the continuity of the church did not lie in them, but in the word and the sacraments and in the confession of faith.

LUTHER'S CRITIQUE OF THE CHURCH YEAR

The Protestant principle at work in Luther's view of the liturgy is also evident from his attitude toward the church year. Although

[1] See p. 16, note 2 above.
[2] Cf. Pelikan, *Luther the Expositor*, p. 91.
[3] Rudolf Stählin, 'Die Geschichte des christlichen Gottesdienstes von der Urkirche bis zur Gegenwart', *Leiturgia*, I, 60.
[4] Cf. p. 96, note 6 above.
[5] Jungmann, *op. cit.*, II, 343ff.

he was the enemy of radical subjectivism, he never lost sight of how important 'the receiving side'[1] of revelation was. He is, after all, the man through whom faith once more became a major theological issue. False objectivism was therefore as foreign to his thought as false subjectivism. As he never tired of saying, the word and faith belong together.[2] And it was the function of the liturgy to give expression both to the word of grace from God to man and to the responding word of faith and thanksgiving from man to God —to neither without the other.

When this principle was applied to the church year, it meant that the several sections of the church year were not to be fenced off too rigidly from one another. As Luther said as early as 1518, 'the truly righteous man resembles God so much that just as God is indifferent to every day, every place, and every person, so also for the righteous man every day is a festival.'[3] There was a wholeness to Christian faith and experience which did not correspond to the current portion of the ecclesiastical calendar. Luther's preaching makes this abundantly clear. He complained of those who were good Easter preachers, but poor Pentecost preachers.[4] He himself preached Christmas sermons in which the message of the cross had a prominent place, while his sermons about the suffering and death of Christ did not neglect the Easter gospel.[5] Luther employed the particular part of the church year in which he happened to be preaching as an occasion to proclaim the wholeness of the Christian message. For him and for his hearers, every day was Christmas and Good Friday and Easter and Pentecost. No arbitrary division of the church calendar could violate that wholeness. Luther did not have his attacks of despair, his *Anfechtungen*, only during Holy Week!

Luther was not satisfied with the propers of the church year either. Chapter V has already mentioned that he proposed to replace the introits with entire psalms. He was especially displeased with the traditional pericopes. In the *Formula of the Mass* he accused the compiler of the epistle lessons of laying too great an

---

[1] Paul Tillich, *Systematic Theology*, I, 111.
[2] See my comments, *LW* 13, 88, note 21.
[3] *The Ten Commandments Preached to the People of Wittenberg*, WA 1, 436-437.
[4] *On the Councils and the Church*, WA 50, 599 (*WML* 5, 234).
[5] Cf. *The Martin Luther Christmas Book*, ed. Roland H. Bainton (Philadelphia, 1948), for examples.

emphasis upon works and of skipping those sections in the Pauline epistles which treat of faith;[1] this 'singularly ignorant and superstitious partisan of works' had thus obscured the heart of St Paul's message. Luther was much more satisfied with the gospel lessons, which seemed to him to stress faith in Christ more consistently than did the epistle lessons. Luther nevertheless retained the standard pericopes, both the gospels and the epistles. His sermons on them show that for a pulpit virtuoso like him the system of fixed lessons in the church year was no great hindrance. But they also show his skill in addressing the proclaimed word to the needs and experiences of his audience, rather than adhering to the meaning of the festival at hand.

A special problem in the church year were the saints' days. In the *Formula of the Mass*, as has already been pointed out, Luther says that Wittenberg was abolishing all the saints' days. In 1520, writing to the German nobility, he even urged the abolition of all holy days except Sunday.[2] It does not require extensive study of the Lutheran church orders of the sixteenth century to show that these suggestions of Luther's were not carried out.[3] Many of the major days were retained, even days of non-biblical saints. Indeed, several of the feast days of the Blessed Virgin Mary were celebrated by many Lutherans in the sixteenth century.[4] But the suspicion of saints' days remained as part of the Protestant principle in the liturgical thought of Luther's Reformation. Luther felt that saints' days diverted attention from Christ, whose life and work were our exemplar, to the saints, whose lives and works were merely examples—and sometimes not very good examples at that. As our exemplar, Christ showed how God deals with man, not for man to imitate him but to demonstrate that in our own lives, with their suffering and their exaltation, we are brought into conformity with him.[5] Thus objective history and subjective experience were brought together in Christ, and even the church year could not be a hindrance to that.

[1] *Formula of the Mass*, *WA* 12, 209 (*WML* 6, 87).
[2] *An Open Letter to the German Nobility*, *WA* 6, 445-446 (*WML* 2, 127-128).
[3] See, for example, the Church Order of Hamburg of 1556, *Die evangelischen Kirchenordnungen des 16. Jahrhunderts*, ed. Emil Sehling, V (Leipzig, 1913), 553-554.
[4] Cf. Reintraud Schimmelpfennig, 'Die Marienfeste im Luthertum', *Oekumenische Einheit*, III-1 (1952), 94-102.
[5] See the comments, *LW* 22, 117, note 90.

A CAPITULATION TO NATURALISM?

The problem of 'cultus and culture' does not, of course, appear in this form in Luther. But as we have seen, he brought his aesthetic awareness and his sense of propriety to bear upon his liturgical work, too. At their best, Luther's hymns are probably the most successful combinations of 'cultus and culture' in his work. In the preface to his *Spiritual Songs* of 1524, Luther reiterated his desire to keep the arts in the church, in opposition to the left wing reformers.[1] But he was Protestant enough to be aware of the dangers of aestheticism in the liturgy and to avoid it.

For one of Luther's accusations against the liturgy was that it had lost its soul by its intimate identification with culture. As Luther complains in the *Formula of the Mass*, all the crafts of the artisans were making a profit from the mass.[2] The indiscriminate ornamentation of the churches and the services had so encrusted them that their fundamental purpose was being obscured. The outline of the liturgy had originally been the drama of redemption, the yearning in the Old Testament and the fulfilment in the New. But natural religion had so strongly influenced the evolution of the liturgy that the inner dynamics of the church's faith in redemption no longer controlled and shaped it. Just as Luther maintained that the church's invasion of the secular order had secularized the church instead of Christianizing the secular order, so he interpreted the identification of the cultus with the culture as an accommodation to the culture and a blurring of the distinction between nature and grace, between creation and redemption. The naturalism of late medieval liturgies was an expression of their identification with the folk life of Western Europe, especially as the sacramentals of the church—relics, salt, holy water, and the like—came to be regarded as cures and talismans to be employed for warding off demons, diseases, and the terror of the Turks.

Such an identification with folk life did indeed make the liturgical and sacramental life of the church a genuine part of the culture, but in so doing it deprived the liturgy of its specifically Christian character. As a student of the Old Testament, Luther knew the dangers in too close a link between naturalism and reli-

---

[1] *Spiritual Hymn Booklet, WA* 35, 475 (*WML* 6, 284).
[2] *Formula of the Mass, WA* 12, 208 (*WML* 6, 86).

gion. The apostasy of Israel to false gods was frequently a capitulation of the religion of the covenant to the worship of man's natural vitalities, symbolized by Baal and Ashteroth.[1] Much as he was concerned to make the liturgy live and much as he was interested in the world of nature, Luther was a true Protestant in his anxiety lest the liturgy dethrone the very thing it was intended to celebrate.

From what has been said in these chapters, it might well appear that Luther was guilty of equivocation or at least of ambiguity. In fact, it is possible to construct a *Sic et Non* from Luther's works, lining up statements on both sides of many crucial questions. As Erich Seeberg said of Luther in another connection, 'What is there that a man like Luther could not have said?'[2] But the liturgical ambivalence described here is a direct expression of the critical reverence with which Luther interpreted the whole Christian tradition and his role in it. The Roman Catholics of his day and ours have frequently interpreted him as the Protestant *par excellence*, the wild boar in the Lord's vineyard, heedless of tradition and scornful of custom, whose careless snout had uprooted the heritage of centuries.[3] The left-wing Protestants of his day and ours, on the other hand, have been unable to understand how he could tolerate and even defend Catholic doctrines and customs, and they have portrayed him as a reactionary who could not bear to see the established order disturbed and whose heart remained with the old even when he was bringing the new into existence. And it is the genius of Luther's Reformation, as this book is intended to show, that in it both Catholic substance and Protestant principle came to voice. In his treatment of the dogmatic, conciliar, and liturgical tradition of Catholic Christianity, Luther proved to be an obedient rebel—or, to use terms coined in quite another context, 'an orthodox heretic, a respectable agitator, an intellectual Philistine, a conservative revolutionist'.[4]

---

[1] *Against the Falsely So-called 'Spiritual' Estate of the Pope and the Bishops*, *WA* 10-11, 120.

[2] Erich Seeberg, *Studien zu Luthers Genesisvorlesung* (Gütersloh, 1932), p. 45.

[3] Cf. Roland H. Bainton, *Here I Stand. A life of Martin Luther* (New York, 1950; London, 1951), pp. 136-150: 'The Wild Boar in the Vineyard'.

[4] Henry Steele Commager and Richard Brandon Morris, 'Editors' Introduction' to George E. Mowry, *The Era of Theodore Roosevelt and the Birth of Modern America* 1900-1912 (London, 1958; New York, 1962), p. x.

PART TWO

UNITY DESPITE SEPARATION

THE concern of Luther and his Reformation for the catholicity and the unity of the church, which has been summarized in Part One, did not remain a matter only of theology and of books, but expressed itself in repeated efforts to discover, or to recover, a unity beyond the separations on the right and on the left. These separations have been discussed much more thoroughly in the history books than have the efforts at reunion, and even today the record of 'unitive Protestantism' (to use the name of a fine history of these efforts)[1] is too little known and studied. Luther at Worms bidding defiance to papacy and empire, or Luther at Marburg refusing fellowship to a fellow Protestant—these pictures are familiar to every student of the Reformation. In the following chapters another picture of Luther's Reformation will become evident: Luther the irenic churchman. By the nature of the case, actions will speak more loudly than words in these chapters, although ideas and doctrines will be as decisive here as they were in Part One. It is interesting to note that the negotiations and compromises discussed here all took place between the German Reformation and Eastern Europe. This does not mean that there were no irenic movements or events closer to the home of Luther's Reformation; the Wittenberg Concord of 1536 is a prime example of such an event. But the history of Luther's Reformation in the Slavic lands is, if anything, even less familiar than is the history of his striving for unity despite separation. Therefore a study of the irenicism of Luther's Reformation among the Slavs may illumine two dark corners simultaneously.

[1] John T. McNeill, *Unitive Protestantism* (New York, 1930).

VII

FATHERS AND REFORMERS

WHEN Luther discovered, to his amazement, that his ideas had started a revolution, he also found himself linked with earlier reformations and with earlier reformers. Among these the most important was the reformation of John Hus; for as Chapter IV has pointed out, Luther developed his critical attitude toward church councils largely on the basis of his study of the Council of Constance, which had condemned Hus in 1415. Luther's deepening affinity with 'St John Hus', as he came to call the Czech reformer, forms a significant chapter in the history of the Reformation.[1] Hus emerged in Luther's thought as a medieval father who was also a reformer, as a Catholic who was also a Protestant, in short, as an 'obedient rebel'. In addition, the affection and respect in which Luther held Hus helped to cement relations between Luther and the Hussites of his own time, with the result that in 1538 Luther published a Hussite confession, the *Confessio Bohemica*, with his endorsement. The negotiations leading up to that confession and the factors responsible for its publication by Luther will concern us in Chapters VIII and IX.

LUTHER'S EARLY KNOWLEDGE OF HUS

Just when Luther first heard of Hus, and from whom, cannot be determined. Nevertheless, it seems safe to say that his first knowledge of Hus and of the Hussites must have come when he was quite young. Luther's father was a miner, and the German miners of the latter half of the fifteenth century were in constant contact

---

[1] Cf. Jaroslav Goll, 'Jak soudil Luther o Husovi?' *Časopis musea kralovství českého*, 54 (1880), 69ff.; E. Novikof, *Gus i Luter* (2 vols.; Moscow, 1859). Independent of the previous two, because, as he says, he was unable to read 'Hungarian' (*sic*), is Walter Koehler, *Luther und die Kirchengeschichte*, pp. 162-236.

with Bohemia.[1] German noblemen also hired Czech artists, and *vice versa*. The contact between Germany and Bohemia, moreover, can be judged through a study of the Czech, Moravian, and Silesian students at various German universities in this period. One can get some indication of the meaning of this academic contact for Luther by paying particular attention to those who attended at Wittenberg.[2]

Much more conclusive than this tenuous evidence for an awareness of Hus and the Hussites among Luther's contemporaries are the signs that the memory of the Hussite Wars was still alive in the places and among the people with whom Luther spent his early life. Several times in his writings, Luther indicated an acquaintance with German participation in those wars; this is not surprising, for the city of Erfurt, whose university Luther entered early in 1501, has been a collecting-place for the anti-Hussite taxes of the early and middle fifteenth century.[3] In the lower classes, too, the social upheavals of the Hussite period served as an encouragement in their difficult lot.[4] The extent of the awareness of the Hussites in sixteenth century Germany may well be gauged by an examination of the part played by John Žižka, the Hussite warrior who had died in 1424, in the writings of Luther's contemporaries. Thus, for example, a coloured picture of Žižka and of the Hussite armies decorates the cover of a sixteenth-century book about the Turks.[5] The German anti-clericals of the same time, notably Ulrich von Hutten, used Žižka as proof that an anti-clerical revolt could be successful. This enthusiasm for

---

[1] On the extent of these contacts, cf. S. Harrison Thomson, *Czechoslovakia in European History* (Princeton and Oxford, 1943), pp. 101-102.

[2] J. O. Novotný, *Střední Slovensko* (Prague, 1937), I, 150-159; Ferdinand Menčík, 'Studenti z Čech a Moravy ve Wittemberku od r. 1502 až do r. 1692', *Časopis českého musea*, 1897, 250-268. For a handy summary, see E. G. Schwiebert, *Luther and His Times*. The Reformation from a New Perspective (Saint Louis and London, 1950), pp. 254ff.

[3] *Warning of Dr Martin Luther to His Dear Germans*, WA 30-III, 218; cf. his reference to the Germans as those 'who killed him [Hus]', *Message to the Bohemian Estates*, WA 10-II, 174; *Concerning the Ministry*, WA 12, 171 (*LW* 40, 16); and Schäfer, *Luther als Kirchenhistoriker*, p. 459. On Erfurt's role in the Hussite Wars, see František Palacký, *Dějiny národu českého* (Prague, 1921), p. 624.

[4] Wilhelm Vogt, *Die Vorgeschichte des Bauernkrieges* (Halle, 1887), pp. 57-83.

[5] Karel Hrdina, 'Žižka v humanistickém písemnictví XV. a XVI. století', *Sborník Žižkuv 1424-1924*, ed. Rudolf Urbánek (Prague, 1924), pp. 196-199 and Plate 120.

Žižka was shared by others in the same period, as well as by Luther's followers of a generation later.[1]

As the Hussite Wars had not been forgotten, so, too, it was rumoured here and there that the condemnation of John Hus at Constance had not been completely legal and fair. Luther became acquainted with these rumours from at least two sources. One of them was John Greffenstein, from whom Luther claimed to have heard that 'Hus had not been overcome with written arguments', but with force; diligent study by various scholars has failed to identify Greffenstein, but it seems safe to take 1505 as the latest possible date of the utterance.[2] Similarly, he heard 'from Andrew Proles' that Hus was defeated in debate by the use of a corrupted Bible. Although Luther is said to have met the aged Proles in Magdeburg in 1497, it was probably not from Proles himself, but from John Staupitz that Luther heard the story.[3] Ever since the sixteenth century, it has been customary to speak of Proles as a 'pre-reformer', to compare him to John the Baptist as a 'preparer of the way'. On the basis of the data quoted above and similar indications, modern scholars have sought to find such a 'pre-reformer' especially in Staupitz, but with uneven results. It would seem nearer to the truth to see in these facts an indication of an active spiritual life in the Augustinian order, a spiritual life which may well have recognized John Hus as the loyal son of the church that he was despite his rebellion.[4]

Such an interpretation is strengthened by the availability of books by John Hus in certain places where they could be read. It is apparent that this was true either of Luther's monastery or of his university. Despite his claims never to have read anything by

[1] Ulrich von Hutten, 'Monitor', *Gespräche von Ulrich von Hutten übersetzt und erläutert*, Part III of David Friedrich Strausz, *Ulrich von Hutten* (Leipzig, 1860), 209; cf. Paul Held, *Ulrich von Hutten*. Seine religiös-geistige Auseinandersetzung mit Katholizismus, Humanismus, Reformation (Leipzig, 1928), pp. 146-147. Martin Bucer (?), *Gesprechbiechlein neüw Kartshans*, ed. Ernest Lehmann (Halle, 1930), p. 15; cf. Hajo Holborn, *Ulrich von Hutten and the German Reformation*, tr. Roland H. Bainton (New Haven, 1937), p. 179. For Luther's followers, cf. Matthias Flacius Illyricus, *Catalogus testium veritatis* (Frankfort, 1672), p. 733.
[2] *On the New Bulls and Lies of Eck*, WA 6, 591; cf. Otto Scheel, *Martin Luther. Vom Katholizismus zur Reformation*, I (Tübingen, 1921), 306.
[3] *On the New Bulls and Lies of Eck*, WA 6, 590; Melchior Adamus, *Vitae Germanorum theologorum* (Heidelberg, 1620), p. 6; cf. *WA Ti* 5, 654.
[4] Flacius, *Catalogus*, pp. 849-850; H. A. Pröhle, *Andreas Proles ein Zeuge der Wahrheit kurz vor Luther* (Gotha, 1867); Scheel, *op. cit.*, II, 75-104, 193-209.

Hus before 1519, Luther showed at Leipzig in that year that he had read something of the Acts of the Council of Constance and had remembered passages from Hus's book *On the Church* not contained in the condemnatory decrees of that Council, though they may well have been recorded in other anti-Hussite writings.[1] Nor is the possibility excluded that the books of John Wesel, of which Luther spoke highly, provided him with information, for Wesel had been in close contact with the Bohemians and had addressed some treatises to them.[2]

Luther's early knowledge of and attitude toward John Hus therefore, can be summarized thus: Although he was taught that Hus was a heretic to be avoided, there were nevertheless influences in his early life which gave him a proclivity for the Czech reformer that made itself more prominent as his thought progressed. The first of Luther's opponents to recognize that proclivity seems to have been either John Tetzel or Sylvester Prierias, who concluded upon reading some of Luther's words that if he were to make his opinions public, people would get the impression that he was about to emigrate to Bohemia.[3] There were probably others among Luther's opponents early in 1518 who hurled the name 'Hussite' at him; indeed, the use of that name may well have been a common polemical device in the early sixteenth century.[4]

JOHN ECK AND THE LEIPZIG DEBATE

Effective use was not made of the similarity between Hus and Luther, however, until the entry of John Eck into the controversies which had sprung up as a result of Luther's theses. Somewhat younger than Luther—he was born on November 14, 1486—Eck was pro-chancellor at the University of Ingolstadt and inquisitor for Bavaria and Franconia. The publication of the ninety-five theses caused him to lose his earlier respect for Luther and to write

---

[1] Cf. Luther to Staupitz, October 3, 1519, *WA Br* 2, 514; *On the New Bulls and Lies of Eck*, *WA* 6, 587-588. Cf. Luther and Carlstadt to the Elector Frederick, August 18, 1519, *WA Br* 2, 470; Kolde, *Luthers Stellung zu Konzil und Kirche*, p. 47.

[2] Cf. *On the Councils and the Church*, *WA* 50, 600 (*WML* 5, 236); also *Luther's Response*, *WA* 6, 184.

[3] *Reply of Brother Sylvester Prierias, Master of the Sacred Palace, to Brother Martin Luther of the Order of Hermits*, *WA* 2, 51; on the possibility of Tetzel, cf. Köhler, *op. cit.*, p. 172.

[4] Cf. Luther to Johann Lang, March 21, 1518, *WA Br* 1, 154; and Luther's sermon on John 8, *WA* 4, 614.

Obeliscs against him sometime early in 1518. Here he took exception to Luther's view of the church, labelling it 'Bohemian poison'; although his *Asteriscs*, written in reply, do not refer to this charge, Luther was struck by it.[1] In May, 1519, Luther published a reply to Eck's accusations. At this time he criticized the Council of Constance and ridiculed Eck's accusation of Hussitism by a reference to an inscription on the Church of St John Lateran in Rome.[2]

Strengthened by this in his conviction that Luther was in league with the Hussites, Eck came to Leipzig in June, 1519, and on the twenty-seventh day of that month began his debate with Andrew Carlstadt. Rumour had it that there were some Bohemians in Leipzig for the disputation, who wanted to support Luther as a follower of Hus.[3] When Luther was asked to preach, all the churches were closed to him and he used the debate auditorium. His sermon, delivered on June 29, St Peter's and St Paul's Day, dealt with grace and free will, and with the primacy of Peter. Because of its treatment of this latter point, the sermon seemed to Eck to be Hussite.[4] It is not surprising, therefore, that when Luther chanced into the Paulist church one morning while the fathers were reading mass, they ran away with their monstrances for fear of being contaminated by the heretic.[5]

On July 4, 1519, after the preliminary bout between Eck and Carlstadt was over, the debate between Eck and Luther began. Before the morning has passed, Eck took occasion to refer to the Hussites; Luther's reply mentioned the Bohemians, and no more.[6] But the next day Eck pressed his point, acknowledging himself as an enemy of the schismatic Bohemians and citing the resemblance between their position and Luther's on the controverted points. While granting that the Bohemians had sinned by breaking

---

[1] Eck, *Obeliscs*, No. 18, *WA* 1, 302; Luther to Johann Sylvius Egranus, March 24, 1518, *WA Br* 1, 158; Carlstadt to Eck, June 11, 1518, *StL* 15, 805.

[2] *Dispute and Defence of Brother Martin Luther Against the Accusations of Dr John Eck*, *WA* 2, 159, reading *Constantipolitanam* rather than *Constantinopolitanam*.

[3] Eck to Georg Hauen and Franz Burckhardt, July 1, 1519, *StL* 12, 1228; cf. pp. 123-124 below.

[4] The sermon is reprinted *WA* 2, 246-249; cf. Eck to Jakob Hochstraten, July 24, 1519, *StL* 15, 1227; also Eck to Hauen and Burckhardt, July 1, 1519, *StL* 15, 1228.

[5] Such is the report of Sebastian Fröschel in the preface to his *Vom Königreich Jesu Christi und seinem ewigen Priesterthum* of 1566, *StL* 15, 1208.

[6] *The Leipzig Debate*, *WA* 2, 262 (Eck); Luther's response, *WA* 2, 266.

the highest law of Christian love, Luther expressed his amazement that so avid an opponent of the Bohemians as Eck had never taken the time to write against them.[1] At first he attempted to sidestep the issue about his agreement with Hus and his disagreement with the Council of Constance.[2] Eventually, however, he was forced to defend Hus and even to grant that the Bohemians had been wronged, for many of Hus's articles were 'most Christian and evangelical'. With inexorable logic, Eck concluded that if Luther supported Hus, whom Constance had condemned, then Luther was putting his own judgment above that of the council.[3] The significance of this conclusion has been weighed in Chapter IV.

Eck's strategy had worked, his suspicions were confirmed: Luther was a Hussite, and at Leipzig he had been forced to admit it. Now that Luther's identity with the Hussites was established, Eck determined to take full advantage of the situation. A few months after the debate he tried to use the Hussite bogey to intimidate Luther's protector, Frederick, but the attempt failed.[4] Less than a year later, in October, 1520, Eck published a tract in criticism of what Luther had said and written since Leipzig. There were many things of which he did not approve, and Luther's growing friendship for Hus and the Hussites was one of them. Such a friendship was not surprising, for Luther seemed to have much in common with the Bohemian heretics.[5] In June, 1520, Luther had urged that attempts be made to conciliate the Czechs, since an injustice had been done them—a charge that irked Eck very much.[6] Luther's pamphlet on the Lord's Supper of December,

---

[1] Cf. Eck's *Ad malesanam Lutheri venationem* (1519), leaf 4B; Eck to the Elector Frederick, November 18, 1519, *StL* 15, 1317. On Luther's criticism of the Bohemians, Erich Seeberg, *Luthers Theologie*, II (Stuttgart, 1937), 226.

[2] 'It is not true that I have spoken against the Council of Constance', *The Leipzig Debate*, *WA* 2, 283; on Hus, cf. *ibid.*, *WA* 2, 288.

[3] Eleven years later Eck referred to this admission in the thirtieth of his *Theses 405*, reprinted in *Quellen und Forschungen zur Geschichte des augsburgischen Glaubensbekenntnisses*, ed. Wilhelm Gussmann, II (Kassel, 1930), 107. Cf. also Hartmann Grisar, *Martin Luther*, I (Freiburg, 1911), 295; and Holl, *Luther*, p. 312, note 3.

[4] Eck to Frederick, November 18, 1519, *StL* 15, 1317.

[5] Johann Eck, 'Des heilgen concilii tzu Costentz, der heylgen Christenheit und hochlöblichen keyszers Sigmunds, und auch des teutzschen adels entschüldigung', *Vier deutsche Schriften gegen Martin Luther, den Bügermeister und Rat von Konstanz, Ambrosius Blaurer und Konrad Sam*, ed. Karl Meisen and Friedrich Zoepfl *cc* 14 (Münster in Westfalen, 1929), 17-18.

[6] *Open Letter to the Christian Nobility*, *WA* 6, 454 (*WML* 2, 140 ff.); these words are quoted both on the title page and on p. 14 of Eck's 'Entschüldigung'.

1519, had even suggested that communion might be administered under both kinds, although, as Chapter VI has indicated, Luther himself did not act on his own suggestion until much later.[1] According to Eck, this suggestion proved that Luther preferred the practice of the heretics to the custom of the orthodox church.[2] Worst of all, Luther had recommended compromise with those Bohemians who doubted the Roman Catholic doctrine of transubstantiation and had himself declared that doctrine to be a fiction.[3] It was, therefore, with renewed confidence in the correctness of his tactics at Leipzig that Eck could throw the approval of Hus up to Luther in the presence of the emperor at the Diet of Worms. As late as 1530 he referred to Luther's previous denunciation of the Bohemians and called him a supporter of the 'Picards', insisting that 'it is to Luther that we are indebted for the new Hussites'.[4]

LUTHER A 'HUSSITE'

Once established by Eck, Luther's affinity with Hus and the Hussites was exploited by his enemies; it soon became the usual practice in a polemic against Luther to refer to his 'Hussitism'. Thus, at Luther's fateful admission about Hus during the Leipzig Debate, Duke George of Saxony (who was himself said to be of Czech blood) arose with arms akimbo and cried: 'A plague on that!'[5] When the above-mentioned pamphlet on the Lord's

---

[1] *The Blessed Sacrament of the Holy and True Body of Christ and the Brotherhoods*, WA 2, 742-743 (*LW* 35, 49). Luther lived to regret some of the phrases in this pamphlet; cf. his letter to Frankfort of 1533, *WA* 30-III, 563. For its effect on Duke George, see p. 113 note 1 below. In this respect, as in others, Carlstadt was more eager than Luther to apply the Protestant principle, saying that 'those who receive the bread and the cup of Christ are not Bohemians, but true Christians': Hermann Barge, *Andreas Bodenstein von Karlstadt* (Leipzig, 1905), I, 291, note 118; also the Wittenberg faculty to the Elector, October 20, 1521, *CR* 1, 469. For Luther's interpretation of the incident, cf. *Receiving Both Kinds in the Sacrament*, WA 10-11, 17 (*LW* 36, 248).

[2] Eck, 'Entschüldigung', p. 4; cf. Henry VIII, *Adsertio septem sacramentorum*, StL 19, 146.

[3] *Open Letter to the Christian Nobility*, WA 6, 456 (*WML* 2, 144).

[4] Eck listed this sympathy as one of Luther's worst offences, *WA* 7, 836-837. Cf. also his *Christenliche erhaltung der stell der geschrifft für das Fegfeür wider Luthers lasterbüchlin* (Augsburg, 1530), leaf 4B and 16B; and 'Praefatio' to *Theses* 405, Gussmann, *op. cit.*, II, 101.

[5] On the ancestry of Duke George, cf. Luther to Amsdorf, January 2, 1526, *WA Br* 4, 3, and the note to J. K. Seidemann, 'Schriftstücke zur Reformationsgeschichte', *ZHT*, 44 (1874), 120. For the account of Duke George's reaction at Leipzig, cf. K. Köhler, 'M. Sebastian Fröschel', *ZHT* 42 (1872), 535.

Supper appeared, and when Luther published essays and books praising Hus, Duke George feared that the heresiarch's influence would assert itself in his land, too.[1] Royalty was joined to nobility in that denunciation when Henry VIII of England expressed the thought that perhaps Luther would flee to the Bohemians if the situation in Germany grew too hot for him—a rumour that had been current for some time. Henry used the example of the Bohemians to warn the Saxon dukes of what continued toleration of Luther might mean.[2]

The rumour which had come to Henry's ears about Luther's trips to Bohemia grew, until Luther was said to be Czech himself, born and reared in Prague.[3] Although this rumour was an obvious misrepresentation, that did not prevent its dissemination; many of those who knew that Luther was not a Czech were still inclined to suspect that he might be a Hussite. In 1528 a book appeared under the name of J. Faber, comparing Luther unfavourably with Hus; George Witzel took Luther's Smalcald Articles of 1537 as an occasion to remind Luther of what he had written to the Bohemians in 1523; eventually even Erasmus joined in the denunciation of Luther as a Hussite.[4] John Fisher summarized the feeling of many when he declared that Luther was, if anything, a worse heretic than Hus had been.[5]

Sooner or later, however, someone was bound to see the dangers connected with identifying Luther and the Hussites. Despite its

[1] Duke George to Luther, December 28, 1525, *WA Br* 3, 648; Duke George to the Elector Frederick, December 27, 1519, *StL* 19, 450-451; Frederick to George, December 29, 1519, *StL* 19, 452.

[2] Henry VIII, *Adsertio septem sacramentorum, StL* 19, 149; also Conrad Pellicanus to Luther, March 15, 1520, *WA Br* 2, 67; Silvester von Scharmberg to Luther, June 11, 1520, *WA Br* 2, 121; Luther to Spalatin, July 10, 1520, *WA Br* 2, 137. Henry to Elector Frederick, Dukes John and George, February 20, 1523, *StL* 19, 357.

[3] Luther first heard of the rumour early in 1520; Luther to Spalatin, January 10, 1520, *WA Br* 1, 608; it became stronger a few days later, Luther to Spalatin, January 14, 1520, *WA Br* 1, 610; see also Luther to Johann Lang, January 26, 1520, *WA Br* 1, 619; and *Explanation of Doctor Martin Luther of Several Articles in his Treatise on the Blessed Sacrament, WA* 6, 81-82.

[4] J. Faber, 'Nonaginta articuli, in quibus Joan. Hus et Pighardi, Waldenses ac Wesselius tractabiliores ac meliores Martino Luthero inveniuntur', Gussmann, *op. cit.*, II, 45; Witzel, *Antwort auff Martin Luthers letzt bekennete artickel, unsere gantze religion und das concili belangend*, ed. Hans Volz, *CC* 18 (Münster, 1932), 106; Erasmus, 'Purgatio adversus epistolam non sobriam Lutheri', quoted in Grisar, *op. cit.*, I, 82.

[5] Fisher, 'Epistola dedicatoria', *Sacri sacerdotii defensio contra Lutherum*, ed. Hermann Klein Schmeink, *CC* 9 (Münster, 1925), 6; also p. 117, note 5 below.

disadvantages for the theory of papal supremacy, the Bohemian schism did prevent the formation of a bloc against Rome. But if Luther were to take Hus's part in the controversy, that might effect such a bloc, brought on by the loyal churchmen who had used the Hussite stratagem to force Luther into a heretical position.

The danger was real, and something had to be done about it. One way to accomplish this was to play one Bohemian group against another and thus to aggravate the disunity in the Bohemian situation as a lever against the possibility of Luther's uniting with the Czechs. Such a thought seems to have occurred already to Eck, since he was concerned about the pious Czechs.[1] But it remained for Jerome Emser, one of Eck's associates, to take concrete steps in that direction. While in the service of Duke George, Emser had had an opportunity to travel in Bohemia. Feeling that his intimate connection with Bohemia imposed upon him the duty of setting Czech affairs straight, Emser wrote an essay for the faithful Czechs a month after the Leipzig Debate. After calling Bohemia a 'land . . . of superstition and confusion' and lamenting that the religious situation had even divided families, the treatise went on to show that there was no connection between Luther's position and that of the Czechs, and that Luther had repudiated the role of being a patron of Hus and of the Czechs.[2] Luther recognized the significance of Emser's treatise, exclaiming: 'Will miracles never cease? Eck rages against me as a Bohemian, but Emser, who is a worse enemy to me than many Ecks, denies that I am a Bohemian!' But he went on condemning the schismatic Bohemians and so did not enter into the alliance of which Emser and his co-religionists were so afraid.[3]

THE WORK OF COCHLAEUS

Nevertheless, as Luther's contacts with the Czechs grew, Emser's fears spread among other opponents of Luther. Illustrative of the situation in which Luther's opponents found themselves

[1] Eck to Elector Frederick, November 8, 1519, *StL* 15, 1324.
[2] Cf. Gustav Kawerau, *Hieronymus Emser*, *SVR* 61 (Halle, 1898), 18; Luther's jibes about Emser's connections with Bohemia, *Martin Luther's Addition to the Goat Emser*, *WA* 2, 661, and Kawerau, *op. cit.*, p. 119, note 69. Emser, *De disputatione Lipsicensi, quantum ad Boemos obiter deflexa est*, leaf 1A, 3A; also Barge, *Karlstadt*, I, 395.
[3] Luther, *Addition*, *WA* 2, 658, 661-663.

is John Cochlaeus, whose biographical screed against Luther has shaped Roman Catholic polemics for four hundred years.[1] He may himself have come from a Slavic family—his real name was Dobneck—and was in contact with Bohemia, both through personal visits and particularly through correspondence with various people there. He carried on an extensive correspondence especially with Peter Paul Vergerio, papal legate in Prague, from whom, among other things, he sought financial help from the legacy of a wealthy Czech for historical and polemical writing, chiefly against Luther. The character of that writing is apparent from his history of the Waldenses, in which he set down 'the doctrines of the heretics which our antipope [Luther] approves'.[2]

More important than his Waldensian study, however, was Cochlaeus's research in Hussite history. In his *magnum opus* in this field, which is useful even today and which caused him much grief while he was writing it, he purposed 'to edit the history of the Hussites old and new'. As a result of these researches, Cochlaeus was quite free in applying the name 'Hussite' to Luther and in blaming Hussite influence for Luther's doctrinal aberrations; he seems nevertheless to have had fears similar to those of Emser, with whom he was in contact and whose opinion and work he respected very highly.[3] Certain factors in the religious and political situation,

[1] See p. 12, note 2 above.

[2] Cf. Cochlaeus to Aleander, written from Prague, April 12, 1534, *ZKG* 18, 247; Friedensburg's note, *ZKG* 18, 270; and Cochlaeus to Cardinal Farnese, June 18, 1540, *ZKG* 18, 433. See Cochlaeus's letters to Vergerio: December 24, 1533, *ZKG* 18, 242; March 14, 1534, *ZKG* 18, 243; April 27, 1534, *ZKG* 18, 249; July 27, 1534, *ZKG* 18, 254. On his manuscript about the Waldenses, cf. Cochlaeus to Aleander, May 5, 1521, *ZKG* 18, 111; Cochlaeus to Aleander, June 11, 1521, *ZKG* 18, 115; his complaint to the Pope, June 19, 1521, *ZKG* 18, 117; and his desire to revise the manuscript, Cochlaeus to Aleander, September 27, 1521, *ZKG* 18, 125. On Luther as 'antipope', cf. Cochlaeus to Aleander, May 11, 1521, *ZKG* 18, 112, and Cochlaeus to Morone, March 19, 1538, *ZKG* 18, 284.

[3] On the progress of his history of the Hussites, cf. Cochlaeus to Aleander, June 25, 1535, *ZKG* 18, 265; Cochlaeus to Johann Faber, October 28, 1534, *ZKG* 18, 258. On its purpose, see Cochlaeus to Aleander, September 8, 1534, *ZKG* 18, 256-257; Cochlaeus to Vergerio, July 27, 1534, *ZKG* 18, 254. Luther is referred to as 'the new Hussite', Cochlaeus to Pope Leo, June 19, 1521, *ZKG* 18, 116; Hus is referred to as Luther's 'master' in Cochlaeus, *Articuli CCCCC Martini Lutheri ex sermonibus eius sex & triginta* (1526), art. 63. Hus is responsible for Luther's aberrations: on the church, *ibid.*, art. 159; on purgatory, *ibid.*, art. 109 (cf. p. 112, note 4 above); on miracles at holy places, *Articuli*, art. 154; on the mass, *ibid.*, art. 220; in general, Luther and his followers preach 'Hussite dogmas that have long since been condemned', *ibid.*, art. 113. On Emser, cf. Cochlaeus to Aleander, September 27, 1521, *ZKG* 18, 124; and Cochlaeus to Aleander, May 22, 1521, *ZKG* 18, 114.

moreover, made Cochlaeus even more apprehensive than was Emser about driving Luther and the Czechs together.

Perhaps chief among these factors was the Polish question. Emser had feared an alliance of Luther and the Czechs; Cochlaeus feared the influence of the Lutheran movement upon other lands throughout Europe, especially upon Poland. He frequently stated that one of the chief purposes of his writing was to prevent the spread of the Lutheran heresy outside Germany, as well as to counteract the influence of Luther's translated books. Being probably quite aware of the many Hussite churches in Poland, Cochlaeus may have known of the intense struggle that had been going on in Poland for over a century: the lower clergy supported the Hussites, while the higher clergy, with German backing, advocated the eradication of the Hussite heresy.[1] The situation was still in a state of flux in the sixteenth century; and as Chapter X will show, any strong unifying force might have brought about a re-alignment in Poland. Of this Cochlaeus was afraid—of an alliance between Poland, Bohemia, and Lutheran Saxony against Rome.

He therefore became alarmed when a number of young Polish noblemen were enrolled at Wittenberg and were being encouraged by Melanchthon.[2] When it was further rumoured that one of the Polish bishops was inviting Melanchthon to Poland and that even the young Polish king was 'infected with the Lutheran ferment', he began to write profusely.[3] He was overjoyed when the Polish king forbade his nobles to send their sons to Wittenberg to study, and he attributed the success of this to his books and to the grace

[1] Cochlaeus to Ottonello Vida, July 26, 1536, *ZKG* 18, 268; Cochlaeus to Vergerio, June 2, 1534, *ZKG* 18, 253; Cochlaeus to Aleander, September 8, 1534, *ZKG* 18, 257. Cf. E. D. Schnaase, 'Die böhmischen Brüder in Polen und die Reformierten in Danzig', *ZHT* 37 (1867), 125-156 for a general summary. See also Josef Macek et al., *Mezinárodní ohlas husitství* (Prague, 1958). On Polish opposition to Hus, see Hans Bellée, *Polen und die römische Kurie in den Jahren 1414-1424*, Heft 2 of 'Ost-Europäische Forschungen' (Leipzig, 1914), 5-37; on Polish support of Hus, Karl Völker, *Kirchengeschichte Polens*, VII of 'Grundrisz der slavischen Philologie und Kulturgeschichte' (Bielefeld and Leipzig, 1930), 96-101.

[2] The earliest report was about December 24, 1533; cf. *Nuntiaturberichte aus Deutschland nebst ergänzenden Aktenstücken*, I (Gotha, 1892), 156; by the following spring Cochlaeus was sure, letter to Aleander, April 12, 1534, *ZKG* 18, 246. On Melanchthon, cf. Cochlaeus to Aleander, September 8, 1534, *ZKG* 18, 255; Cochlaeus to Johann Faber, October 28, 1534, *ZKG* 18, 260.

[3] Cochlaeus to Aleander, April 23, 1534, *ZKG* 18, 248; on the arrangements being made by Andrew Krzycki to invite Melanchthon, cf. Theodor Wotschke, *Geschichte der Reformation in Polen* (Leipzig, 1911), p. 27. On the king, see *Nuntiaturberichte*, I, 291; also Cochlaeus to Vergerio, July 27, 1534, *ZKG* 18, 255.

of God. But what he had feared almost happened anyway in 1537, when reports came that some of Melanchthon's noble Polish pupils were plotting a rebellion.[1]

Because of such fears, it is not surprising to learn that Cochlaeus was careful about how he dealt with the parallels between Hus and Luther in his polemics. As noted above, he did call Luther a Hussite. And while he could not avoid seeing and pointing out affinities between Luther's position and that of the Hussites, notably on the eucharist, he took every chance to point out that Luther was now advocating what he had criticized in the Czechs, namely, the perversion of the Scriptures in proof of a position and particularly the sectarianism which Luther had often attacked.[2] Like Emser, he did this to show the Czechs that Luther was different from them. Another strategy he employed for that same purpose was his aid to Roman Catholic Czechs. Among them was John Hasenberg, for whom he secured financial assistance; he performed the same favour for four Czech noblemen; and the provost of All Saints' Church in Prague, Simon Villaticus, managed to publish his poems in Leipzig through Cochlaeus's intercession.[3] So concerned was Cochlaeus about the problem of Luther's alliance with the Hussites that he hoped to use the Czechs as a lure to bring the Germans back to the church and wanted to revise his history of the Hussites to avoid offending the Czechs.[4] Though he pretended to be shocked at Luther's statement that 'if [Hus] was a heretic, I am ten times more a heretic', it actually gave him an opportunity to continue this strategy by granting Luther's point.[5]

[1] Cochlaeus to Aleander, June 25, 1535, *ZKG* 18, 265; Cochlaeus to Aleander, October 7, 1537, *ZKG* 18, 275-276.

[2] *Articuli CCCCC*, art. 422; Cochlaeus to Morone, August 31, 1537, *ZKG* 18, 272. Cochlaeus, *Confutatio XCI. articulorum* (Cologne, 1525), art. 66; *Ein nötig und christlich bedencken auff des Luthers artickeln, die man gemeynsamen concilio fürtragen sol*, ed. Hans Volz, *CC* 18 (Münster, 1932), 7.

[3] Cochlaeus to Vergerio, March 14, 1534, *ZKG* 18, 243; Cochlaeus to Vergerio, May 29, 1534, *ZKG* 18, 252, on Hasenberg. On the noblemen, Cochlaeus to Giberti, January 31, 1540, *ZKG* 18, 422-423. On Villaticus, Cochlaeus to Morone, January 12, 1538, *ZKG* 18, 282; and Johann Metzler in *Tres orationes funebres in exequio Iohannis Eckii habitae*, *CC* 16 (Münster, 1930), p. Lv, with Villaticus's poem, *ibid.*, p. 7.

[4] Cochlaeus to Johann Faber, October 28, 1534, *ZKG* 18, 259; Cochlaeus to Vergerio, November 16, 1535, *ZKG* 18, 266.

[5] *Defence of All the Articles Condemned by the Bull of Leo X*, *WA* 7, 135; Cochlaeus, *Commentarius de actis et scriptis Mt. Lutheri* (German edition, 1581), p. 550.

LUTHER'S FRIENDS AND HUS

But Cochlaeus's attempts were in vain. The forces which Eck had set into motion at Leipzig were too strong to be checked; and by the time Luther's enemies had become aware of the dangers latent in the Hussite myth, Luther's friends and Luther himself had willingly accepted the charge and were acquainting themselves with Hus and his views. In 1522, to be sure, some of Luther's friends were still defending him against that charge. But soon after, Otto Brunfels became the first of the Protestants to publish some of Hus's work.[1] Much more significant than the work done by Otto Brunfels were the efforts made by John Agricola to acquaint himself and others with the person and significance of Hus. In 1529 he collaborated with Nicholas Krumbacher in the publication of a collection of documents—letters, reports, and speeches—dealing with Hus's defence at Constance. In 1536, after moving to Wittenberg, Agricola published a German translation of Luther's edition of some of Hus's letters; the next year there appeared an edition of various tracts by Hus; and in 1538 Agricola wrote a five-act drama on Hus's martyrdom.[2] Aroused by this drama, Cochlaeus composed a dialogue between Luther and a friend proving that the Council of Constance had been correct in condemning Hus.[3] Because of all this activity on Agricola's part, it is not surprising that it should have been he who wrote the preface to the Apology of the Unity of Bohemian Brethren when that document appeared in 1538.[4]

[1] Cf. the anonymous, 'Ein kurze anred zu allen misgunstigen doctor Luthers, und der christenlichen Freiheit' in *Satiren und Pasquille aus der Reformationszeit*, ed. Oskar Schade (2nd ed.; Hannover, 1863), II, 191. See Luther to Otto Brunfels, October 17, 1524, *WA Br* 3, 359. He had heard of Brunfels through Nicholas Gerbel; cf. Luther to Gerbel, November 1, 1521, *WA Br* 2, 398, also Bucer to Luther, August 2, 1520, *WA Br* 2, 160. There is a print of Brunfels's edition of the works and letters of Hus in the library of The University of Chicago.

[2] Agricola's activities are summarized in the chapter 'Hussitica' in Gustav Kawerau, *Johann Agricola von Eisleben*. Ein Beitrag zur Reformationsgeschichte (Berlin, 1881), pp. 118-128. Jan Jakubec, *Dějiny literatury české*, I (Prague, 1929), 316. What appears to be a second edition is in the library of Concordia Seminary, Saint Louis; it is anonymous and bears the title *Die in Huszen bekriegte doch unbesiegte Wahrheit* (Frankfort and Leipzig, 1686), claiming to have been based on Agricola (p. 4). Cf. Otto Clemen's reference to Agricola's original, *WA* 50, 17-18.

[3] *Ein heimlich gespräch von der tragedia Johannis Hussen*, ed. Hugo Holstein, *NDL* 174 (Halle, 1900); cf. also Kawerau, *Agricola*, p. 122, note 2, on the authorship, and Cochlaeus to Aleander, October 7, 1537, *ZKG* 18, 277.

[4] Cf. Georg Loesche, *Luther, Melanthon und Calvin in Oesterreich-Ungarn* (Tübingen, 1909), p. 55.

Such were the forces which brought Luther to a conviction that he was supporting the same cause for which, a hundred years before, John Hus had lived a hero's life and died a martyr's death. Here was a man who, like Luther, had loved the church so much that he was forced by his conviction to speak out against its churchly enemies. Church councils were not the infallible voice of the true church, for the Council of Constance had condemned the Catholic truth in the doctrines of Hus. Nor was the antiquity of a man any measure of his true standing in the church. John Hus, who had died early in the same century in which Luther was born, had been a saint, a reformer, and a church father—all at the same time. By adopting him as such, Luther both affirmed his continuity with 'the succession of the faithful' and, as Chapter VIII will show, took a long step toward healing a schism that had preceded his own Reformation.

VIII

NEGOTIATIONS TOWARD UNITY

IN the Leipzig Debate of 1519 Luther was forced to admit publicly that certain teachings of John Hus, condemned at the Council of Constance in 1415, had been truly Christian. Chapter IV has described the eventual outcome of this admission, the combination of Catholic substance and Protestant principle in Luther's view of church councils. Chapter VII has traced the development of Luther's attitude toward Hus, which is perhaps the most striking illustration of the effect that 'Catholic substance and Protestant principle' had upon Luther's reinterpretation of the Christian past. The relation between Catholic substance and Protestant principle became much more complex during Luther's negotiations with the spiritual descendants of John Hus. For as a recent summary has put it, 'Hus was no sectarian or founder of a sect, neither an innovator as a theologian . . . nor a radical reformer'; but his followers, 'the Hussites, were united only in their opposition [to Rome], not in their faith or in their goals'.[1] Despite the dissensions among them, however, there was a messianic hope alive in their midst. Since they had cut themselves off from Rome, they felt the need of establishing unity with another church. Like Luther, they needed a way of affirming both Catholic substance and Protestant principle. Therefore, when Luther arose as a powerful opponent of the papacy, the Hussites eagerly investigated him and his teaching in the hope that he would fill that need.

FACTIONS AMONG THE HUSSITES

Certainly something was needed in Bohemia. Not only had the results of Hus's work so divided the country that, as Emser

[1] Herbert Grundmann, *Ketzergeschichte des Mittelalters*, 'Die Kirche in ihrer Geschichte', II-G (Göttingen, 1963), 63-64.

observed, even married couples were split up; but there was not even unity among those who had broken off from Rome. The centrifugal tendency in the Protestant principle, which was to become evident in the Reformation of the sixteenth century and in its descendants, produced various factions among the Hussites, each claiming to be loyal to the New Testament and insisting that it alone had preserved the teachings of John Hus in an unadulterated form. Two of these factions are pertinent to our discussion: the Calixtines and the Unity of Bohemian Brethren.[1]

The Calixtines or Utraquists were a partly aristocratic, partly middle-class group, conservative both politically and religiously. They derived their name from their practice of administering the communion *sub utraque specie*, 'under both kinds', granting the chalice to the laity. This practice was condemned by the Council of Constance; nevertheless, it took deep root in Bohemia in 1417, when the preachers at Charles University in Prague proclaimed that Christ had ordained the Supper in both kinds. Beyond this, however, the Calixtines were unwilling to go; they did not repudiate the authority of the pope in principle, and if they had been granted the cup, they would readily have gone back to Rome.[2] Thus, when, in 1437, the Council of Basel gave them permission to use the chalice, the Utraquists thought that a reconciliation with Rome was in sight. The so-called *Compactata* of 1433, which Luther's Reformation used in its propaganda a century later,[3] granted them certain concessions, especially the chalice, with the stipulation that the priests were to remind their people that Christ

[1] The interpretation of these factions in Anglo-Saxon scholarship has been significantly affected by the discussion of Troeltsch, *Social Teachings*, I, 362 ff., which, despite its complete dependence on secondary sources, is quite perceptive. See also the illuminating comments of Norman Cohn, *The Pursuit of the Millennium* (2nd ed.; New York, 1961), pp. 217-251.

[2] Clemens Borowy, 'Die Utraquisten in Böhmen', *Archiv für österreichische Geschichte*, 36 (1866), 239-289; Leopold Krummel, 'Utraquisten und Taboriten', *ZHT* 41 (1871), 163-256, 311-413, 465-530; Palacký, *Dějiny*, pp. 710-717.

[3] Cf. Christian Adolph Peschek, *Geschichte der Gegenreformation in Böhmen* (Leipzig, 1850), I, 25-26. On the view of the *Compactata* among Luther's opponents, cf. Cochlaeus to Johann Faber, October 28, 1534, *ZKG* 18, 259; for Luther's use of it, cf. his *Report to a Good Friend on Both Kinds in the Sacrament*, *WA* 26, 600. In 1539 Prince George of Anhalt was at the convent of St Ludmila, where he saw 'missals, which the Bohemians cited at the Council of Basel, in which it is indicated that after distributing the body of the Lord, the priest should also distribute the chalice': 'Bericht an den Churfürsten Bericht von der Lehr und Ceremonien so zu Dessaw gehalten werden' in *Des Hochwirdigen . . . Georgen Fürsten zu Anhalt . . . Predigten und andere Schrifften* (Wittenberg, 1555), fol. 351A.

was wholly present in either kind; they were also to keep the faith as far as all other doctrines were concerned. Because of the unrest caused by the *Compactata*, Pope Pius II, who had travelled in Bohemia and written a book on the Czechs, eventually revoked the decree of the Council of Basel.[1] But the Utraquists continued in their practice of communion under both kinds.

Dissatisfied with both Roman Catholicism and Utraquism, a group of Hussites, under the influence of Peter Chelčický and under the leadership of a certain Gregory, met in Kunwald in 1459 and formed the Unity of Bohemian Brethren. Into this body there came various Hussite groups. Requiring a strict biblicism of its adherents and no more, the Unity caught up many (though not all) of the radical, sectarian elements which could find no religious satisfaction elsewhere. As a result, when Luther arose as a defender of John Hus, the Unity appeared to have very little unity in its religious convictions.[2]

On two convictions, however, there seems to have been unanimity in Bohemia at the opening of the sixteenth century: that the Roman Catholic position on the Lord's Supper was wrong, and that there was a necessity for Czech Christians to open negotiations toward unity with some other Christian group. In 1450 the Utraquist estates held a synod at which it was decided to send a delegation to Constantinople for negotiation with the ecumenical patriarch. The result was that the Orthodox, expressing their joy over the unity of faith which had been established, promised to ordain the Utraquist priests; obtaining that promise had been the main purpose of the delegation.[3] Similarly, the Unity agreed in 1486 to send out four men all over Christendom, to try

---

[1] See the Jesuit historian, Blahoslavus Balbinus, *Epitome historica rerum bohemicarum* (Prague, 1677), pp. 528-530, with citations of original documents; Ludwig Pastor, *History of the Popes from the Close of the Middle Ages*, tr. F. I. Antrobus *et al* (London, 1907-1938), III, 228-229.

[2] Cf. Matthew Spinka, 'Peter Chelčický, the Spiritual Father of the *Unitas Fratrum*', *Church History*, XII (1943), 271-291. The standard manuals on the history of the Unity of Bohemian Brethren are: Anton Gindely, *Geschichte der böhmischen Brüder* (2 vols., 2nd ed.; Prague, 1861-1862); Bernhard Czerwenka, *Geschichte der evangelischen Kirche in Böhmen* (2 vols.; Bielefeld and Leipzig, 1869-1870); Ernest de Schweinitz, *History of the Church Known as the Unitas Fratrum* (Bethlehem, Pa., 1885); Joseph Müller, *Geschichte der böhmischen Brüder* (2 vols.; Herrnhut, 1922-1931). There is an excellent survey and summary of the historical materials in Rudolf Říčan, *Die böhmischen Brüder*, tr. Bohumír Popelář (Berlin, 1958).

[3] Peschek, *op. cit.*, pp. 31-32.

to find a church group with which the Unity could associate itself. When the men returned with the report that they had found no such church, the Brethren dispatched others, restricting themselves this time to Western Europe. This embassy found some Waldensians here and there; and relations between the Unity and the Waldensians, which had been going on for some time, were thereby strengthened.[1] Although neither the *rapprochement* with Constantinople nor the unity with the Waldensians ever came to fruition, they do serve to illustrate the longing which the Czechs felt and for which they ultimately came to believe that Luther was the fulfilment.

THE HUSSITES AND THE LEIPZIG DEBATE

The hope that Luther was indeed the fulfilment of their longing seems to have come to the Czechs quite early, first of all to the Utraquists, probably because they were strong in Prague. Some of their number were present at the Leipzig Debate and brought back favourable reports concerning Luther's support of Hus against Eck, thus substantiating the impression which Luther's writings had made in Bohemia.[2] On the strength of these reports, two Utraquists, John Poduška and Wenceslaus Rožďalovský, wrote to Luther soon afterward to express their sympathy with his stand. Congratulating Luther on his position, both writers exhorted him to stand firm. They backed up their exhortation with kind words about Elector Frederick and with gifts: Poduška sent cutlery, and Rožďalovský a copy of Hus's book *On the Church*.[3] Rožďalovský promised to send a biography of Hus, too, should Luther desire it; there is no record of what came of that promise, and

---

[1] F. M. Bartoš, 'Z počátku Jednoty bratrské', *Časopis českého musea*, 1921.

[2] On Luther and the Utraquists, cf. Josef Čihula, 'Luther a Čechové podoboji', *Český časopis historický*, 3 (1897), 274 ff.; Loesche, *Luther, Melanthon und Calvin in Oesterreich-Ungarn*, pp. 36-42. On the attendance of some Utraquists at the Leipzig debate, cf. Wenzel Rožďalovský to Luther, July 17, 1519, *WA Br* 1, 419, on 'a certain James, an organist', who had attended. See also Jan Poduška to Luther, July 16, 1519, *WA Br* 1, 417: 'Many and various treatises of yours have come into our hands.' See also P. Dedic, 'Verbreitung und Vernichtung evangelischen Schrifttums in Innerösterreich im Zeitalter der Reformation und Gegenreformation', *ZKG* 57 (1938), 433-458.

[3] On the Elector, cf. Rožďalovský to Luther, July 17, 1519, *WA Br* 1, 419; Luther to Staupitz, October 3, 1519, *WA Br* 1, 514; and Luther's message to the Utraquist estates, *WA* 10-II, 173. Almost a year later, Luther sent Spalatin a copy of this treatise by Hus, perhaps the same copy that Rožďalovský had sent him; cf. Luther to Spalatin, March 19, 1520, *WA Br* 2, 73.

Luther did not refer to it when he reported the letters to Staupitz with the remark: 'They are amazingly Erasmian both in their ideas and in their language.'[1]

Luther's contacts with the Utraquists are obscure for the next few years, but there may have been some communication between them. So, at least, it seems from the report that in the summer of 1522, when some of the Utraquists were planning a reconciliation with Rome, a dissenting group sent a 'legate' to Luther. A diet of the Utraquist estates was scheduled to decide on the question in June, 1522. That formed the occasion for Luther's open letter to the Czech estates. Luther opened the letter with a description of how he had once felt about the Hussites and of how his attitude had changed to such an extent that rumour was making him a Czech native who was preparing to flee to Bohemia. After assuring the Utraquists that the German princes were well-disposed to them, he went on to suggest a union between the Utraquists and the Lutherans; but this could not be accomplished without patience.[2] The whole treatise is important for the light it sheds on Luther's views of unity beyond separation, particularly on his attitude toward the question of unity with the Hussites. First the parties would have to be united in their beliefs, only then in their name. Union would have to be a gradual process of patiently permitting the gospel to work on both groups. And the Utraquists were not to be so afraid of becoming a sect that they returned to Rome and thus blemished Hus's memory.[3]

THE CAHERA FIASCO

Because of Luther's appeal and the other writings that were circulating among them, the Utraquists were split into two parties, one pro-Lutheran, the other pro-Roman. As the representative and hopeful leader of the former, Gallus Cahera came to Wittenberg

---

[1] Luther to Staupitz, October 3, 1519, *WA Br* 1, 514.
[2] Cf. Luther to Lang, July 16, 1522, *WA Br* 2, 579 (if, as the Weimar editors suggest, *blasphemos* should be *Bohemos*); *Message to the Bohemian Estates*, July 15, 1522, *WA* 10-II, 172-174.
[3] Quite consistently, Luther stressed this view of unity beyond separation. Thus he said in a sermon in 1525: 'A tiny faith is a faith, too. That was why he [Christ] came into the world, to accept, bear, and show patience to the weak. . . . Even though they are not strong today, in a single hour it can happen that such a person grasps the word [of God] more richly than we', *WA* 17-I, 458-459. Even in the bitterness of his later years this was true: *Brief Confession on the Blessed Sacrament*, *WA* 54, 158.

in the summer of 1523. After gaining Luther's confidence, Cahera prevailed upon him to write a treatise on ordination for the Utraquists. He returned to Prague with the treatise in the fall of 1523. It appeared first in Latin and was then translated into German by Paul Speratus. The treatise was a systematic review of the prerogatives which Roman Catholicism claimed for the priest, and a demonstration that all of them belonged to individual Christians, since they were priests.[1] Discouraging the practice of private communion in the home, Luther attempted to show that the Lord's Supper was inferior in importance to the preaching of the word and to baptism, both of which belonged to the layman as priest. He also included a strong recommendation of Cahera, who had been legitimately ordained; thus, he said, the Utraquists could overcome the qualms of those who were still reluctant to establish a separate ministry.[2]

On the basis of this recommendation, Cahera was elected administrator of the Utraquist estates. But he soon began negotiating with the papal party, and his actions aroused much antagonism among his fellow-Utraquists. In the subsequent tumult Cahera seems to have given up his position and to have gone into exile. Luther wrote to him to express his bitter disappointment, and by the early part of the year he was sufficiently wrought up to refer to Cahera as 'that monster among the Bohemians'.[3]

LUTHER AND THE UNITY OF BOHEMIAN BRETHREN

With that fiasco the contacts between Luther and the Utraquists seem to have ended. Meanwhile, Luther had begun his negotiations with the Unity of Bohemian Brethren; out of these negotiations was to issue Luther's preface to the irenic Czech Confession of 1538, discussed in Chapter IX. As has already been mentioned, the Brethren were earnestly seeking commendation and

[1] *Concerning the Ministry*, WA 12, 169-196 (*LW* 40, 7-44). For a comprehensive summary, cf. A. W. Dieckhoff, *Luthers Lehre von der kirchlichen Gewalt* (Berlin, 1865), pp. 90-96, and the critique, pp. 97-106 and *passim*.
[2] *Concerning the Ministry*, WA 12, 194 (*LW* 40, 41).
[3] The chronicle of Burianus narrates: 'Gallus Cahera, the Lutheranizer, was sent into exile by King Ferdinand I; he went to Ansbach and there took a wife', quoted in Balbinus, *op. cit.*, p. 586. Cf. Luther's bitter letter to Cahera of November 13, 1524, *WA Br* 3, 370-371; also Luther to Burian Sobek von Kornitz, October 27, 1524, *WA Br* 3, 363. The phrase *Bohemorum portentum* appears in Luther to Nicholas Hausmann, February 2, 1525, *WA Br* 3, 431.

approval from other Christians who seemed to be opposing the papal system. Thus they had approached Erasmus in 1511 with a request that he approve their confession of 1508. Excusing himself because of too much work, Erasmus expressed his fears concerning the impression such approval might make and declined to offer it, though he seems to have referred to the Brethren approvingly in the preface to the second edition of his New Testament.[1]

But the Brethren were still hopeful of making some sort of contact, and Luther's rise as a Reformer seemed to offer a possible fulfilment of that hope. As he had condemned Hus in his early days, so Luther had also condemned the Brethren. Throughout his early life he regarded them as heretics. We have seen that he was quite violent in his censure of them as late as 1519. Although it is a problem whether the name 'Pickards' always refers to them, it is clear that he often used that name for the Bohemians.[2] His chief criticism of them, as at Leipzig, was directed at their supposed pride and lovelessness; and in at least one place in his commentary on Romans he referred to their views on sin and grace. For Luther, as for the entire church, they were 'distorters of Scripture and crafty slanderers of our piety'.[3] As Luther's opposition to the papacy increased, however, and as he began his association with the Utraquists, his view of the Bohemian Brethren also underwent revisions. Late in 1519 he came into possession of an anti-papal tract, which may have been the work of Brother John Lucas, bishop of the Unity. By June, 1520, he was less derogatory than he had been of the 'Pickards', and this in a letter to a man

[1] In addition to the histories cited in note 6 above, cf. F. M. Bartoš, 'Das Auftreten Luthers und die Unität', *Archiv für Reformationsgeschichte*, 31 (1934), 103-120; Josef Čihula, 'Poměr Jednoty Bratří Českých k Martinovi Lutherovi', *Věstník královské české společnosti nauk*, 1897; J. Ružička, 'Čechové a doktor M. Luther, s poznamenáním o ostatcích bratrstva', *Českobratrský věstník* (Prague, 1850), pp. 281ff.; Loesche, *Luther, Melanthon und Calvin*, pp. 43-60; Erhard Peschke, *Die Theologie der böhmischen Brüder in ihrer Vorzeit*, I, *Das Abendmahl*, 1. *Studien* (Stuttgart, 1935), 307-380. On the correspondence with Erasmus, cf. F. M. Bartoš, 'Erasmus a česká reformace', *Křestanská Revue, Theologická příloha* (1956).
[2] *The Ten Commandments Preached to the People of Wittenberg*, WA 1, 506; *Commentary on Psalm* 109, WA 1, 697. Cf. Köhler, *Luther und die Kirchengeschichte*, p. 171.
[3] *The Ten Commandments Preached to the People of Wittenberg*, WA 1, 426. Cf. *Lectures on Romans*, WA 56, 494, tr. Wilhelm Pauck, 'Library of Christian Classics', XV, (Philadelphia, 1961), p. 381; see Peschke, *op. cit.*, pp. 338-340, on other passages in the *Lectures on Romans*. Cf. also Luther to Spalatin, December 31, 1516, *WA Br* 1, 82; Sermon on the Chains of St Peter (August 1, 1516), *WA* 1, 69; *Lectures on the Psalms*, WA 3, 334; *ibid.*, WA 4, 361.

prominent in anti-Hussite activity.[1] Nevertheless, they remained heretics in Luther's opinion because of their doctrine of the Lord's Supper.[2] It was chiefly around this doctrine that future discussions between Luther and the Unity were to move.

THE PROBLEM OF THE EUCHARIST

The doctrine of the Lord's Supper was the focal point of Hussite piety and thought for a full two centuries. It was an especially troublesome point to Lucas, whose extensive literary output was largely devoted to positive and polemical discussion of the eucharist. Lucas's view of the Lord's Supper caused Luther much difficulty; and small wonder, for it is quite complicated.[3]

In the form it had before his first encounter with Luther, Lucas's doctrine of the eucharist was postulated on a detailed theory of the modes of being in Christ. He gave best expression to it in his treatise of 1520 on the adoration of the sacrament. Christ had fundamentally two modes of existence: the personal, essential, real [*bytný*] mode; and the spiritual mode. According to the personal mode he had walked on the earth, suffered, died, and risen from the dead. The spiritual mode, on the other hand, was divided into the essential spiritual existence and the ministerial spiritual existence. By the essential spiritual existence Christ existed in himself and in the believer, in this world and in the next. By the ministerial existence he served through the ministers of the church and also through its ministrations; chief among these latter were the word of the gospel and the sacraments, most particularly, of course, the Lord's Supper, in which his presence was directly asserted.[4] Working on the basis of such a theory, Lucas could come to what Peschke summarizes as 'a definite rejection of transubstantiation, consubstantiation, and the theory of signification'.[5]

---

[1] Cf. Luther to Johann Lang, December 18, 1519, *WA Br* 1, 597; Luther to Hieronymus Dungersheim, June 1520, *WA Br* 2, 126; and Karl Schottenloher, *Jakob Ziegler aus Landau an der Isar* (Münster, 1910), pp. 380ff.

[2] Luther enumerates various parties among the Hussites, *Explanation of Doctor Martin Luther of Several Articles in his Treatise on the Blessed Sacrament*, *WA* 6, 80.

[3] Cf. Jan Jakubec, *Dějiny literatury české*, I, 630-635, 646-647; Rudolf Vindis, 'Bratra Lukáša Pražského názory o eucharistu', *Věstník královské české společnosti nauk* (Prague, 1922-1923); Peschke, *op. cit.*, pp. 227-304.

[4] *Sepsánie duovoduov z najjistčích písem . . . o klaněnie a klekánie před svátostí Těla a krve božie, a to pod spuosobem pohádky*, 27af, quoted in Peschke, *op. cit.*, p. 275, note 4; cf. also Jakubec, *op. cit.*, I, 633.

[5] Peschke, *op. cit.*, p. 287.

If Peschke has caught his meaning, Lucas taught that the spiritual body received in the sacrament was not the same body betrayed by Judas and crucified on Good Friday, but that by the reception of that spiritual body one participated in the natural body as well. And so the presence of Christ in the Lord's Supper was neither spiritual nor symbolic nor sacramental nor real, but all of these.

Luther was, of course, confused by such a viewpoint. As has already been pointed out, the Bohemian Brethren were known to have peculiar ideas on the sacrament, and this was one of Luther's objections to them. It was therefore natural that Luther should speak of the sacrament in his dealings with the Brethren. The situation was brought to a head through the difficulties encountered by Paul Speratus in his work as the preacher at Iglau in Moravia. After arriving in Iglau early in May, 1522, Speratus had begun to make inquiries of the Utraquists and Brethren in the vicinity concerning their doctrinal position. Interviews and research produced a group of articles, which he sent to Luther for his opinion. The letter reached Wittenberg just as Luther was entertaining a delegation from the Unity, headed by John Roh. Luther's conversations with Roh and his companion convinced him that despite their somewhat peculiar manner of speaking, the Brethren did not deny the true presence of Christ in the sacrament. They did, of course, teach that the body which was present in the sacrament was different from that which was sitting at the right hand of the Father; not knowing that he would eventually address himself to the problematics of just that relationship, Luther expressed the pious wish 'that one should not be too concerned about these matters, but should have a pure and simple faith'.[1]

MICHAEL WEISSE ON THE PRESENCE OF CHRIST

In the same letter Luther gave voice to his displeasure at the report that the Brethren, as quoted in Speratus's theses, were still applying the sixth chapter of St John to the eucharist, an exegesis that Luther rejected.[2] The indication that there was an almost

---

[1] Luther to Speratus, May 16, 1522, *WA Br* 2, 531. Cf. James Mearns, 'Roh', *A Dictionary of Hymnology*, ed. John Julian (London, 1925), pp. 972-973; and the preface to the hymnal of the Bohemian Brethren, reprinted in *Das deutsche Kirchenlied von der ältesten Zeit bis zu Anfang des XVII. Jahrhunderts*, ed. Philipp Wackernagel, I (Leipzig, 1864), 727.
[2] Cf. Pelikan, *Luther the Expositor*, pp. 174-190.

completely symbolic interpretation of the Lord's Supper in some sections of the Unity, even during Lucas's period of prominence, is substantiated by the views expressed in the hyms of Michael Weisse; and it is well to recall Wilhelm Dilthey's winged word that the religiousness of a group cannot be gauged from its theological treatises alone, but also from its prayers and hymns.[1] Weisse's hymnody quite plausibly represents a considerable section of popular piety within the Unity.

Although he was not averse to employing metaphysical terminology in his hymns, Weisse's allusions to the Lord's Supper show that he wished to avoid the Christological speculation which had marked Lucas's approach to the problem of the real presence. Weisse therefore emphasized the point that having personally ascended into heaven, Christ could be present in only one place at a given time; and since his transfigured and exalted body was glorious, his presence only before the throne of God was a source of comfort. The logical conclusion from these facts, thought Weisse, was a spiritualistic and somewhat moralistic conception of the Lord's Supper. Warning the believers against false prophets who taught Christ's personal presence in the eucharist, Weisse stressed the testamental character of the Supper. His views are well summarized in these verses:[2]

> The sacrament is bread and wine
> And is not changed to things divine;
> Though it be called Christ's body and blood,
> This must be spiritually understood.
>
> By itself, Christ's body and blood
> Makes no one righteous before God.
> But the Spirit's power can impart
> Balm to every thirsting heart.

That such was actually Weisse's position is evident from Roh's criticism of him in the preface to the 1544 edition of the hymnal

---

[1] Wilhelm Dilthey, *Weltanschauung und Analyse des Menschen seit Renaissance und Reformation, Gesammelte Schriften*, II (Leipzig, 1914), 515.

[2] Hymn No. 413, st. 8-10, Wackernagel, *op. cit.*, III, 347; other hymns upon which the above summary is based are, in the order referred to: No. 314, st. 9 (*ibid.*, p. 276); No. 411, st. 6 (*ibid.*, p. 346); No. 297, st. 8 (*ibid.*, p. 265); No. 409, st. 2 (*ibid.*, p. 344); No. 305, st. 4 (*ibid.*, p. 271); No. 414, st. I (*ibid.*, p. 348).

of the Brethren, as well as from the changes that Roh made in Weisse's hymns for that edition.[1]

With due realization of the hazards in such a parallelization, it can be suggested that Weisse represented a view similar to that of Zwingli, and that Lucas's position was closer to that of Calvin. The inconsistency which that implies was very significant in Luther's dealings with the Unity: he was repelled or attracted by their doctrine because of the view of the man or group with whom he was dealing at a particular time. Thus, when Roh visited him, Luther came to believe that the Brethren were closer to his own position than many of them actually were.

THE ADORATION OF THE HOST

Understandably, then, Speratus was not satisfied with Luther's answer of May 16. A discussion with Beneš Optát had convinced him that there was more to the doctrine of the Brethren than Luther had supposed from his conversation with Roh, that, in short, Luther had been duped. Optát was curious about the adoration of Christ in the sacrament and about the doctrine of concomitance, which underlay that custom. Though he regarded such questions as 'foolish and inappropriate', Luther replied that the veneration of the host was an adiaphoron, and that they should hold to the simple faith of simple people in the true presence of Christ in the elements. He was sure that 'no one denies, not even the Brethren, . . . that the body and blood of Christ are present there'.[2] In a short time, however, Luther was to see that Speratus's suspicions about the Unity were justified. Sometime late in 1522 or early in 1523, the Brethren published a catechism in Czech and German. It seems to have been written partly at Luther's request for clarification of their doctrine of the sacrament. Lucas sent a Latin translation to Luther and asked him to edit and publish it; this Luther agreed to do. But a more thorough investigation of the contents of the brochure convinced him that he should first determine the view of the Brethren on Christ's presence in the sacra-

---

[1] Thus, for example, in Hymn No. 409 (Wackernagel, *op. cit.*, III, 345), Roh inserted the words: 'truly thy body and blood'; cf. also No. 412, st. 6 (*ibid.*, p. 346).
[2] Luther to Speratus, June 13, 1522, *WA Br* 2, 560-561; cf. Müller, *Geschichte*, I, 403ff.

ment before going ahead with the publication.[1] In order to clarify matters, Luther composed an extensive treatise on the adoration of Christ in the sacrament, addressed to the Unity.

The treatise is highly significant for an understanding of Luther's relations with the Unity and of his stand in the later sacramentarian controversies. In the first part he listed four possible errors on the sacrament and attempted to refute each one exegetically. Some Christians 'held that in the sacrament there is merely bread and wine, such as people otherwise eat and drink. They have taught nothing more than that the bread signifies the body and the wine signifies the blood of Christ.' The second group supposed that 'the sacrament is nothing else than a participation in the body of Christ, or, better, an incorporation into his spiritual body'. The other extreme was taken by the doctrine of transubstantiation, the theory 'that in the sacrament no bread remains but only the form of the bread'. And the fourth theory, 'the worst of all and the most heretical', was that the sacrament was 'a sacrifice and a good work'.[2] Either the first or the second of these possibilities seemed to Luther to have led the Brethren astray. As the cause of their error Luther suggested the existence of a rationalistic tendency among them, and he warned them against it. Though one of the most biblicistic of Luther's earliest works, the treatise on *The Adoration of the Sacrament* was very careful to avoid the logomachy caused by linguistic differences. Luther sent it to the Brethren with the hope 'that my German may perhaps be clearer to you than your German and Latin are to me'. He also recommended that they cultivate the classical languages and promised that the Germans would strive to do something about the low level of piety and morality in their midst.

The treatise was well received by the Unity, and in a letter to Luther[3] the Bohemian elders expressed their appreciation for his

[1] Cf. *Die deutschen Katechismen der böhmischen Brüder*, ed. Joseph Müller, 'Monumenta Germaniae Paedagogica', VI (Berlin, 1887); cf. Luther's *The Adoration of the Sacrament of the Holy Body of Christ*, WA 11, 431 (*LW* 36, 276), on the background of the catechism.
[2] *The Adoration of the Sacrament*, WA 11, 434, 437, 441 (*LW* 36, 279, 282, 287-288); cf. Julius Köstlin, *The Theology of Luther in Its Historical Development and Inner Harmony*, tr. Charles E. Hay (2 vols; Philadelphia, 1895-1897), II, 65-67. See Luther's reference to the treatise three years later in his *Message to John Herwagen*, WA 19, 471.
[3] The Elders of the Bohemian Brethren to Luther, before June 23, 1523, WA Br 3, 98-99.

generous treatment of the points on which the Brethren differed
with him. They promised to think the points through carefully and
to try to formulate a clearer statement of their position. Despite
this tone of friendship, there was an undertone of formality in the
letter, indicative of the alienation that was already beginning. Such
was the nature of that sudden alienation that there seems to have
been little or no contact between the Unity and Luther for almost
an entire decade. Both Luther and the Unity were deeply involved
in determining their future course, and the only relation there was
between them seems to have been through the Bohemian students
who came to Germany.[1] When contacts were re-established, the
man chiefly responsible was John Augusta.

RENEWED NEGOTIATIONS

Born in 1500 as the son of a Utraquist hatter, Augusta rose
to the leadership of the Unity without the benefit of an extensive
formal education. He nevertheless joined that group in the Unity
which felt the need for an educated clergy, the same group which
attempted to break with Lucas's policy of isolation and to re-
establish friendly contacts with Luther's Reformation. Under his
leadership that group prepared a confession of faith in 1532 for
presentation to the Margrave George of Brandenburg. The confession was translated into German, presumably by Michael
Weisse, and published in Zurich in 1532; the tone of the translation was almost Zwinglian. Alarmed at what this might mean for
their relations with Luther, the elders of the Brethren quickly tried
to stop the translation, but to no avail. They therefore did the next
best thing and retranslated the confession.[2] This second translation came somehow into Luther's hands; and in 1533 he published
it in Wittenberg, together with his own preface to it.[3] The preface
emphasized the principle 'that one should not quarrel over words
and ways of speaking'. Despite their strange manner of speaking,
Luther was convinced that the Brethren 'basically agree with us
and believe that in the sacrament the true body and blood of Christ

---

[1] See p. 107, note 2 above.
[2] Cf. Otakar Odložilík, 'Two Reformation Leaders of the *Unitas Fratrum*'
Church History, IX (1940), 253-263; Müller, *Geschichte*, II, 45-48.
[3] The preface appears in *WA* 38, 78-80; see the introduction, *ibid.*, pp. 76-77,
for a brief account of the events preceding the publication of the second version.

are received'. Expressing the hope that the publication of this confession would lead to more unity, Luther sent it on its way.

Nevertheless, the confusion caused by the differing translations persisted. To clear up the confused situation as well as to inform themselves about the moral convictions and conditions among the German Lutherans, the Brethren sent out a delegation in 1535.[1] Although the delegation was intended as an embassy to both the Lutherans and the Zwinglians, it never got beyond Wittenberg. Here the delegates spent four weeks, from March 21 till April 18, in theological discussion. The chief subjects of the dialogue were justification by faith and, as always, the sacraments. Particular attention was devoted to the meaning of the confession of 1532, which had described the presence of Christ in the Lord's Supper as 'consecrated, spiritual, powerful, and true'.[2] When the dialogue was over, both Luther and Melanchthon were so pleased that they sent cordial letters back to Bohemia with the delegates.[3] Luther's reaction to the visit was particularly enthusiastic. He had always maintained, he said, that 'it is sufficient if the church Catholic agrees in faith and doctrine', and more explicitly that 'where these two sacraments [baptism and the Lord's Supper] are correctly administered, the observance of everything else is easy'. According to this definition of unity, whose implications we have examined in Part One of this book, Luther and the Unity of Bohemian Brethren were now one. On the controverted issue of the Lord's Supper, Luther said, 'I do not see how we differ, even though we use different words. But as the saying goes, it is vain to dispute about words when there is agreement on the issues.' Nor did differences in practice militate against that essential agreement; 'for it is doctrine that makes men Christians or heretics, while life makes them saints or sinners.'

A NEW CONFESSION

Encouraged by this warm reception, the Brethren proceeded to work up a new confession of their faith and to present it to King

[1] Cf. the chronicle of N. Slanský, *Quellen zur Geschichte der böhmischen Brüder*, ed. Anton Gindely, 'Fontes Rerum Austraicarum', XIX (Vienna, 1859), 16-71.

[2] '... poswátně duchowně mocně a prawě', *ibid.*, p. 46. The Latin translation of the *Rechenschaft* appears in Balthasar Lydius, *Waldensia* (Rotterdam, 1616), Ib, 92-367, which I have used in the library of Columbia University.

[3] Melanchthon's letter, *CR* 2, 854, was probably written at this time; Luther to Benedict Baworinský, April 18, 1535, *WA Br* 7, 175-177.

Ferdinand. This was the Czech Confession of 1535. Although the monarch did not even deign to read the document, its publication by Luther in 1538 was the culmination of the negotiations toward unity between Luther and the Hussites. The confession was presented to Ferdinand on November 14, 1535, as the official doctrinal position of the Unity. Almost a year later the Brethren sent John Augusta, Erasmus Sommerfeld, and George Israel to Luther with the confession and a letter of introduction.[1] The letter is a model of evangelical Catholicity. In presenting their confession to Luther for his reaction and, if possible, his assistance with its publication, the Brethren were willing to be corrected, as they had been on the question of rebaptism, or to have Luther indicate his disagreement with any particular point by means of marginal glosses. As a reason for requesting his aid in publishing the confession, they referred to the lack of printers and of Latin type and to the restrictions on printing in Bohemia; they were, of course, also very eager to receive endorsement from the leader of the Reformation.

Such an endorsement was not immediately forthcoming. Luther was grateful to the Brethren for their willingness to clarify the issues, as well as for their gifts.[2] With the confession he found himself in substantial agreement. Only two minor points were unclear to him: The Brethren taught that someone who deferred repentance until his deathbed was not to be absolved; they also had men in their midst who preferred a celibate life. Luther expressed the desire that they clarify the first point and make it plain with regard to the second that this was a purely personal and optional matter. On both these points the Brethren gave in to Luther. In June, 1537, they sent another delegation to him with the revised Czech Confession and a Latin translation of their confession of 1532, now called Apology. Luther promised to have them both printed, though he added the warning that it might take some time. On the strength of that promise, the Brethren circulated the report of the Reformer's intended action all over Bohemia.[3] But Luther did not get the job done as soon as the Brethren had ex-

---

[1] Müller, *Geschichte*, II, 59-77; the original of the letter perished in the fire at Litoměřice in May 1546, but a German translation of a Czech translation of the Latin original appears, *WA Br* 7, 559-563.

[2] Luther to the Elders of the Bohemian Brethren, November 5, 1536, *WA Br* 7, 585-586.

[3] Cf. the Bohemian Brethren to Luther, November 27, 1537, *WA Br* 8, 147-148.

pected and hoped. They therefore wrote to him on November 27, 1537, to repeat and emphasize their request and to remind him of his promise. No printer had been willing to undertake the printing at his own expense, Luther explained, but he would keep trying.[1]

Though he tried to find a printer, he did not succeed. Of making books, as the Preacher had pointed out, there was no end; and bad books were finding a more ready market than good ones.[2] Therefore, Luther felt obliged regretfully to return the manuscripts to the Brethren with a word of deep admiration and sympathy for their patience and perseverance. But the Brethren would not be stopped by any monetary considerations, now that Luther's approval of the confession was assured. They sent the books back with a statement of their readiness to underwrite the printing. Now Luther engaged George Rhau, the Wittenberg printer, and saw the Apology, with Agricola's preface, and the Czech Confession, with his own preface, through the press.

With no other group of fellow-Protestants did Luther negotiate as long, as patiently, and as successfully as he did with the Hussites. The publication of his preface to the Czech Confession came almost two decades after he had begun to transform John Hus from a heretic and schismatic into a reformer and church father. The history of these negotiations documents the thesis that the Protestant principle as Luther defended it was not divisive but unitive, not sectarian but Catholic. As Chapter II and Chapter VI have pointed out, Luther's Reformation was concerned to base the unity of the church upon its divine charter and to subordinate both the polity and the liturgy of the church to this charter. As this chapter has shown, Luther was eager to subordinate the language of the church's theology to the same judgment. Separation from Rome did not mean separatism, any more than the Protestant principle of loyalty to Scripture meant a repudiation of Catholic substance. What such separation and loyalty did mean, as Chapter I has said, was an evangelical Catholicity that accepted the unity of the church, together with her holiness, as a gift from God and then pursued it as a goal. Luther's negotiations with the Bohemian Brethren make clear that in the question of church unity, as in the question of personal holiness, 'Become what you are' was a *leit-motiv* of Luther's Reformation.

[1] Slanský, *op. cit.*, p. 25.
[2] Luther to the Bohemian Brethren, December 7, 1537 *WA Br* 8, 161.

IX

THE IRENIC REFORMER

NEITHER the Catholic substance nor the Protestant principle in Luther's Reformation appeared to leave much room for an irenic attitude toward other Christians. Standing as he did in the Catholic tradition, Luther regarded, for example, any denial of the perpetual virginity of the Blessed Virgin Mary as an insult.[1] Convinced as he was of the correctness of his doctrine of the Lord's Supper, Luther took the Protestant principle of biblical authority to imply that he could not join forces with those who erred in this doctrine. Thus he was sharply critical both of the latitudinarian tendency in medieval Catholicism and of the doctrinal indifference in many of his fellow-Protestants.[2] Yet in his negotiations with the Hussites he consistently showed a willingness to put the best construction on their equivocal statements and to let the worse appear the better reason. An irenicism more often associated with Philip Melanchthon than with Martin Luther characterized the entire relationship between Luther and the followers of Hus, especially his contacts with the Unity of Bohemian Brethren. Luther's endorsement of the Czech Confession, whose history has been sketched in Chapter VIII, is probably the most irenic chapter in the whole tragic history of fission and schism in Luther's Reformation. Thus it becomes necessary to dig more deeply to find the sources of that irenic spirit.

LUTHER'S REGARD FOR HUS

One of the factors which brought about Luther's endorsement of the Czech Confession was the regard for Hus traced in Chapter

---

[1] Cf. *That Jesus Christ Was Born a Jew, WA* 11, 323-325; Smalcald Articles, Part I, *Bek.* 414, Latin text (*BC* 292).

[2] On the latitudinarian tendencies of medieval Catholicism, see *Against Henry the King of England, StL* 19, 345; on other Protestants, *Brief Confession on the Blessed Sacrament, WA* 54, 158.

VII. Closely connected with it was Luther's sense of gratitude to Hus and to Hus's church for the historical continuity which they provided. 'The church is hidden', wrote Luther to Erasmus in 1525. He was equally sure, however, that 'the holy Christian church will not perish, even to the end of the world'. That applied to the Middle Ages, too; and Hus was a proof to Luther that there had been a church also under the papacy.[1] In short, though Hus was not, as has sometimes been maintained, the source for Luther's view of the church as invisible, or hidden, he was an indication of the continuity of the church despite the 'apostasy' of medieval Catholicism. In addition, the memory of Hus had considerable significance for Luther's sense of mission and vocation. Like other 'pre-Reformers', Hus had prophesied of Luther's coming; and later Lutheranism was quite in keeping with Luther when it saw in Hus's predictions 'oracles and prophecies about the work of the Reformation'.[2]

THE PRIORITY OF THE SPOKEN WORD

Also worthy of consideration as a factor in Luther's irenic treatment of the Czech Confession is his appreciation of semantic difficulties involved in the composition of a creed or confession. Luther's insistence upon doctrinal conformity does indeed give the impression as though, to use Brunner's striking phrase, 'the word of God is again made compassable'.[3] Nevertheless, he criticized the Roman Catholic system for its objectivism and absolutism—at the same time that he was himself 'objectifying'! The same paradox is apparent also in his attitude toward the possibility of expressing the Christian faith in language. As Chapter III has shown, he criticized the ecumenical creeds and

---

[1] *The Bondage of the Will, WA* 18, 652; cf. *Answer . . . to the Book . . . of Catharinus, WA* 7, 722. Large Catechism, Part IV, par. 50, *Bek.* 701 (*BC* 443), which links Hus and Gerson. See also Karl Holl, *Luther,* pp. 369-370.

[2] Johann Gerhard, 'De vocatione beati Lutheri', *Loci Theologici* (1610-1622), ed. E. Preuss (Berlin, 1867), VI, 87. On other 'pre-Reformers', especially John Hilten, cf. Friedrich Myconius to Luther, December 2, 1529, *WA Br* 5, 191-192 also Apology, XXVII, 1-3, *Bek.* 377-378 (*BC* 268-269). On Hus's prophecy that though his enemies were burning a goose at the stake (*hus* means 'goose' in Czech), there would come a swan, which they would not be able to burn, cf. Adolf Hauffen, 'Husz ein Gans—Luther ein Schwan', *Prager deutsche Studien,* IX (1908), 1-28.

[3] Emil Brunner, *The Divine-Human Encounter,* tr. Olive Wyon (Philadelphia and London, 1943), p. 31.

conciliar decisions; and yet he could be completely orthodox in his treatment of them. Luther's sensitivity for the conditioned character of even the ecumenical descriptions of the Christian faith was due at least partially to his own version of an ancient theory of semantics and knowledge. Propounded by Plato and occupying a prominent place in Hebrew thought as well, the theory of the superiority of the spoken to the written word has had an interesting history. Luther adapted it to his view of the dynamic character of the Christian gospel; 'I am speaking of the oral, not the written, gospel.' His favourite word for the gospel was 'proclamation', and in a fascinating, if philologically question-able, exposition of the word 'Bethphage' he expounded his view that the church was a place where the lips, not the pen, held sway.[1]

Nowhere was Luther more conscious of the relation between the written and the spoken word than in his dealings with other Protestants, especially in the 1530s. Probably this was because of the logomachy that had resulted from the sacramentarian con-troversies. Luther was moved, for example, to write to the clergy in Augsburg in July of 1535:[2] 'Dearest brethren, how happy I was to receive your letter! I would rather come to know you on the basis of a living epistle, which is your Dr Gereon and Caspar Hueber, than on the basis of these words.'

That mood asserted itself even more effectively while Luther was dealing with the Unity of Bohemian Brethren. As we have seen in Chapter VIII, their writings had often made him suspicious of their views, but a personal interview had set things straight. This he attributed to the excessively close identification between their faith and their language; hence, anyone who did not read and understand Czech could not understand them.[3] And though he he did not particularly like that fact, he did take account of it. It seems clear that in his endorsement of the Czech Confession of

---

[1] Cf. Plato, *Phaedrus*, 276 A; the brief but suggestive note of Agathe Thorn-ton, 'The Hebrew Conception of Speech as a Creative Energy', *The Hibbert Journal*, XLIV (1946), 132-134. Luther, *Response to . . . Ambrosius Catharinus*, *WA* 7, 721; Elert, *The Structure of Lutheranism*, pp. 67-68, 188-189.

[2] Luther to the Clergy in Augsburg, July 20, 1535, *WA Br* 7, 213. See their answer to him, September 8, 1535, *WA Br* 7, 257: 'In relation to our letter you should have no doubt that we have sent you not some dead writing, but our liv-ing heart; thus also we are surely persuaded that we have received from you not some dead letters, but the living heart of Christian love.'

[3] *German Mass*, *WA* 19, 7 (*WML* 6, 172).

1535, Luther was striving to go beyond the written word of the confession to the meaning behind it.

THE BRETHREN AS 'WEAK BRETHREN'

Yet another factor accounting for Luther's irenic stand on the Czech Confession was the change that had come about in the theological tenor of the Unity because of their association with him. One by one, all the objectionable tendencies among them were removed; by 1538 they were all gone, and so he could and did endorse their confession. He had, for example, taken sharp issue with Lucas's view of the function of reason in theology.[1] He had expressed similar compunctions about their mysticism, which evidently made the Brethren despise education in general and the study of foreign languages in particular.[2] Their practice of rebaptizing converts from Roman Catholicism displeased him, too. But at Luther's suggestion they added a condemnation of mysticism to their Apology.[3] They strove to make it clear to him that they had abandoned the practice of rebaptizing and that they were willing to make almost any concession—as indeed they did—to win his approval. All this marked them as open-minded men, 'weak brethren', according to Luther's definition.[4] That attitude of teachable humility must certainly be taken into account as a factor in Luther's endorsement of the Czech Confession of 1535.

Each of these considerations was instrumental in moving Luther to treat the Czech Confession with sympathy. But the fundamental problem in his dealings with the Brethren had been that of the Lord's Supper, and this is the crux in a discussion of Luther's endorsement of the confession. Why was Luther willing to tolerate the view of the Brethren and yet unwilling to accept Ulrich Zwingli's formulation? This was difficult for his contemporaries to understand, and modern interpreters have not had less difficulty with the problem.

---

[1] Cf. Luther's *Exposition of Psalm 110* of 1518, *WA* 1, 696; cf. the interesting comments of Thomas Garrigue Masaryk, *Světová Revoluce* (Prague, 1925), pp. 589-590.

[2] *To the Councillors of All Cities in Germany, WA* 15, 42-43.

[3] It condemned those who 'put their foundation in some sort of spirit and in some sort of substantial or essential things with which they have struggled, that is, in the visions of their own imagination', Lydius, *Waldensia*, Ib, 246; cf. Luther, Sermon on Matt. 8:1-13, *WA* 17-II, 81.

[4] See the passage quoted on p. 124, note 3 above.

AFFINITIES OF ZWINGLI AND THE BRETHREN?

Was the doctrine of the Brethren similar to that of Zwingli? If so, why did Luther accept the one and reject the other? Assuming such a similarity, some of Luther's contemporaries urged that he reconsider the stand he had taken at Marburg in 1529. Such objections made themselves heard shortly after that colloquy, and when the Apology appeared with Luther's preface, some of Zwingli's followers hoped that now Luther would revise his previous position. With a similar interest in mind, a modern scholar has used Luther's dealings with the Brethren as substantiation for the possible historicity of a disputed conversation between Luther and Melanchthon about Zwingli.[1] Faced with the same problem, other interpreters have suggested that the Czech Confession of 1535 represented a completely Lutheran position. So, for instance, Martin Chemnitz tried to explain Luther's embarrassing conduct by stating that when the Zwinglians sought to substantiate their position on Christ's presence only at the right hand of the Father by reference to the Czech Confession of 1506, the Brethren 'testified publicly, by a repetition and clarification of their confession, that they approved Luther's doctrine of the Lord's Supper as in agreement with the word of God, and that they disagreed with Zwingli'. Similarly, a standard manual on Luther's theology suggests that despite their somewhat dubious modes of expression, the Brethren were in substantial agreement with Luther.[2]

If there is little difference between Zwingli's view of the Lord's Supper and that of the Brethren, how can one explain the paradox that, from the late 1520s on, Luther consistently condemned the

---

[1] Cf. Gregory Brück, 'Ursachen warumb man sich mit den schwermern nit in verstentnus noch ander handlung zu beschutzung des irrsals geben sol', written in November or December 1529, reprinted in Hans von Schubert, *Bekenntnisbildung und Religionspolitik 1529-1530 [1524-1534]* (Gotha, 1910), p. 145; see the English translation by J. Bodensieck in M. Reu, *The Augsburg Confession* (Chicago, 1930), II, 60; cf. Ambrosius Blaurer to the Bürgermeister and City Council of Constance, December 18, 1536, *Briefwechsel der Brüder Ambrosius und Thomas Blaurer 1509-1548*, ed. Traugott Schiess (Freiburg, 1908), I, 838, and Ambrosius Blaurer to Heinrich Bullinger, May 23, 1533, *ibid.*, pp. 395-396. See also Th. Diestelmann, *Die letzte Unterredung Luthers mit Melanchthon über den Abendmahlsstreit* (Göttingen, 1874), pp. 141-147.

[2] Martin Chemnitz, *Fundamenta sanae doctrinae de vera et substantiali praesentia, exhibitione, et sumtione corporis et sanguinis Domini in Coena* (1569; Frankfort, 1690), p. 102; Julius Köstlin, *Theology of Luther*, II, 192-194.

first and tried to sympathize with the second? In 1533, the same year that he published the Apology of the Brethren, he wrote to the Protestants in Frankfort: 'If anyone definitely knows that his pastor teaches Zwinglian doctrine, he should avoid him and rather dispense with the sacrament all his life than receive it from such a person—yes, rather die and suffer everything on this account.'[1] And in 1544, only two years after his cordial letter to John Augusta, he wrote one of his bitter and violent books against Zwingli, who had died more than a decade earlier.[2] Luther had objected to some formulations of the Unity as violently as he had to Zwingli's, for he saw their similarity; but to the formulation in the Czech Confession he did not object. But that is not because the confession was completely Lutheran. The Brethren still insisted, as much as Zwingli had, upon Christ's presence at the right hand of the Father and quoted the Apostles' Creed to prove their point, and they were careful to state very explicitly their rejection of any physical presence of Christ's body in the Lord's Supper.[3] Their willingness to join with Calvin a few years later also shows that the thirteenth article of the Czech Confession was not completely Lutheran.

The first interpretation referred to above, the agreement of the Brethren and Zwingli, is usually preferred by Refor.ned interpreters; the second, agreement with Luther, usually by Lutheran interpreters. But both interpretations, as we have seen, involve themselves in inconsistencies and historical inexactitudes. Rather, the solution of the problem of Luther's irenic attitude toward the Czech Confession seems to lie in the relationship of the position of the confession to the position of Martin Bucer, particularly as this was being formulated in the Wittenberg Concord of 1536. It is noteworthy that the Czech Confession and the Wittenberg Concord should have appeared within one year of each other. An analysis of Luther's irenic treatment of the Czech Confession must take account of the Wittenberg Concord as well.

---

[1] *Message to Those in Frankfort, WA* 30-III, 561.
[2] Compare Luther to Augusta, October 5, 1542, *WA Br* 10, 152, with his *Brief Confession on the Lord's Supper, WA* 54, 141-167.
[3] Cf. *Confessio Bohemica*, VI, *Collectio Confessionum in Ecclesiis Reformatis Publicatarum*, ed. H. A. Niemeyer (Leipzig, 1840), p. 792.

BUCER AND THE BRETHREN

There is a striking similarity between the theological development of the Brethren and that of Martin Bucer, especially in the doctrine of the Lord's Supper and in the effect which that doctrine had on Luther. Like the Brethren, Bucer attempted to occupy a mediating position between Luther and Zwingli.[1] The Brethren had sent legates at the same time to Luther and to the Zwinglians.[2] The compromise suggested by that action appears in Bucer, too; although his view of the Lord's Supper seems to have been much akin to Zwingli's, particularly from 1524 on, he was throughout more consistent than Zwingli in regarding the sacrament as a means of grace.[3] For our purpose the most important stage in the development of Bucer's doctrine of the Lord's Supper was that which culminated in the Wittenberg Concord of 1536.

In the Wittenberg Concord there was articulated the pro-Lutheran, but still mediating position to which Bucer had come by 1536, and the desire for union which had come upon Luther in the same period.[4] Luther gave frequent expression to that desire in prayers like this:[5] 'Farewell in Christ. Be persuaded that as much as lies within me, I shall faithfully and gladly perform and suffer everything possible for the achievement of this concord. For as I have written previously, there is nothing I desire more passionately than to conclude this life, which is soon to end, in peace,

[1] See Wilhelm Pauck, *Das Reich Gottes auf Erden. Utopie und Wirklichkeit. Eine Untersuchung zu Butzers 'DE REGNO CHRISTI' und zur englischen Staatskirche des 16. Jahrhunderts* (Berlin and Leipzig, 1928), p. 100; Hastings Eells, 'Sacramental Negotiations at the Diet of Augsburg 1530', *Princeton Theological Review*, XXIII (1925), 213-233; Walther Köhler, 'Zum Religionsgespräche von Marburg 1529', *Festgabe für Gerold Meyer von Knonau* (Zurich, 1913), pp. 359-381.

[2] '. . . yes, also among the Zwinglians', N. Slanský in Gindely, *Quellen*, p. 46.

[3] Cf. August Lang, *Der Evangelienkommentar Martin Butzers und die Grundzüge seiner Theologie* (Leipzig, 1900), pp. 237-250. Hopefully, the new edition of Bucer's works now in progress, *Martini Buceri Opera Omnia* (Strasbourg, 1955 ff.), will finally make it possible to assign him his rightful place in the history of the Reformation; cf. Pauck, *The Heritage of the Reformation*, pp. 73-99.

[4] Cf. Ernst Bizer, *Studien zur Geschichte des Abendmahlsstreits im 16. Jahrhundert* (Gütersloh, 1940); Walther Köhler, *Luther und Zwingli*, II (Gütersloh, 1953), esp. 432ff.; Hastings Eells, *Martin Bucer* (New Haven, 1931), pp. 190-224, and Lang, *op. cit.*, pp. 269-282.

[5] Luther to the Clergy in Augsburg, October 5, 1535, *WA Br* 7, 290; also Luther to Bucer, January 22, 1531, *WA Br* 6, 25-26; Luther to the Clergy in Augsburg, July 20, 1535, *WA Br* 7, 213; Luther to the Clergy in Strasbourg, October 5, 1535, *WA Br* 7, 286-287; Luther to Gereon Seiler, October 5, 1535, *WA Br* 7, 293.

charity, and the unity of the Holy Spirit with you. May Christ
Jesus, the author of life and of peace, join us together by the bond
of his Spirit in perpetual unity. Amen.' Moved by his conviction
that he was soon to die, Luther was eager for reunion with the
alienated Protestants; he was nevertheless suspicious of anything
that looked like compromise.

In addition to this general attitude, there are certain specific
factors in Luther's motivation to sign the Wittenberg Concord
which offer an interesting parallel to those involved in his dealings
with the Bohemian Brethren. One of them was his high personal
regard for Bucer, despite the latter's having tampered with
Lutheran books in translation and despite the appearance of a
preface by Bucer to a collection of Zwingli's letters published
while negotiations were going on.[1] As with the Czech Confession,
so with the Wittenberg Concord, the problem of logomachy
entered in. Several times Bucer had suggested that perhaps the
controversy was at least partly semantic, a suggestion that Luther
rejected defensively; after the discussions, however, Luther, too,
granted that it was not necessary that parties be united in their
mode of expression.[2] Again, he was more kindly disposed toward
Bucer and his supporters because they had declared themselves
in agreement with the Augsburg Confession and its Apology and
because they had admitted the error of their previous ways.[3]

But the principal aspect of Bucer's thought on the Lord's
Supper was his insistence—despite the difference between him
and Luther on the mode of Christ's presence in the sacrament—
that the Supper was principally a gift of God, not an action of

[1] Cf. Luther to Bucer, March 25, 1536, *WA Br* 7, 379; Justus Jonas to the
Clergy in Augsburg, July 19, 1535, *StL* 17, 2067. On the translations, see Eells,
Bucer, pp. 76-81; the report of Frederick Myconius, *StL* 17, 2092-2093, and
Bernardi's explanation, *StL* 17, 2104-2105; Bucer to Brück, July 1530, *StL* 17,
1986; Luther to Bucer, January 22, 1531, *WA Br* 6, 25.
[2] Luther to Duke Ernest of Braunschweig-Lüneburg, February 1, 1531,
WA Br 6, 28-20; Bernardi's report, *StL* 17, 2103, and Bucer's discussion, *ibid.*,
2106-2107. Luther to the Swiss cities, December 1, 1537, *WA Br* 8, 150-153; cf.
Melanchthon's conviction that the parties were united 'in re', letter to Urbanus
Rhegius, February 3, 1535, *CR* 2, 843.
[3] Elector John Frederick to Luther, May 14, 1536, *WA Br* 7, 411, demanding
agreement with the Augsburg Confession; *idem* to Brück, n.d., *StL* 17, 2087;
Melanchthon to John Agricola, February, 1535, *CR* 2, 827; Myconius, 'Bericht',
StL 17, 2086-2087, 2097; Clergy in Ulm to Luther, October 31, 1536, *WA Br*
7, 577; and Clergy in Strasbourg to Luther, January 18, 1537, *WA Br* 8, 10-11;
Bucer to Luther, July 21, 1536, *WA Br* 7, 472.

men. In a treatise addressed to the Czechs, Luther had branded
as 'the worst . . . and most heretical' misinterpretation of the Lord's
Supper, not the refusal to agree on the nature of Christ's presence,
but the treatment of the sacrament as 'a sacrifice and a good work.'[1]
Already in 1531 Luther was glad that Bucer saw the sacrament as
a food for the soul; and in 1535-36 Bucer's party continually
emphasized that a valid sacrament was dependent not upon man,
but upon God, who through Christ was given in the sacrament.[2]
When, finally, even the staunchly Lutheran John Brenz was convinced and satisfied, it was clear that, at least for the moment,
the union was acceptable; and 'Zwinglians and Lutherans ate
and drank together of the body of the Lord'.[3]

The Wittenberg Concord contributes two insights to our
knowledge of Luther as an irenic Reformer. For one thing, it
illustrates Luther's attitude toward those who differed with him
at the time when he was considering the Czech Confession.
Hence Luther's treatment of the Wittenberg Concord is perhaps
our most important clue to his irenic view of the Czech Confession. But the Wittenberg Concord is important, or at least extremely
intriguing, for another reason as well: it suggests how Luther and
Calvin were related in their views of the sacrament. And since the
Brethren dealt extensively with Calvin, but not so extensively
with Bucer, Calvin's doctrine of the Lord's Supper, as laid down
in the 1536 edition of his *Institutes*, demands a brief examination
for the light it sheds on Luther's attitude toward the Czech
Confession.[4]

---

[1] See p. 131; cf. Wilhelm Hopf, 'Die Abendmahlslehre der evangelisch-
lutherischen Kirche', *Abendmahlsgemeinschaft?* (Munich, 1937), pp. 159-160.

[2] Luther to Bucer, January 22, 1531, *WA Br* 6, 25; Theologians of Strasbourg
to Luther, August 19, 1535, *WA Br* 7, 236; Myconius, 'Bericht', *StL* 17, 2105;
Bucer to Melanchthon, *CR* 3, 78; Gereon Seiler to Luther, September 8,
1535, *WA Br* 7, 261.

[3] Eells, *Bucer*, p. 202. On the attitude of Brenz, cf. Theologians of Stras-
bourg to Luther, August 19, 1535, *WA Br* 7, 235; Caspar Hedio to Brenz,
August 18, 1535, *Anecdota Brentiana*, ed. Th. Pressel (Tübingen, 1868), pp.
148-149; Joachim Camerarius to Brenz, August 22, 1535, *ibid.*, pp. 149-150;
Jacob Otther to Brenz, August 26, 1535, *ibid.*, pp. 151-152; Brenz to John
Luthmann, June 26, 1536, *ibid.*, pp. 186-187; and Julius Hartmann, *Johannes
Brenz* (Elberfeld, 1862), pp. 159-160.

[4] The most authoritative study is that of Wilhelm Niesel, *Calvins Lehre vom
Abendmahl* (2nd ed.; Munich, 1935); cf. also Walther von Loewenich, *Vom
Abendmahl Christi* (Berlin, 1938), pp. 90-98; and Jaroslav Pelikan, *Luther the
Expositor*, Part II, with bibliographical footnotes.

THE RELEVANCE OF CALVIN

Luther's doctrine of the real presence, it must be remembered, is to be interpreted in the light not so much of his Christology as of his doctrine of the Holy Spirit.[1] So it is, too, with Calvin. As a means of granting 'a taste of his sweetness', God had provided the sacraments. Their purpose was 'to be of service to our faith, namely to nourish, exercise, and increase it'.[2] Calvin insisted that to accomplish this, Christ's body and blood 'are shown forth truly and efficaciously, though not naturally'. Important here is the word 'efficaciously', for a fear of blaspheming the body of Christ had often kept men from communing. When that happened, men were placing the responsibility for the effectiveness of Christ's presence into their own hands, instead of leaving it in God's hands, where alone the entire matter had meaning.[3]

Because of this basic orientation toward the sacraments, Calvin was unable to accept Zwingli's formulations. But it is interesting as well as highly significant for our study that Calvin found an affinity with Bucer and in the Wittenberg Concord.[4] It was to Bucer, in turn, that Luther addressed his highly controverted words: 'Greet Dr John Sturm and John Calvin, whose [*quorum*] books I have read with singular pleasure.'[5] Luther may have been referring to Calvin's *Institutes*; perhaps he read also Calvin's *Little Treatise on the Holy Supper*, published a year after the letter.[6] If he read either, he must have seen, and correctly, that Calvin's doctrine of the Lord's Supper was close to that of the Wittenberg Concord and to that of the Bohemian Brethren, both of which he had approved. Calvin, Bucer, and the Brethren were considerably closer to Luther than to Zwingli, despite their varying formulations; therefore, Luther could and did deal with them approvingly.[7]

[1] Perhaps more clearly than anyone else, Helmut Gollwitzer has pointed this out; see 'Luthers Abendmahlslehre' in *Abendmahlsgemeinschaft?*, pp. 94-121, and *Coena Domini* (Munich, 1937).

[2] *Institutiones religionis christianae* (1536), *CR* 29, 101-103.

[3] *Ibid.*, pp. 103, 128.

[4] Cf., among other accounts, François Wendel, *Calvin*—The Origins and Development of his Religious Thought, tr. Philip Mairet (London and New York, 1963), pp. 138-139.

[5] Luther to Bucer, October 14, 1539, *WA Br* 8, 569, and note 14.

[6] *CR* 33, 433-460.

[7] See the summary statement of Reinhold Seeberg, *Lehrbuch der Dogmengeschichte* (5th ed.; Basel, 1953), IV-2, 607-608.

The difference between Luther's hostility to Zwingli and his irenic posture in the Wittenberg Concord and in the Czech Confession is so intriguing because it raises the question: What would the ecumenical situation within Protestantism have been if Luther had met with Calvin in 1539 rather than with Zwingli in 1529? This is, of course, an academic and hypothetical question. Yet surely Luther could not have said of Calvin, as he did of Zwingli, 'that he goes ahead smugly, spitting out whatever comes to his mouth and not looking at a thought ten times over to see whether it is correct in the eyes of God'.[1] Such an indictment was a misrepresentation of Zwingli's position, but Zwingli had never been able to persuade Luther that he placed the word of God above reason and private judgment. The Unity of Bohemian Brethren did persuade Luther of this. Alongside the usual picture in the textbooks of church history, which portray Luther in his intransigence against Zwingli and against the Anabaptists, must be placed this portrait of his pliant and irenic negotiations with the Hussites. The evidence of these negotiations must be part of any answer to the question raised in Chapter I: Which Luther was 'the real Luther'?

[1] *This Is My Body*, *WA* 23, 71 (*LW* 37, 17).

X

A REFORMATION CONSENSUS

THE decades that immediately followed Luther's death were not a good time for holding Catholic substance and Protestant principle together. As we have seen, Luther's Reformation did hold them together in creative tension. But both the Protestantism that emerged from the Reformation and the Roman Catholicism that spoke in the Counter-Reformation tended to separate what the Reformation had joined together. Yet even in the second half of the sixteenth century there were exceptions. At least some of the theologians who participated in the Council of Trent said both/and rather than either/or on the questions we have reviewed in Part One: the nature of the church, the relation of Scripture and tradition, the authority of councils, the meaning of worship and sacraments. As its very name indicates, the Formula of Concord of 1577, adopted by the contending parties among Luther's followers, was intended as a plan for unification.

One of the least known and most interesting irenic efforts of the sixteenth century took place in Poland. From April 9 to 14, 1570, representatives of Polish Calvinism, of Polish Lutheranism, and of the Unity of Bohemian Brethren met in the city of Sandomierz in southwestern Poland and signed a document acknowledging each other's confessions and doctrines as orthodox and looking forward to the time when all three could be united in one confession and one national Polish church; that document was the so-called *Consensus Sendomiriensis*, the Consensus of Sandomierz.

THE TEXT OF THE CONSENSUS

The synod of Sandomierz opened on Sunday, April 9, 1570, with common worship and the election of the officers.[1] On Monday,

[1] For my account of the events of the synod, I am indebted chiefly to Oskar Halecki, *Zgoda sandomierska 1570 r.* (Warsaw, 1915), and to Jerzy Lehmann,

the leaders of the Lutheran delegation began the actual negotiations with an admonition to 'strengthen the sacred bonds that we might be, as we also are, one kingdom of Christ and one vineyard of the Lord of hosts'. In a similar vein, Andrew Pražmovský, plenipotentiary representative of the *Unitas Fratrum*, expressed the hope of his communion for the establishment of peace and suggested that perhaps the Czech Confession of 1535 might be the ideal confession for the united churches. As Chapter IX has shown, it was well suited to the irenic purpose of the synod of Sandomierz. But Paul Gilowski, one of the leaders of the Reformed Church in Poland, had another suggestion, namely, that the Second Helvetic Confession of 1566, already translated into Polish and provided with an appropriate preface, would be more suitable.[1] The rest of the day was devoted to the Lutheran objections to both the Bohemian and the Helvetic confessions, and to the defence of the former by Simon Turnowski.

After this inauspicious beginning, the sessions of the synod were opened on Tuesday with the report that the Lutherans and Reformed of Lithuania had come to an agreement in Wilno on March 2. Spurred on by this report, the synod returned to the reading of the Polish translation of the Helvetic Confession and to a debate on the accuracy and adequacy of its formulations, particularly on the Lord's Supper, with both the Bohemian Brethren and the Lutherans objecting to certain words and phrases.

Finally, on Wednesday, the reading and discussion of the Confession were completed, and the matter of adopting it came to a vote. Though still desirous of having their own confession adopted for the entire group, the representatives of the Bohemian Brethren stated their satisfaction with the Helvetic Confession and their willingness to accept it as the basis of union. 'The eyes

---

Konfesja sandomierska na tle innych konfesji w Polsce XVI wieku (Warsaw, 1937). See also, Daniel Ernest Jablonski, *Historia consensus Sendomiriensis* (Berlin, 1731), pp. 39-60; and Kai Eduard Jordt Jørgensen, *Ökumenische Bestrebungen unter den polnischen Protestanten bis zum Jahre 1645* (Copenhagen, 1942), pp. 252-279. The principal account is that of Simon Bohumil Turnowski, a leader of the Unity of Bohemian Brethren in Poland; cf. Theodor Wotschke, 'Joh. Turnowski. Ein Senior der böhmischen Brüder', *Aus Posens kirchlicher Vergangenheit*, I (1911), 73-111.

[1] The Second Helvetic Confession is reprinted in Philip Schaff, *Creeds of Christendom* (3 vols.; New York, 1919), III, 233-306; on the Polish translation of it, cf. Lehmann, *op. cit.*, pp. 105-129.

of all', writes Jablonski, 'were now turned on the Saxons.' Under the pressure of this switch in the tactics of the Bohemians and of the earnest exhortations of all present, the Lutherans agreed to the composition of a new confession, with the proviso that they be allowed to retain the Augsburg Confession as a separate creedal statement; to this everyone consented.

As an incentive and model for their efforts, the agreement of the Reformed and Lutherans in Wilno was read the following day; and on April 14, as a climax to the synod, all three communions adopted and signed the following statement, the Consensus of Sandomierz. The text is presented here in English for the first time.[1]

Since, after many long conflicts with sectarians, Tritheists, Ebionites, and Anabaptists, we have nevertheless emerged, by the grace of God, from so many great struggles and deplorable contentions, it was decided by those reformed and orthodox churches of Poland which seemed to the enemies of the truth and of the gospel to be in least agreement in certain articles and formulas of doctrine to call a synod in the interest of peace and concord and to attest their mutual consensus. Therefore, after a friendly and Christian conference, we agree to these articles with minds thus joined and agreed.

First. As both we who in the present synod have published our confession and the Bohemian Brethren have never believed that those who adhere to the Augsburg Confession feel otherwise than piously and orthodoxly about God and the Holy Trinity, also the incarnation of the Son of God and our justification and other principal articles of our faith; so also those who follow the Augsburg Confession have openly and sincerely confessed that they, on the other hand, know of nothing in the confession of our churches or that of the Bohemian Brethren concerning God and the Holy Trinity, the incarnation of the Son of God, justification, and other primary articles of the Christian faith which would be contrary to the orthodox truth and the pure word of God. And there we have mutually and unanimously promised according to the rule of God's word that we shall defend this mutual consensus in the true and pure religion of Christ against Papists, against sectarians, against all the enemies of the gospel and the truth.

Moreover, as far as the unfortunate difference of opinion on the Lord's Supper is concerned, we agree on the meaning of the words of our Lord Jesus Christ, as they have been orthodoxly understood by the fathers, and especially by Irenaeus, who said that this mystery consists of two elements, namely, an earthly and a heavenly one.[2]

[1] Cf. H. A. Niemeyer, *Collectio Confessionum*, pp. 553-561.
[2] *Sancti Irenaei episcopi Lugdunensis Libri quinque adversus Haereses* IV, xxxi, 4, ed. W. Wigan Harvey (2 vols; Cambridge, 1857), II, 206-209, with a

Nor do we assert that those elements or signs are bare and empty; we state, rather, that at the same time by faith they actually [*re ipsa*] exhibit and present that which they signify. Finally, to put it more clearly and expressly, we have agreed to believe and confess that the substantial presence of Christ is not merely signified, but that the body and blood of the Lord are represented, distributed, and exhibited to those who eat by the symbols applied to the thing itself, and that the symbols are not at all bare, according to the nature of the sacraments. But lest the diversity of manners of speaking bring forth another controversy, we have decided by mutual consent, in addition to the article which is inserted into our confession, to add the article of the confession of the Saxon churches on the Lord's Supper, sent to the Council of Trent in 1551, which we acknowledge as correct and have accepted. These are the words of that confession:[1]

'Also men are taught that sacraments are actions instituted of God, and that without the use whereunto they are ordained the things themselves are not to be accounted for a sacrament; but in the use appointed, Christ is present in this communion, truly and substantially, and the body and blood of Christ is indeed given to the receivers; that Christ does witness that he is in them and does make them his members and that he does wash them in his blood, as Hilary also says, "These things being eaten and drunk do cause both that we may be in Christ and that Christ may be in us." Moreover, in the ceremony itself we observe the usual order of the whole ancient church, both Latin and Greek. We use no private masses, that is, such wherein the body and blood of Christ is not distributed; as also the ancient church, for many years after the Apostles' times had no such masses, as the old descriptions which are to be found in Dionysius, Epiphanius, Ambrose, Augustine, and others do show.'

We have decided to be bound by this holy and mutual consensus, and have agreed that just as they regard us, our churches, our confession published in this synod, and that of the Brethren as orthodox, so also we shall treat their churches with the same Christian love and acknowledge them as orthodox. We shall avoid the extreme and impose utter silence upon all bickering, disagreement, and controversy by which the course of the gospel is impeded to the great offence of many pious people, and from which there comes a severe calumny by our adversaries and contradiction to our true Christian religion. Rather let the occasion be provided to strive for public peace and tranquillity, to exercise mutual charity; we should also offer our labours for the building up of the church in our fraternal union.

---

lengthy and learned footnote. These words of Irenaeus were quoted also in the opening sentence of the Wittenberg Concord of 1536, *CR* 3, 75, and thus found their way into the Formula of Concord, Solid Declaration, VII, 14, *Bek.* 977 (*BC* 571).

[1] There is a sixteenth-century translation of the Saxon Confession into English in Reu, *Augsburg Confession*, II, 411-418.

For this reason we have agreed by mutual consent to persuade all our brethren with utmost zeal and to invite them to increase, build up, and conserve this Christian and unanimous consensus, to nourish it and testify to it, especially by the hearing of the word (by attending the services first of one, then of another of the confessions) and the use of the sacraments, observing the proper order and manner of the discipline and custom of each church.

We leave the rites and ceremonies of each church free by this concord. For it does not matter much what rites are observed, as long as the doctrine itself and the foundation of our faith and salvation are kept intact and incorrupt. So the Augsburg Confession itself and the Saxon Confession teach on this matter;[1] and in this our confession published in this synod of Sandomierz we have expressed the same thing.

We have therefore promised and decided to compare counsels and works of charity among ourselves, and in the future to consult about the conservation and growth of all the pious, orthodox, and reformed churches of the entire realm of Lithuania and Samogitia, as well as [the formation of] one body. And if they ever hold general synods, let them inform us; and when called to our general synods, let them feel free to come. And to put a colophon to this consensus and mutual concord, we do not think it would be inappropriate for the saving and assuring of this fraternal society to gather in a certain place, where, forced to this by the improbity of the enemies of truth, we would draw up a compend of the body of doctrine (one out of the several confessions) and publish it, that the mouths of evil men may be stopped to the great comfort of all the faithful in the name of all the Polish, Lithuanian, and Samogitian reformed churches which agree with our confession.

Having given and joined our right hands, therefore, we have sacredly promised and mutually agreed that we want to build up and nurture faith and peace and to strive more and more for the building of the kingdom of God, avoiding all occasions for the alienation of the churches. Finally, we agree that unmindful and forgetful of ourselves, as is proper for true ministers of God, we shall promote the glory solely of Jesus Christ our Saviour and contend for the truth of his gospel in word and deed.

That this might be fixed sure and firm forever we pray with ardent petitions to God the Father, the author and abundant fountain of all consolation and peace, who rescued us and our churches from the morass of the papacy and endowed us with the pure and holy light of of his word. May he deign to bless this our holy peace, consensus, conjunction, and union to the glory of his name and the building up of the church. Amen.

[1] See pp. 30-31 above.

THE SITUATION OF POLISH PROTESTANTISM

Like every statement of faith, the Consensus of Sandomierz was an answer to a need, in this case the need of a solid Protestant front against Roman Catholicism on the one hand and Socinianism on the other. An understanding of the Consensus involves a consideration of this need as well as a discussion of the attitudes of the three communions involved.

In the quarter century between 1548 and 1573, designated by Paul Fox as the period of the 'triumph and dominance' of Protestantism in Poland,[1] the attempts of the Roman Catholic Church to win back lost ground in Poland grew in size and intensity. In 1556 the pope had sent Aloysius Lippomani to Poland as his nuncio, and in 1563 Francesco Commendone. Their hand was strengthened in 1569 by the introduction of the Society of Jesus, one of whose members, Antonio Possevino, remembered for his work in Russia, provided much of the literature of the Polish Counter-Reformation.[2] Also prominent in the effort to save Poland from Protestantism was Luther's opponent, John Cochlaeus. We have assessed the importance of his historical work in Chapter II.[3] In Chapter VII we have also described the concern of Cochlaeus over the prospects of an alliance, encouraged by Melanchthon, between Saxony, Poland, and Bohemia against Rome.[4] And though he was quite sure by 1540 that Poland was aved,[5] he nevertheless travelled there and continued to supply literature for Poland as late as 1550.[6]

In Poland itself, meanwhile, the outstanding proponent of what came later to be known as 'ultramontanism' was the Bishop of Ermland, Stanislaus Hosius.[7] Zealous in his hatred of everything Protestant, Hosius ought perhaps to receive most of the

[1] Paul Fox, *The Reformation in Poland,* Some Social and Economic Aspects (Baltimore, 1924), p. 40.

[2] Cf. Carl Sommervogel (ed.), *Bibliothèque de la Compagnie de Jésus,* Part I, *Bibliographie,* (Brussels, 1890ff.), VI, 1061-1093, for a list of his writings, most of them directed against Protestantism and Eastern Orthodoxy; see also Oskar Halecki, 'From Florence to Brest', *Sacrum Poloniae Millennium.* Rosprawy—Szkice—Materialy historyczne, V (Rome, 1958), 203-213.

[3] See pp. 27ff. above.

[4] See pp. 114ff. above.

[5] Cochlaeus to Bishop Giberti of Verona, January 31, 1540, *ZKG* 18, 423.

[6] Cochlaeus to Cardinal Cervini, November 24, 1540, *ZKG* 18, 438; and April 27, 1550, *ibid.,* p. 633.

[7] Cf. Joseph Lortz, *Kardinal Stanislaus Hosius* (Braunsberg, 1931); J. Smoczyński, *Bibliographia Hosiana* (Pelplini, 1937).

credit for the ultimate return of Poland to Roman Catholicism. Testimony of this hatred as well as to his zeal in expressing it are his collected works, published in two large volumes, and especially such a work as his *Confutatio Prolegomenon Brentii*, directed, as the title indicates, against a work by the Swabian reformer, John Brenz.[1]

Polish Protestantism was, then, under great pressure from the Roman Catholic side, 'the enemies of truth and of the gospel', as the Consensus calls them. Equally great, however, and much more embarrassing to the three communions which participated in the synod was the Socinian left, the 'sectarians, Tritheists, Ebionites, and Anabaptists' to whom reference is made in the opening sentence of the document. While dealing with the Roman Catholics, the Polish Protestants were always aware of the Unitarians, too; and in making clear their anthithesis to the Catholic view, they had to keep clear of the Unitarian or Socinian view. And although our concern in this book is not with 'their [Socinians'] more parlous situation as a consequence of the Consensus',[2] a brief review of their development is in order.

The Socinianism of the sixteenth century began in Italy, but soon thereafter moved to Poland.[3] In interpreting this fact, we may well adopt the explanation suggested by Harnack: 'That the Italians were attracted to Poland cannot be explained merely from the great freedom that prevailed there in consequence of the permanent anarchy (sovereignty of the great landed proprietors); we must rather remember that there was perhaps no other country in Europe in the sixteenth century whose towns were so Italian as those of Poland.'[4]

In Poland the Unitarians had gained new converts not only from Roman Catholicism, but also from the Reformed and Lutheran camps.[5] Objecting to much of the Catholic substance still retained in Protestant dogma and worship, they revised the

[1] *D. Stanislaui Hosii Opera omnia*, ed. Stanislaus Rescius (Cologne, 1584), I, 417-609; cf. Brenz to Duke Albert of Prussia, September 24, 1558, *Anecdota Brentiana*, p. 451.
[2] George Huntston Williams, *The Radical Reformation* (Philadelphia and London, 1962), p. 699.
[3] See Tadeus Grabowski, *Literatura aryanska w Polsce* (Posen, 1908).
[4] Adolf Harnack, *History of Dogma*, VII, 135.
[5] See Theodor Wotschke's refutation of the claim that the Unitarians came only from Calvinism: 'Wittenberg und die Unitarier Polens', *Archiv für Reformationsgeschichte*, XIV (1917), 123-142.

classic Protestant estimates of sin, of free will, of the person of Christ, and, therefore, of the Trinity. Others in Poland, meanwhile, had become so aroused over the 'Sabellianism' of Francesco Stancaro that they had stressed the distinction between the persons of the Trinity at the expense of the unity of the Godhead, thus laying themselves open to the charge of Tritheism.[1]

The Consensus of Sandomierz was called forth, then, not only by the vigorous counter-reformatory activity of Roman Catholicism, but also by the embarrassing presence of Socinianism. Both of these made it politically necessary for the Protestants of Poland to declare their faith; for despite his Protestant sympathies[2] Sigismund Augustus, the Polish king, had been urging that they adopt a unified confession. Indeed, as Jaroslav Biblo summarizes the situation, 'the king was willing to grant the Protestants freedom for that faith or confession on which they would agree so that they would make up only one religious party'.[3] And just as the Lublin Union of 1569 between Poland and Lithuania had called forth the Wilno agreement referred to above, so the political situation in Poland called for united Protestant action. In view of these circumstances, we may agree with the great Polish historian Józef Szujski that the Consensus of Sandomierz 'became the reason why in the next election the dissident party did not play any role. It was primarily a political union.'[4]

THE CALVINISTS AND THE BOHEMIAN BRETHREN

Such were the political and religious circumstances which produced the Consensus of Sandomierz; it remains now to analyse the reasons why each of the participating churches agreed to the Consensus, considering first the Calvinists.

[1] Cf. Williams, *op. cit.*, pp. 653-669; also the resolution against the teachings of Stancaro adopted at Sandomierz in Jablonski, *Historia*, pp. 56-57.

[2] More perhaps than any other Western scholar, Karl Völker has helped to elucidate the complex interrelations between the political and the religious situation in the Polish Reformation. Most relevant to this book are three studies: 'Der Protestantismus in Oesterreich und Polen im Ringen um seine Rechtsstellung', *ZKG* 53 (1934), 542-570; 'Die Glaubensfreiheit in den Städten Polens', *Zeitschrift für osteuropäische Geschichte*, IX (1934), 67-88; 'Der Kampf des Adels gegen die geistliche Gerichtsbarkeit in seiner Tragweite für die Reformation in Polen', *Harnack-Ehrung zum 70. Geburtstag* (Leipzig, 1921), pp. 317-327.

[3] Jaroslav Bidlo, *Jednota bratrská v prvním vyhnanství*, II (Prague, 1903), 146.

[4] Józef Szujski, *Dzieje Polski*, II (Kraków, 1894), 399.

'We may certainly say', writes Hermann Dalton, 'that the famous union formula of Sandomierz is the late and mature fruit of Laski's work; in its content we see again the beautiful spiritual features of our friend.'[1] Best known for his work in England during the Edwardian Reformation in 1551,[2] John a Lasco or Laski had worked for ideal of a united Polish Protestantism all his life. This ideal he was willing to achieve even at the expense of theological accuracy; thus, it took Brenz considerable time to persuade Laski that his Calvinistic view of the Lord's Supper was not the same as that of the Augsburg Confession.[3] He was nevertheless a thoroughgoing Calvinist; this is evident from his treatise on the Lord's Supper of April 15, 1558, in which the traditional Calvinistic objections to the Lutheran view were rehearsed: it conflicted with the doctrine of the ascension, with the doctrine of Christ's true humanity, and with the general doctrine of the sacraments.[4]

From this fact it is apparent that what Laski wanted was not only compromise: he sought a national Polish church with a new confession. That was the ideal of the Consensus, too. The Consensus attempted to set up that church on the basis of equal participation by all three communions; but, like Laski, the Reformed sought what Karl Kratzke has called 'subordination of the Lutherans to the Calvinists'.[5] Having once persuaded the Polish Lutherans to go along with them in the Consensus, the Polish Calvinists tried to make the Second Helvetic Confession of 1566 the official confession of the new Polish national church.[6] Because the Consensus made such a strategy possible, the Polish Calvinists agreed to the Consensus of Sandomierz.

But in many ways the most significant aspect of the Consensus is the fact that it brought about some degree of understanding between the Lutherans and the Unity of Bohemian Brethren.

[1] Hermann Dalton, *Johannes a Lasco. Beitrag zur Reformationsgeschichte Polens, Deutschlands und Englands* (Gotha, 1881), p. 570.

[2] Cf. M. M. Knappen, *Tudor Puritanism* (Chicago, 1939), pp. 90-92, for his activity in England; on his early career, see p. 75, note 5.

[3] Cf. Brenz to Hartmann Beyer in Frankfort, September 2, 1556, *Anecdota*, pp. 432-433; for a commentary on the attitude of Brenz toward Laski, see Dalton, *op. cit.*, p. 520.

[4] Joh. a Lasco, *Opera*, ed. A. Kuyper, II (Amsterdam, 1866), 755ff. For a detailed discussion of Laski's eucharistic theories see Karl Hein, *Die Sakramentslehre des Johannes a Lasco* (Berlin, 1904).

[5] Karl Kratzke, *Johannes a Lasco und der Sacramentsstreit* (Leipzig, 1901), p. 172.

[6] Cf. Bidlo, *op. cit.*, p. 162.

From its very inception, the Unity had looked for co-operation with other groups which wanted to be Christian without being Roman Catholic—with the Waldensians, the Eastern Orthodox, and, ultimately, the Protestants of Germany and Switzerland. With Luther, as Chapter VIII has shown, they carried on extensive negotiations. Similarly, the Brethren corresponded with John Calvin[1] and Henry Bullinger,[2] and continued to figure prominently in the struggle for the unity of the church well into the seventeenth century.[3]

Always strong in the Unity, the irenic and ecumenical spirit grew even stronger during their stay in Poland.[4] Faced with an active Lutheran party and an energetic Calvinist group, they sought various possible means of effecting a *rapprochement* among the various churches. It is interesting to note, however, that the role of the Unity in such a *rapprochement* had radically changed in one generation. In the 1530s, as we have seen, the Unity had acted as the mediating party between the Lutheran and the Reformed extremes. But in Poland the Brethren often seemed to represent a position farther removed from the Lutherans than was the Reformed view.[5] Thus, two months before the synod of Sandomierz, on February 14-17, 1570, the Polish Lutherans and the Brethren had met in Poznań for discussion; but the comparison of the Augsburg Confession and the Czech Confession had led to a debate on ubiquity, on pedobaptism, and on the presence of Christ in the sacrament, which sharply divided the conference.[6]

As a result, the Brethren were pleased to find in the Consensus of Sandomierz a formula on which the three communions could agree as a basis for discussion; and even though they were frustrated in their attempt to have the Czech Confession of 1535 adopted by the other groups, they were willing to co-operate in the Consensus because it brought about the possibility of an understanding with the Lutherans.

[1] Cf. E. Doumergue, *Jean Calvin. Les hommes et les choses de son temps*, VII (Neuilly-sur-Seine, 1927), 479-507.

[2] Carl Pestalozzi, *Heinrich Bullinger* (Elberfeld, 1858), pp. 455-458.

[3] The Brethren were represented by John Amos Comenius (1591-1670) at the *collegium charitatis* in Thorn in 1647; cf. Matthew Spinka, *John Amos Comenius, That Incomparable Moravian* (Chicago, 1943), pp. 101-115.

[4] Cf. Jerzy Śliziński, *Z dzialaności literackiej braci czeskich w Polsce XVI-XVII w.* (Warsaw, 1959), and the bibliographical data cited there.

[5] See Ján Kvačala, 'Styky Jednoty Bratov Českých s Flaciom a Laským', reprinted in his collected essays, *Viera a Veda* (Liptovský Svätý Mikuláš, 1911), pp. 241-281.

[6] Jablonski, *Historia*, pp. 31-35; Bidlo, *op. cit.*, pp. 147-149.

THE LUTHERANS AND THE CONSENSUS

These circumstances might explain the attitude of the Polish Calvinists and of the Bohemian Brethren. But what of the Lutherans? How account for the fact that they went along on a plan to form a federation, or union, of the various Protestant communions in Poland? At least two considerations help to explain the Lutheran position.

For one thing, the Consensus—indeed, the entire union movement of which the Consensus is the climax—had the blessing of the theological faculty of the University of Wittenberg. Philip Melanchthon had been very influential in Poland and had carried on extensive correspondence with Polish Protestant leaders.[1] Testimony to this abiding influence is the inclusion in the Consensus of his Saxon confession of 1551. The men who were prominent at Wittenberg during this time—Paul Eber, Caspar Peucer, Melanchthon's son-in-law, George Major—were all Melanchthonian in their orientation and therefore inclined to look with favour upon any movement for church union.

As pointed out, the chief obstacle in the way of union in Poland was the relation between the Lutherans and the Bohemian Brethren. In 1568 the Wittenberg faculty had said of the Brethren: 'We have read your confession before and recognized that in most parts of doctrine and in all the chief articles it agrees with the confession of our church, although certain things are expressed in less detail and there is some variety in church practices. Since we do, however, agree in the foundation and in the doctrine necessary for salvation, we have never held that your church and our church are alien.'[2]

What effect such a statement from the Wittenberg faculty could have on the Polish Lutherans can be gauged from an examination of the Polish students who had been at Wittenberg and who were now old enough to participate in Polish affairs. From 1554 to 1565, inclusive, there had been at least forty-seven Polish noblemen and sixty-eight Polish commoners—a total of 115 men—in

[1] Loesche, *Luther, Melanthon und Calvin in Oesterreich-Ungarn*, pp. 167-172; Theodor Wotschke, 'Zum Briefwechsel Melanchthons mit Polen', *Archiv für Reformationsgeschichte*, VI (1909), 350-357.
[2] Quoted in Wotschke, *Geschichte der Reformation in Polen* (Leipzig, 1911), p. 241; cf. the similar statements of February 8, 1573, quoted at length in Jablonski, *Historia*, pp. 68-69, and of November 3, 1575, *ibid.*, p. 73.

residence at Wittenberg.[1] This meant that a considerable segment of Polish Lutheranism was under the influence of Wittenberg at the time of the Consensus. Nor dare the fact be ignored that there is really nothing in the Consensus to which a Lutheran could not subscribe, though that document ignores certain things which a Lutheran would have been obliged to include.[2] Its statement on the chief point of controversy, the doctrine of the Lord's Supper, was Lutheran in origin and scope. The Consensus is not a confession; it is an agreement to co-operate until a confession can be drawn up, with the proviso that the Lutherans may retain the Augsburg Confession as their own statement of faith.

How and why the Consensus failed is part of the tragic history of the Counter-Reformation in Poland and therefore outside the scope of this book. But the Consensus of Sandomierz does document the continuing concern of the generation after Luther to work for a healing of the schism. Placed into the context of the Catholic theology summarized in Part One of this book and into the setting of the irenic efforts described in Part Two, the Consensus reinforces the thesis that Catholic substance and Protestant principle were inseparable in the thought and programme of Luther's Reformation. Because they are inseparable still, Part Three of this book will have to turn to a consideration of 'Catholic substance and Protestant principle today'.

[1] This figure is based upon the records of the Wittenberg roster reprinted in Karl E. Förstemann (ed.), *Album Academiae Vitebergensis*, I (Leipzig, 1841) and II (Halle, 1894). The largest registration in any single year came in 1554, when there were twelve noblemen and twenty-one commoners.
[2] Cf. Johann George Walch, *Historische und theologische Einleitung in die Religionsstreitigkeiten . . . ausser der Lutherischen Kirche*, III (Jena, 1734), 1047.

PART THREE

CATHOLIC SUBSTANCE AND PROTESTANT PRINCIPLE TODAY

I F 'Catholic substance and Protestant principle' is a formula for understanding Luther's Reformation, as Parts One and Two of this book have been arguing, neither Roman Catholicism nor Protestantism can afford to ignore the implications of this formula for their thought and life today. As a colleague has said, 'it is becoming increasingly difficult, if not absurd, to try to describe the fundamental difference between the theologies of the confessions in terms of some universal contrast such as "Word *versus* Sacrament", or "the Catholic *versus* the Protestant principle".'[1] Both the critical reverence toward tradition that characterized the Reformation and the efforts of the Reformation to recover or discover a unity beyond separation are directly relevant to this changed situation. In Part Three of this book, therefore, we shall attempt to draw some lines from the Catholic substance and Protestant principle in the Reformation of the sixteenth century to the dialogue of the twentieth century between Protestantism and Roman Catholicism. That dialogue must be interpreted, not as an attempt to undo the Reformation, but as a fulfilment of its deepest meaning. Not by going around the message of the Reformation, but by going through it to both Catholic substance and Protestant principle, the Roman Catholic and the Protestant churches today can confront each other in a way that is simultaneously more candid and more charitable. In the following chapters we shall consider the implications of this evangelical Catholicity for Roman Catholicism today and for the task of Protestant theology.

[1] George A. Lindbeck, 'The Future of Roman Catholic Theology in the Light of the First Session of the Second Vatican Council', *Dialog*, II (1963), 251.

XI

EVANGELICAL CATHOLICITY AND CONTEMPORARY CATHOLICISM

CATHOLIC is a synonym for 'universal'.[1] So is 'ecumenical'. Yet in the judgment of many American Protestants or non-Christians, and apparently of a considerable group of American Roman Catholics as well, there is nothing more sectarian and less universal than the Roman Catholic Church, specifically the Roman Catholic Church in the United States. The isolationism of the American church has frequently been caricatured, but parts of the church have often worked hard to live up to the caricatures. If 'Catholic' is to be synonymous with 'universal' and with 'ecumenical' and is not to be merely a denominational label, the dimensions of authentic Catholicity will have to become more evident than they are now in the American church. There is good evidence for the supposition and hope that the Roman Catholic Church in America is becoming more conscious of these dimensions. As we pointed out in the introduction to Part One, Christian universality must extend into at least three dimensions to be authentically Catholic: It must have a universality in space, a universality in time, and a universality in faith, hope and charity.

AN IMMIGRANT CHURCH

Roman Catholicism in the United States accounts for somewhat less than one tenth of the entire Roman Catholic Church. Its contributions to the total life of the Roman Catholic Church include the most comprehensive educational system in Christian history and considerably more than one tenth of the church's

[1] The term occurs first in Ignatius, *Letter to the Smyrneans*, VIII, 2; cf. the comments of P. Th. Camelot (ed.), *Ignace d' Antioche Lettres*, 'Sources chrétiennes' (3rd ed.; Paris, 1958), p. 162, note 2; Jaroslav Pelikan, *The Riddle of Roman Catholicism*, pp. 21-33, with accompanying notes.

gross income, but only one saint (Mother Cabrini, born in Italy) and pathetically few theologians, artists, or composers. So it is understandable if the attitude of the American church toward Roman Catholicism in other lands is an attitude of simultaneous and ofttimes exaggerated attraction and repulsion.[1]

Scholars who have studied immigrant society have noted all sorts of gestures of obeisance to the old country. Its ways were somehow more meaningful, its piety more genuine, and its liturgy holier. Perhaps no outsider can grasp the existential pathos of this mood, subtler by far than mere nostalgia. When immigrants put on their mantillas or babushkas and went to church, they fastened upon visitors or items of news from the church in the motherland with eagerness and personal involvement. Even the Roman Catholic *literati* of the United States seem addicted to what one American critic has termed 'the assumption that the ultimate intellectual achievement for American Catholicism is to bring to completion an exhaustive raid on what Europeans are saying and to make all this available to the man in the American street'.[2] When an American Roman Catholic does write a solid book, the fashionable reaction in some circles of the church is to cut it down to size by calling it an *oeuvre de vulgarisation*, based on a monograph published in France or Germany ten years ago.

Beneath all the oratory and the diffidence, however, is the immigrant's version of the myths of the exodus and the new frontier. Remembering how things used to be in Ireland or eastern Europe during his grandfather's childhood, the Roman Catholic in America fancies himself to be in the vanguard of the church. It is a shock to discover that ecclesiastically European Christianity is far in advance of the church in the New World. A drive for greater lay participation, not in societies or sodalities but in the actual life and liturgy of the church; a fresh approach to the Bible that has put fundamentalism behind and has discovered a new biblical theology; adoption of a strategy of penetration into secularized industrial society—these and similar avant-garde movements have

---

[1] The pioneering study was that of Gerald Shaugnessy, *Has the Immigrant Kept the Faith?* (New York, 1925); cf. the recent researches of Andrew M. Greeley, *Religion and Career. A Study of College Graduates* (New York, 1963), pp. 99-109, on the role of ethnicity.
[2] Walter Ong, *Frontiers in American Catholicism* (New York, 1957; London, 1961), p. 5.

been flourishing on the Continent but have only begun to sprout in the United States. To say that the American church is far behind is to recognize the present stage in the Americanization of the immigrants and of their descendants.

Here it would be easy to equate Americanization with a loss of religious identity. There has been considerable loss, or 'leakage', as church sociologists have shown.[1] But more impressive historically and more significant religiously are the conservation of the second and third generations and the creation in them of the recognition that as members of the church they live and worship in a universal context. The clichés about modern transportation and communication do have a point, and for the life of the American church the point is that at no time in the history of Catholic Christianity have so many Christians in one country known the universality of the church by personal experience. The Roman Catholic Church in the United States has been coming of age at the very time when the United States as a country has committed itself irrevocably to its international responsibilities. Thus 'Hansen's law', which states that what the children of immigrants reject, the grand-children of immigrants seek to repossess, has been at work to help the American church discover the richness and variety of Roman Catholicism today.[2]

One can only hope that it has not come too late. For Pan-Atlanticism may soon become as obsolete as colonialism, and the wave of the future, also for the church, may belong to those movements that can forge a link between the world of the white man and the new worlds of Asia and Africa. Those who are sure that the Roman Catholic Church has forged such a link, and those who are sure that it cannot, must pause before the coincidence, within a period of less than a month, of lay resistance to racial integration in the diocese of New Orleans and the canonization of St Martin de Porres, a mulatto.[3] Historians of the early church still wonder whether St Augustine was a Negro,[4] but it does not take much

---

[1] Cf. Gerald J. Schnepp, *Leakage from a Catholic Parish* (Washington, 1942).

[2] Will Herberg, *Protestant, Catholic, Jew* (New York and London, 1955), is an effort to apply this 'law' specifically to religious life.

[3] Cf. Felician A. Foy (ed.), *1936 National Catholic Almanac* (New York, 1963), pp. 118-120 on New Orleans; on St Martin de Porres, see p. 64.

[4] It seems unlikely, but the only evidence available is really quite late; cf. Door K. Smits, 'Rond St Augustinus' Beeltenis', *Miscellanea Augustiniana* (Amsterdam, 1930), pp. 197-211, and accompanying plates.

historical erudition to recognize the truth in this thesis: If Christianity is to survive, it will have to be reminded that it began as a Near Eastern religion and that its intellectual and cultural centre in the first three or four centuries was not Europe but North Africa. Under the strains of the 1960s it may be difficult to imagine an America that has outgrown 'the race question' or an American Christianity that has realized in its concrete life the gift of oneness in Christ. Yet the long-range implications of the Catholic vision of universality demand that the American church and its members open themselves to the redeeming power of a Christ in whom there is neither Jew nor Greek, neither bond nor free. And that applies to all the American churches.

UNIVERSALITY IN TIME

For the Roman Catholic Church in America to achieve such a universality in space, it will have to discover a universality in time, too. Theoretically it may be possible for a portion of the Christian community to become worldwide in its sympathies and yet not to regain the continuity of Christianity through time and history, but in practice a liberation from the tyranny of the here and now makes Christians aware not only of their contemporaries but also of their ancestors. If the American church has missed the full range of what it means to be Roman Catholic in the twentieth century, it has certainly neglected to come to terms with all that it has ever meant to be a Catholic Christian. At the very least, to be a Catholic Christian means to know a universality that extends to the saints and fathers of all the Christian centuries. When Roman Catholics from abroad visit the United States, they often comment upon the absence of a vital sense of tradition both in the parochial life and in the theological thought of the American church.[1] Those who have been working to instil the idea of tradition into American Protestantism have sometimes been inclined to blame the Reformation for destroying the feeling of continuity in their churches and people, but one need only look at Roman Catholicism in the United States to recognize that this is principally a cultural phenomenon, not a religious one. To cite only one instance from Protestantism, the 'old-time religion' memorialized in the

[1] I have sought to point out some of these problems in my 'Introduction' to Otto Semmelroth, *Mary, Archetype of the Church* (New York, 1963), pp. vii-xiv.

gospel song is a form of Christianity that is all of seventy-five years old!

One by-product of the Americanization of Roman Catholicism is the leaching out of the parochial and ethnic traditions of the older generation. Only by pedagogical heroics can the teachers in a parochial school awaken in their pupils an enthusiasm for a patron saint whose name their grandparents invoked almost automatically whenever danger threatened. Even the theologians of the American church have frequently ostracized entire provinces of the communion of saints, preferring the precise formulas of Thomas Aquinas, or rather of nineteenth-century Thomism, to the vagaries of more Platonic and less conventional fathers. A compend of the fathers, properly edited and expurgated, makes a handier syllabus for a seminary course in dogma than does a primary text.

When some awareness of the Catholic heritage rushes into this historical vacuum, that heritage is often equated with a romantic version of the Middle Ages as the age of faith and of homogeneous Christian culture.[1] The term 'Neo-Gothic' applies to more than architecture, although architecture is often a reliable index to the state of the church and to its understanding of history. In the United States the churches bear many traces of the ethnic origins of their parishes. But as the language islands of the church have broken up, the rococo of their buildings has been giving way to some bold and creative designs. No longer is it the ambition of every parish to erect a miniature cathedral. Instead, as one American Benedictine has put it, the church building is seen as a sacred space whose consecrating power will reach 'out from the altar, from the church, to embrace all other areas, all places in which men live and labour, so that all human life and effort may become more directly and consciously part of the great act of sacrificial worship'.[2] Far from being an innovation, this insight is actually a revival of primitive Catholic and even medieval emphases that have

[1] As the German poet Novalis put it, the Middle Ages 'were beautiful and brilliant times, when Europe was a Christian land and when one Christendom inhabited this . . . Continent. One great communal interest bound together the most scattered provinces of this broad spiritual realm': cited in Wilhelm Lütgert, *Die Religion des deutschen Idealismus und ihr Ende* (2nd ed.; Gütersloh, 1923), II, 104.
[2] Godfrey Diekmann, *Come, Let Us Worship* (Baltimore, 1961; London, 1962), p. 54.

been obscured in intervening centuries. What seems most modern is, in fact, the reappropriation of the most hallowed of traditions from the church universal.

TRADITION IN ROMAN CATHOLIC THEOLOGY

There is a cognate reappropriation of tradition in contemporary Roman Catholic theology in the United States. A generation ago, if a Roman Catholic student wanted to read the church fathers in English, he usually had to use editions prepared and translated by Anglicans or Calvinists. And if he wanted to and could consult the fathers in Greek or Latin, most of the modern critical editions were the work of German Lutherans. The situation is changing rapidly. Roman Catholics in America are producing not one but two editions of the fathers in English, and they are doing so just when Calvinists, Lutherans, and even Anglicans have largely abdicated their responsibility for patristic scholarship.[1] Initially it is the Latin fathers, and among these the more orthodox ones, whose treatises are studied. But the first on the list of these orthodox fathers is usually St Augustine, and one does not have to study him very long to learn ideas and expressions that break through the static categories of the catechism. His predecessor in North Africa, Cyprian, is memorable both for his martyrdom in 258 and for his attacks upon the Roman Bishop Stephen I. To learn to know a churchman like Cyprian firsthand from his books and epistles is to acquire a better-informed and more sophisticated sense of the universality of the church.[2]

More sophisticated still is the sense of universality that comes from a study of the Greek fathers. Throughout the Western Middle Ages, Constantinople was what Paris has been to us, the city of lights and of intellectual enlightenment. Even earlier, when Rome was first in the ascendant to its position as the capital city of Christendom, the theological leadership of the church stayed with the Greeks, who were also the source of most early heresies. Thus, the most eminent of the Greek-speaking theologians, Origen, was condemned, albeit centuries after his death, for teaching that all

[1] Cf. Walter J. Burghardt, 'The Literature of Christian Antiquity', *Theological Studies*, 24 (1963), 437-463, summarizing recent research.
[2] See Maurice Bévenot, 'Introduction' to Cyprian, *The Lapsed. The Unity of the Catholic Church* (London and Westminster, Md., 1957), pp. 3-8.

men and even the devil would eventually be saved.[1] Yet the same sort of universalism was propounded by Gregory of Nyssa, a Greek father of the fourth century whom the Roman Catholic Church venerates as a saint.[2] Both Origen and St Gregory of Nyssa are becoming available to Roman Catholics in America,[3] both are being studied, both are helping the American church to plumb the depths of its Catholicity. Similarly, it is impressive to see how Athanasius's use of primordial metaphors such as light and darkness manages to express the message of the gospel to both Roman Catholics and Protestants in America today with a directness and a relevance that are often lacking in the commonplaces of the textbooks sponsored by both sides.[4] Although these commonplaces may indeed require reformulation in the light of the great tradition of the faith, true Catholic orthodoxy can only be deepened and enriched as it pays attention to the voices of the Christian past.

THE VOICE OF THE REFORMATION

Among these voices there is one that has yet to be heard in American Roman Catholicism, and that is the voice of Martin Luther. Here again there is an ironic contrast between the Old World and the New. The historical scholarship of German Roman Catholicism has been taking another look at Luther; one theologian has written a book to measure 'the astonishing gifts of [Luther's] spirit and heart, his brilliant view of the actual elements of Christianity' against the superstition and moral compromise of the sixteenth century.[5] Heretic and rebel he still is, but this Luther is not a figure to be dismissed with the slanders that are found among the tracts in the narthex of many an American church. By some historical twist, the nation in which Roman

[1] Cyril C. Richardson, 'The Condemnation of Origen', *Church History*, 6 (1937), 50-64.

[2] Jean Daniélou, 'L'apocatastase chez Grégoire de Nysse', *Recherches de science religieuse*, 30 (1940), 328-347.

[3] Cf. Johannes Quasten, *Patrology* (Westminster, Md., 1951ff.), II, 37-101 on Origen; III, 254-296 on Gregory of Nyssa.

[4] As I pointed out in the preface to *The Light of the World* (New York, 1962), the lectures on Athanasius in that volume were presented also at Roman Catholic universities; the response to them was an indication of the role that patristic study can play in ecumenical conversations today.

[5] Johannes Hessen, *Luther in katholischer Sicht.* Grundlegung eines ökumenischen Gesprächs (Bonn, 1947).

Catholics and Protestants have been thrown together most intimately is one in which they continue to understand very little of each other's histories. Yet the Roman Catholic Church in the United States cannot grasp what is meant by the historical universality of the church until it comes to terms with the Catholic substance and Protestant principle in the Reformation.

Once there is this sense of universality in time, there will also be a sense of universality in faith, hope and charity. Geographical and historical universality helps to create an awareness of ecumenical universality. Of course, 'ecumenical' is a slippery word in ecclesiastical parlance. When Pope John XXIII announced that there was going to be an ecumenical council, many Protestants and even some Roman Catholics jumped to the conclusion that spokesmen for Protestantism and for Eastern Orthodoxy would meet with representatives of Roman Catholicism for a discussion of the issues that divide them.[1] What the Pontiff meant by 'ecumenical', however, was what he meant by 'Catholic', the total communion of the One Holy Catholic and Apostolic Church, whose visible head is the Bishop of Rome. And that is the only thing he could have meant. To negotiate with Protestant communions as with peers, or even with the schismatic sister churches of the East, would be to betray the very foundation of the church, and then the gates of hell would finally prevail against it. Expecting too much from the ecumenical council, those who yearn for the reunion of Christendom had to be disappointed, and so they ran the danger of missing the genuine progress that could come from the council.

It was, after all, the Holy Office itself that recognized the ecumenical movement among Protestants as a work of the Holy Spirit,[2] and in 1960 Pope John announced the establishment of a Secretariat for the Promotion of Christian Unity. Not since the Counter-Reformation have the highest echelons of the Roman Catholic Church been as aware of the positive features of the Reformation as they are today. Gradually this is happening even in the American church, where there is now widespread discussion of the 'vestiges of the church' in the Protestant denominations.[3]

[1] Cf. Lukas Vischer, 'Report on Second Vatican Council'. *The Ecumenical Review*, XVI (1963-1964), 49ff.

[2] See Gregory Baum, *Progress and Perspectives*. The Catholic Quest for Christian Unity (New York, 1962; London, 1963), pp. 33-43.

[3] Wolfgang Dietzfelbinger, 'Vestigia Ecclesiae', *The Ecumenical Review*, XV (1962-1963), 368-376.

This change does not imply laxity in the Roman Catholicism of America, but rather security. When Roman Catholic immigrants arrived in a largely Protestant America whose literature, traditions, and public schools had a decidedly evangelical and Puritan cast, there was a serious question whether the immigrant would keep the faith. But now that the church is at home in the United States and is acknowledged by all but a shrinking and strident clique as a permanent and positive force in American life, the Roman Catholic Church in America can afford to scrutinize the Christian world beyond its own walls, for it should know by now that it has nothing to lose but its provinciality.

What it has to gain from such scrutiny is nothing less than the fulfilment of the Catholic ideal, a universality in faith, hope, and charity. 'Schismatic churches' as a term for Eastern Orthodoxy is harsh enough. 'Vestiges of the church', on the other hand, may sound not only harsh but condescending as an explanation for the presence of grace and the gospel in Protestant Christianity, and yet its implications reach far into the life and doctrine of the church. If someone is baptized by a Protestant minister in the name of the Father and of the Son and of the Holy Ghost and if, after his baptism, he remains devoted to the Lord Jesus Christ and seeks to teach and live according to the word of God, what can Roman Catholic theology say about such a person except that he has lived and died as a child of God?[1] There is only one church, of which the pope is the head. Baptism is the rite by which a person is initiated into that one church and incorporated into Christ, though it be baptism at the hands of a layman or a Protestant or even a non-Christian—just so that water is used, the name of the Trinity is invoked, and there is the intention to make this act the baptism of the church.[2] In an earlier century St Augustine battled against the extremism of the Donatist heresy and worked out most of the details of this doctrine.[3] It remains for the teaching office of the church, perhaps at the ecumenical council, to make explicit

[1] Cf. Karl Rahner, *Nature and Grace*. Dilemmas in the Modern Church (London, 1963; New York, 1964), pp. 88-105.
[2] As one Jesuit theologian puts it, 'Unless the contrary is proved in each particular case [of Protestant baptism], the presumption favours valid baptism provided flowing water and the Trinitarian formula were used.' John Hardon, *Christianity in Conflict* (Westminster, Md., 1959). p. 190.
[3] Geoffrey Grimshaw Willis, *Saint Augustine and the Donatist Controversy*, (London, 1950), pp. 157-160.

for the twentieth century the full meaning of the universality in this Augustinian doctrine.

There is a significant parallel between many of these changes within Roman Catholicism and the evangelical Catholicity of Luther's Reformation. Thus one student of the liturgical movement within contemporary Roman Catholicism has set its work into the context of the principles we have discussed in Chapters V and VI.[1] Participants in the theological dialogue continually find themselves face to face with the challenge of the Reformation, and both Roman Catholics and Protestants are paying new attention to the thought of Luther. The meaning of this for Protestant theology will engage us in subsequent chapters, but for Roman Catholic theology it means that for the first time since the sixteenth century the Reformation is playing a positive and constructive role. As Karl Barth has said, it would be ironic if the outcome of this change were a greater fidelity to the Reformation in Roman Catholicism than in Protestantism.[2] But even if the results are less dramatic than that, the combination of Catholic substance and Protestant principle in Luther's Reformation has become a fact to be contended with among Roman Catholic theologians. And thus by becoming 'more Protestant', contemporary Roman Catholicism may also become more fully Catholic—as a consequence of the Reformation.

[1] See p. 23, note 4 above.
[2] Karl Barth, 'Thoughts on the Second Vatican Council', *The Ecumenical Review*, XV (1962-1963), 357-367.

XII

CATHOLIC SUBSTANCE IN CONTEMPORARY PROTESTANTISM

THE Protestant theology of the twentieth century has begun to recover the meaning of tradition and thus to modify its Protestant principle by a more positive assessment of the Catholic substance in its past. Initially, this shift in attitude toward history and tradition may appear to be a repudiation of the critical estimate of tradition summarized in Part One of this book; and it is true that the formal anti-traditionalism of Luther's Reformation has been revised as a result of research and debate, even though at the same time some aspects of Reformation traditionalism have also been discarded. The recovery of Catholic substance, therefore, is no simple return to pre-Reformation patterns of thought, but a more mature and critical re-examination of the Reformation itself. Even the reconsideration of Reformation formulas is an an act of fidelity to the Reformation; even the reappropriation of Catholic substance is an expression of the Protestant principle. The Reformation view of history has been revised in at least three ways, which correspond to three senses in which the word 'history' is used in theology: history as events in sequence; history as historical writing; history as an expression of a philosophy of relativism.[1] In all three of these senses, the discussion of tradition in contemporary Protestantism has gone beyond the Reformation and yet has grasped the teaching of the Reformation more profoundly than the uncritical recitation of passages from Luther's writings ever could.

[1] R. G. Collingwood, *The Idea of History* (Oxford, 1946; New York, 1956); H. Richard Niebuhr, *The Meaning of Revelation* (New York, 1941; London, 1946), esp. pp. 43-90.

TRADITION IS INEVITABLE

The history of the church has made the formal anti-traditionalism of the Reformation obsolete. Chapter III and Chapter VII have shown that to defy the accumulated traditions of the medieval church in the name of the freedom of God and of the renewing Spirit, Luther could speak as though traditions were always consequent upon Scripture, both logically and chronologically, and as though it were possible to preclude the development of traditions by firm adherence to the Scriptures as both the source and the norm of Christian teaching. Such defiance makes less and less sense as the several Protestant communions themselves produce traditions of teaching and of usage that are no more (and no less) Scriptural in their origin and validation than were the ecclesiastical customs against whose claim to apostolicity Luther protested so vehemently. Examples from the history of Orthodox, Protestant, and Roman Catholic theology, liturgy, piety, and polity support the thesis that, for better or for worse, or for a combination of the two, traditions are inevitable.[1]

The 'free churches' on the North American continent confirm this thesis in their own histories. They were committed to the principle that 'the Christian tradition . . . must issue in pluralistic representations, each entitled to claim for itself the Christian tradition as ultimately validated by the voluntary identification of that denomination by its members.'[2] In the power of this principle, they broke with traditional patterns not only of Catholic Christianity, but of the very communions and confessional families out of which they themselves had come. So it was that American Christians identified themselves with what has been called 'the North American opportunity to begin anew without being

---

[1] In recent essays I have noted this in two different denominations: 'American Lutheranism: Denomination or Confession?' *The Christian Century*, LXXX (1963), 1608-1610; 'Methodism's Contribution to America', *The History of American Methodism* (New York, 1964), III, 596-614.

[2] Much of the material in this chapter is based on papers presented by various members of the North American Section of the Theological Commission on Tradition and Traditions of the Commission on Faith and Order; most of the papers are unpublished, but I shall refer in the notes to published essays by the same scholars, in which some of the same points are made. Thus, cf. William A. Clebsch, 'Church History' in John A. Coburn and Norman Pittenger (edd.), *Viewpoints: Some Aspects of Anglican Thinking* (Greenwich, Conn., 1959), pp. 58-70.

hindered by custom or misled by tradition'.[1] But, continues the same scholar, 'tradition is not so easily abrogated. America was better: They dwelt on this theme continually in their letters home. Yet it was to home that they wrote; and they preserved the very traditions they left. . . . With the sloughing off of second-generation hesitancies and insecurities not only would the Continental tradition in all of its Evangelical and Catholic ramifications be more deeply cherished, but also the sense of tradition.'

The Disciples of Christ or 'Christians', an indigenously American and consistently Protestant community, opposed tradition so radically that they would not use even the Apostles' Creed— whether as a test of faith or a liturgical confession.[2] Yet this radical biblicism has also justified this anti-traditionalist brotherhood in its tradition of maintaining the necessity of a weekly celebration of the Lord's Supper as the central feature of the church's worship. On the basis of the Protestant principle of the sole authority of Scripture, it affirms this element of the Catholic eucharistic tradition, to which other and more traditionalistic Protestant communions, despite the witness of the Reformers, have come only gradually and with great difficulty, if at all.[3]

Although the data on the Christian churches that have come out of the missionary enterprise are not so easily collected, a similar attitude seems to have manifested itself in their histories.[4] With the Christian gospel they have received many traditions characteristic of the Western communions and cultures that evangelized them. Their growing self-consciousness as churches within nations that are likewise growing in their self-consciousness has made them sensitive to these Western traditions in their faith and life. Some of them, in the name of the freedom of God and of the renewing Spirit, defy their Western tradition and speak as though it were possible to preclude the development of traditions. Mean-

[1] Cf. Sydney E. Ahlstrom, 'Tradition in Transit and Tension: The Continental Inheritance in America; the Lutheran Experience', *Encounter*, XX (1959).
[2] W. E. Garrison and Alfred T. De Groot, *The Disciples of Christ: A History* (Saint Louis, 1948), pp. 231-232, 264-265.
[3] Michael J. Taylor, *The Protestant Liturgical Renewal: A Catholic Viewpoint* (Westminster, Md., 1963), which presents data on the frequency of celebration at the end of each chapter.
[4] See, for one example, Charles W. Forman, 'A Study in the Self-Propagating Church: Madagascar', *Frontiers of the Christian World Mission Since 1938: Essays in Honor of Kenneth Scott Latourette*, ed. Wilber C. Harr (New York and London, 1962), pp. 151-170, esp. pp. 165-167.

while, they have begun to discover that, for all the brevity of their history, they already have traditions of their own. They ask whether they have exchanged one set of traditions for another, or grafted dubious new traditions upon dubious old traditions.

In the very midst of this process of tradition-building many theologians have gone on repeating the formal anti-traditionalism of the Reformers. As a result, there is no tradition more tenacious than the tradition of 'Scripture alone'. Yet theological history has proved that Scripture is never alone.

TRADITION IS PRIMORDIAL

Theological historiography has furnished additional proof for this generalization that Scripture is never alone. Much research into biblical history has been animated by a 'primitivist emphasis on apostolicity which refuses to accept the exegetical authority of the ongoing church or to recognize the weight of traditional precedents in the interpretation and presentation of gospel, sacraments, and ministry'.[1] Despite this emphasis, such research eventually discovered that tradition takes chronological, if not also logical, precedence over Scripture, and that the deeper one's historical study goes into primitive Christianity, the more pronounced the influence of tradition becomes. Theological historiography has, therefore, been obliged by the empirical data to accept these facts: The primitive church expounded its Scriptures in the light of what had been handed down by and about Jesus Christ; the primitive church interpreted what had been handed down in the light of the Scriptures.[2] In short, as Professor Outler summarizes this historiography: 'In the ante-Nicene Church, the notion of *sola Scriptura* does not exist. But then there is also no notion of a tradition which is superior to Scripture, or which alters the essential content of the apostolic message as it is deposited in Scripture. There was simply no way of imagining possible conflict between the Christian Scripture and the Christian tradition—and, therefore, no necessity to choose between them.'[3]

---

[1] Cf. Eugene R. Fairweather, 'Faith and Tradition', *Canadian Journal of Theology*, 3 (1957), 79-86; 'Scripture in Tradition', *ibid.*, 5 (1959), 7-14.
[2] That historiography is well summarized in Ellen Flessemann van Leer, *Tradition and Scripture in the Early Church* (Assen, 1953).
[3] See p. 25 above.

As theological historiography has been obliged to modify, if not to surrender, the traditional dichotomy between Scripture and tradition in the study of Scripture, so it has also been forced to reassess the role of tradition in the very Reformation whose case against tradition it claimed to be espousing. From that reassessment of tradition in the Reformation at least two conclusions have emerged. One conclusion is that although the Reformers were expositors of the Scriptures, none of them could have been the exegete he was without the help of the church's tradition; we shall discuss some of the implications of this in Chapter XIII. The Reformers were traditionalists in spite of themselves. A second conclusion of historical writing about the Reformation is this: 'While agreeing that Calvin's formulation of the doctrine of the *Testimonium* [i.e. *Spiritus Sancti*] is a gift of God to the church that reveals the Reformation as a truly Pentecostal occasion, one must also assert that the Reformers' diagnosis of their experience and their application of the doctrine contained error that produced also deformation in the Catholic Church.'[1] The Reformers did not always choose the right parts of the tradition to accept and reject.

From these two conclusions, one positive and the other negative, there proceeds an interpretation of theological history that differs from the stereotypes of both Roman Catholic and Protestant hagiography. No longer may historians pit the Reformers against the Catholic tradition *à la* David versus Goliath; for we know that many of the stones in David's sling-shot came from Goliath's territory and some of them were stones that Goliath had overlooked. We know, on the other hand, that the Reformers and their descendants may not disclaim all responsibility for the erosion of the Christian tradition during the centuries since the Reformation. This erosion was accompanied by a devaluation of history, which, as one Eastern Orthodox theologian has observed, 'may be regarded as a logical consequence of the reduced conception of the church, which was so characteristic of certain trends of the Reformation. The church was still recognized as the area of an "invisible" action and operation of God, but she was denied

---

[1] Cf. David W. Hay, 'The Reformed Catholic Church' in *The Unity We Seek*, ed. William S. Morris (New York and London, 1963), pp. 98-112; and 'Church Reformation and the World Church', *ibid.*, pp. 113-127.

precisely her historical significance.'[1] This theologian goes on to express the hope that 'the modern recovery of the integral doctrine of the church, which cuts across the existing denominational borders, may lead to the recovery of a deeper historical insight and may restate history in its true existential dimension.' That recovery includes the reassessment by theological historiography of the role that tradition plays both in the Scriptures and in the development of the Christian community.

To interpret the role of tradition in the church, as a result, one may use a formula developed in the Christological tradition: 'There was no time when it was not.' Not only is tradition inevitable in the process of institutionalization by which a prophetic movement develops into established patterns of faith, life, and order; but the prophetic character of the movement itself comes from the tradition, leads to the tradition, and inheres in the tradition. Whether or not one accepts all the conclusions of form criticism in the study of the Old Testament and New Testament, the admission seems unavoidable that the Scriptures, in whose name the Reformers defied traditions, have their roots in tradition. On this issue, as on others, the histories of the separate confessions have not caught up with the findings of their historiography.

TRADITION IS RELATIVE

Ironically, where the Reformation is most traditional, it is also least acceptable to some of its heirs. Luther's notion of the perpetual virginity of Mary or Calvin's doctrine of the relation between the two natures in Christ are echoes of older tradition, but they find little echo in Lutheranism or Calvinism or in most non-Roman Western churches.[2] The reasons for this contrast between the material traditionalism of the Reformation and the anti-traditionalism of some Protestant theologians are many, but one reason is central: the widespread conviction, as formulated by a distinguished Reformation scholar, that 'no historical form of Christianity must be absolutized or regarded as normative or authoritative', for 'truth also undergoes a development, at least in

---

[1] Georges Florovsky, 'The Predicament of the Christian Historian', *Religion and Culture: Essays in Honor of Paul Tillich*, ed. Walter Leibrecht (New York and London, 1959), p. 165.
[2] Cf. p. 136, note 1 above.

connection with the historical forms in which it is held and expressed'.[1] Underlying this conviction is the thesis that 'the Protestant Reformers in principle abolished dogma (e.g., the Trinity, the two natures in Christ, etc.) though in fact they did not realize what they had accomplished when, in the name of the gospel, they denied infallibility to any dogma'.

Such historicism makes the authority of the Reformation's affirmation of tradition inapplicable. Thus, the relativization of tradition, whose beginnings have been described in Chapter IV, forces reconsideration of those traditions which, for both religious and political reasons, the Reformers felt themselves bound to retain. Contemporary interpreters of the Reformation do not agree in their acceptance of the validity of historicism. As a result, their evaluation of the reappropriation of tradition by theological history and theological historiography varies. For some, this relativization serves to reinforce the traditional anti-traditionalism of many American Christians—the implicit negation of the existence of 'a common Christian history which might be held to be longer, larger and richer than those separate histories' of the individual denominations.[2] To others such historicism seems to be radically nominalistic; consistently carried out, it would destroy the quest for a theological consensus and would declare churchly unity unattainable on any grounds save a thoroughgoing pluralism.

Yet theological historiography does not really support such scepticism about either theological consensus or churchly unity. It suggests, rather, that consensus is reached within a community, but that the community expresses its unity through a common confession which bespeaks some sort of common history. When it demonstrates the relativity of particular confessions and parochial traditions, theological historiography performs one of the tasks which, as Chapter II has shown, the Reformation assigned to it: it grinds the golden calves into powder. On the other hand, as the development of theological historicism shows, the battle against idolatry can lead to iconoclasm, which makes the quest for churchly unity yet more urgent. But this does not mean that tradition is only the arithmetic sum total of disparate individual histories. For tradition is the common history of the church, and

---

[1] Wilhelm Pauck, *The Heritage of the Reformation*, pp. 344-345.
[2] Clebsch, *art. cit.*; see p. 171, note 2 above.

the church is never the mere arithmetic sum total of the utterly unique individuals who make it up.

A THEOLOGICAL CONSENSUS ON THE CHURCH

In fact, the very process we have been describing has produced a theological consensus on the doctrine of the church. Nowhere has that consensus been more cogently formulated than in a one-sentence declaration originally framed at St Andrew's, Scotland, in the summer of 1960 and adopted at the New Delhi Assembly of the World Council of Churches in December of 1961:

> We believe that the unity which is both God's will and his gift to his church is being made visible as all in each place who are baptized into Jesus Christ and confess him as Lord and Saviour are brought by the Holy Spirit into one fully committed fellowship, holding the one apostolic faith, preaching the one gospel, breaking the one bread, joining in common prayer, and having a corporate life reaching out in witness and service to all and who at the same time are united with the whole Christian fellowship in all places and all ages in such wise that ministry and members are accepted by all, and that all can act and speak together as occasion requires for the tasks to which God calls his people.[1]

Behind each of these phrases is a generation of efforts by biblical scholars, historians, and theologians to move beyond the cul-de-sac of post-Reformation controversy.

'The unity which is both God's will and his gift to his church is being made *visible*'—this is now the affirmation and the hope of Protestant theology. Of course, unity has always been an attribute of the church in Protestant theology; the Ephesian letter and the Nicene Creed were too explicit to evade. But in conflict with a Post-Tridentine theology that could not always distinguish between the church as organism and the church as organization or, for that matter, between the church and the kingdom of God, the theology of the Reformation made extensive use of the Augustinian distinction between the church as visible and the church as invisible. But while Augustine had invoked this distinction against the Donatists in order to summon them back to Catholic unity in a church whose spotted actuality seemed to belie the idea of the holi-

---

[1] *Commission on Faith and Order: Minutes of the Meeting Held at St Andrews, Scotland* (Geneva, 1960), p. 11.

ness of the church,[1] the Reformers found in the distinction a device for affirming the essential unity of the church amid its existential divisions, or its unity before God despite its schisms before men, or its unity in hope above and beyond its disunity in fact. Luther, as we have seen, spoke of the church not as invisible but as hidden. But both Melanchthon and Calvin made the invisibility of the church a prime attribute, Melanchthon because of the problem of disunity and Calvin because of his definition of the church as the company of the elect.[2]

In the history of Protestant theology after the Reformation, many factors combined to elevate this idea of the invisibility of the church, specifically the invisibility of its unity, to the status of an axiom. Although the thesis of Joseph Lortz that nominalism was a decisive factor is not convincing,[3] it does seem clear that two other movements prominent in Protestant theological history bore a large part of the responsibility: Pietism and Kantian idealism. Beginning as a protest against the externalism and formalism of Protestant Orthodoxy, the Pietist movement emphasized the inwardness of faith and the individuality of the relation between God and man in a manner that made the church more an effect than a cause of the individual's conversion.[4] The Kantian distinction between the noumenal and the phenomenal world— not unrelated, perhaps, to Pietism[5]—facilitated a theological position that made the unity of the church inaccessible to sense-experience and available only to faith, while the disunity of the empirical church was the aspect it presented in the world of phenomena.[6] As the original divisions of the Reformation proliferated, the concept of the invisible unity of the church seemed the only way for a fissiparous Protestantism to make some sort of theological sense out of ecclesiological faith and denominational fact.

[1] Cf. Geoffrey Grimshaw Willis, *Saint Augustine and the Donatist Controversy* (London, 1950), pp. 123-125, 141-143.

[2] See p. 14, note 1 above, but also Thomas F. Torrance, *Kingdom and Church. A Study in the Theology of the Reformation* (Edinburgh, 1956), pp. 148-150.

[3] See, for example, Joseph Lortz, *Die Reformation als religiöses Anliegen heute* (Trier, 1948), pp. 51-61.

[4] Cf. the incisive comments of Emanuel Hirsch, *Geschichte der neuern evangelischen Theologie*, II (Gütersloh, 1960), 128-130.

[5] Cf. Jaroslav Pelikan, *From Luther to Kierkegaard*, pp. 92-96.

[6] See the astute and learned discussion of J. A. Dorner, *System der christlichen Glaubenslehre*, II (Berlin 1880), 887-910.

But now such a rationalization has become impossible. Both the ecumenical experiences of the twentieth century and the theological research of the past generation have made the conclusion unavoidable that the unity of the church must be sought, not in a 'Platonic republic'[1] beyond the empirical realm, but in history. The Declaration of St Andrew's therefore follows the New Testament in linking baptism and the confession of faith as expressions of this visible unity, and it paraphrases the Book of Acts in listing the forms taken by the one committed fellowship of the church: one apostolic faith, one gospel, the breaking of the one bread, common prayer, and a corporate life of witness and service. All of these are visible (or audible) functions of the life of the church. Each demands more specification and definition than this brief formula provides; and Protestant theologians are not equally agreed—either with one another or with Roman Catholicism— about the content of each. Thus there is a long way to go, but the ecumenical consensus achieved thus far is impressive. As Roman Catholic theology proceeds in the direction described in Chapter XI, it should find many points of meaningful contact in this consensus.

THE CHURCH OF ALL AGES

The second part of the declaration also contains a significant affirmation of Catholic substance: 'who at the same time are united with the whole Christian fellowship in all places *and all ages.*' Here the unity of the church is represented as a unity in time as well as in space, and the continuity of the church's tradition thus becomes part of the definition of its unity. This formulation of the doctrine of the church is closely related to the Reformation's understanding of church history, summarized in Chapter II. But as we pointed out earlier in this present chapter, this admission of tradition into the doctrine of the unity of the church can also make possible a study of the tradition in a context more conducive to mutual understanding than were the sixteenth and seventeenth centuries. This phrase 'and all ages' seems to violate the Protestant principle in a fundamental way; for the history of the church, being in the past and therefore unchangeable, cannot participate meaningfully in the dynamic process of establishing

[1] See p. 34, note 2 above.

and articulating that unity 'which is both God's will and his gift to his church'.

The answer to this objection involves several arguments and strikes at the centre of the entire issue. For one thing, the history of the church, while indeed unchangeable as a series of events, is subject to reconsideration as the record of those events. The most important instance of such reconsideration, as far as this issue is concerned, is the discovery that the tradition of the church is exegetical.[1] The fathers of the church spoke as they did because they regarded themselves as interpreters of the Scriptures. Therefore they are not to be made a substitute for the Scriptures; nor can the Scriptures be understood apart from the authoritative interpretation which tradition places upon them. Thus, as we have sought to show in an earlier discussion, tradition is primitive, tradition is inevitable, and tradition is exegetical.[2] This view of tradition suggests, as we have seen, that it is time for both sides to look more carefully at the Reformation attitude toward Scripture and tradition. If tradition is primitive, Protestant theology must admit that 'Scripture alone' requires redefinition. But if tradition is exegetical, Roman Catholic theology must admit that 'Scripture alone', properly understood, is correct. For the writings of the church fathers are expository, even the controversial writings that have been handed down to us.

Until the descendants of the Reformation on both sides face the implications of history and tradition, their mutual discussions will not proceed very far. But now that Protestant theology has acknowledged the necessity of finding unity with the church of all ages, perhaps the elusive 'consensus of the first five centuries', proposed as a basis for unity beyond separation by George Calixtus,[3] can begin to add its influence to the growing pursuit of the church's unity. It is ironic that between Calixtus and the present, Roman Catholicism and Protestantism have in fact grown together on issues like the authority of Scripture and the

[1] Perhaps the outstanding monograph in the contemporary literature on this issue is Jean Daniélou, *From Shadows to Reality*. Studies in the Biblical Typology of the Fathers, tr. Wulstan Hibberd (Westminster, Md., 1960). See also p. 198, note 1 below.

[2] See the generous comments of the late Gustave Weigel, *Catholic Theology in Dialogue* (New York, 1961), p. 40.

[3] Cf. Hermann Schüssler, *Georg Calixt: Theologie und Kirchenpolitik*. Eine Studie zur Ökumenizität des Luthertums (Wiesbaden, 1961), pp. 66-81.

doctrine of justification, even on the doctrine about the church. But in the interim, they have grown apart at some of the very points where the Reformers had retained the Catholic substance. This irony modifies the consensus behind the phrase 'holding the one apostolic faith'. Yet even here the recovery of Catholic substance during the past decades has moved closer to the Reformation. For example, thanks largely to Karl Barth, the doctrine of the Trinity has once more become a central preoccupation of Protestant theology.[1] Thus the revision of Reformation attitudes toward history has produced not only a new understanding of the Reformation, but a new willingness to consider the testimony of Catholic tradition. What this means for the context and the method of Protestant theology will concern us in the final two chapters of this book.

[1] See Claude Welch, *In This Name*. The Doctrine of the Trinity in Contemporary Theology (New York, 1952), pp. 161-208.

XIII

THE CATHOLIC CONTEXT OF
PROTESTANT THEOLOGY

FOR the theologian, one Book is enough and a thousand books are
not too many. This paradox is an epitome of the larger 'paradox
of Luther's Reformation' described in Chapter I. For according
to Luther, the task of the theologian, of every theologian, was the
exposition of the Scriptures. Yet to perform his task of expound-
ing that one Book, the theologian needed a great many books.

It is a basic Protestant principle that theology must be exegetical or it is not theology. The great theologians of the church's past
and present are usually celebrated for their systematic formulations rather than for their exegetical insights. The controversies of
theological history are generally read as conflicts over specific
doctrines, such as the Trinity or original sin, rather than as debates
about the interpretation of the Bible. But a careful study of the
corpus of the writings of Athanasius, for example, reveals that the
central issue and content of his battle against the Arian heresy was
not a dogmatic formulation, not even the famous *homoousios*,
but the interpretation of biblical passages such as the eighth chapter of Proverbs within the context of the church's liturgical
obedience.[1] And what carried the day for Catholic orthodoxy at
Nicaea or at Chalcedon was (apart from the political authority that
was invoked in support of orthodoxy on each of these occasions)
the restoration of exegetical sanity in place of the dogmatic vagaries on both extremes, the victory of biblical modesty over the
high-flown language and thought of the theological left and right.[2]
Yet it has been a continuing temptation of the interpreters of

---

[1] Jaroslav Pelikan, *The Light of the World*, pp. 55ff.
[2] See the creative suggestions of Karl Rahner, 'Chalkedon—Ende oder
Anfang?' in Aloys Grillmeier and Heinrich Bacht (edd.), *Das Konzil von Chalkedon*, III (Würzburg, 1954), 2-49.

Luther's Reformation to substitute concept for function, to battle heroically for the real presence of the body and blood of Christ in the Lord's Supper and then to let the sacramental life of the church dwindle to monthly or even quarterly celebrations, or to suppose that a formal statement of the authority and inspiration of Scripture in the Prolegomena of a dogmatics was some sort of guarantee that the material of the dogmatics would be biblical. Even in the usual interpretation of Martin Luther, a systematizing tendency has predominated, always with the observation that Luther was not altogether systematic.[1] Fundamentally, Luther was a biblical theologian, a *Doctor in Biblia*. It was as *Doctor in Biblia*, not merely as a believer or even as an ordained clergyman, that he felt called 'to expound the Scriptures for all the world and to teach everybody'.[2]

For Luther the theologian, this one Book was enough. But he knew all along, and was reminded over and over in his theological development, that he could not make sense of this one Book nor be obedient to its message without support, criticism, and correction from a thousand books. In 1524, in his letter to the councilmen of Germany, Luther therefore turned his attention to the fitting out of a library in accordance with the principles of his Reformation:

> My advice is not to heap together all manner of books indiscriminately and think only of the number and size of the collection. I would make a judicious selection . . . and furnish my library with the right sort of books, consulting with scholars as to my choice.
>
> First of all, there would be the Holy Scriptures, in Latin, Greek, Hebrew, and German, and any other language in which they might be found. Next, the best commentaries, and, if I could find them, the most ancient, in Greek, Hebrew, and Latin. Then, books that would be helpful in learning the languages, such as the poets and orators, regardless of whether they were pagan or Christian, Greek or Latin. . . . After that would come books on the liberal arts, and all the other arts [including law and medicine]. . . . Among the foremost would be the chronicles and histories. . . . Now that God has today so graciously bestowed upon us an abundance of arts, scholars, and books, it is time to reap and gather the best as well as we can, and lay up treasure in order to preserve for the future something from these years of jubilee, and not lose this bountiful harvest.[3]

[1] Cf. Jaroslav Pelikan, *From Luther to Kierkegaard*, pp. 14-15.
[2] See p. 201, note 2 below.
[3] *To the Councilmen of All Cities in Germany That They Establish and Maintain Christian Schools*, WA 15, 51-52 (WML 5, 128-129).

From the research of Walter Friedensburg and of Ernest Schwiebert it appears that some such schema as this was at the foundation of the collection in the Wittenberg library, established in 1512, the same year that Luther became a Doctor of Sacred Scripture and a professor there.[1]

Careful analysis of Luther's words suggests that if theology is to be faithful to the Protestant principle and to be an exposition of the one Book, it will have to be placed in the context of the Catholic substance represented by three concerns: a deep regard for the theological tradition; a fraternal consideration of contemporary theology; an appreciative attention to non-theological thought.

A REGARD FOR TRADITION

'The best commentaries, and, if I could find them, the most ancient, in Greek, Hebrew, and Latin'—these words of Luther suggest that, next only to the Scriptures themselves, Protestant theology needs to pay attention to the fathers of the church. Yet an examination of theological scholarship in the churches of America would certainly not discover a preponderance of interest in the Catholic tradition. Two tendencies in American theology, which are often set into opposition with each other, militate against a deep regard for the Catholic substance of the theological tradition. One is the proclivity of the American theological public for theological fads, or, as they are usually called, 'current theological trends'.[2] As in Germany, so in the United States ten years later, interest centres not only on the most up-to-date theological author, but on his most recently published book. The study of the church fathers is a defence against this bondage to caprice. For to discover that some members of the Christian community saw more deeply into the message of the Scriptures than we is to learn that the Catholic substance is the context for the Protestant principle. Current trends surely need to act as a counterbalance to the dead weight of the past, and so they deserve a place in theological

---

[1] Cf. Ernest G. Schwiebert, *Luther and His Times*, pp. 244-253, summarizing his own and Friedensburg's findings. For a more detailed study, cf. Ernest G. Schwiebert, 'Remnants of a Reformation Library', *The Library Quarterly*, X (1940), 494-531.
[2] See the essay contributed by Albert C. Outler to *How My Mind Has Changed*, ed. Harold E. Fey (New York and London, 1961), pp. 40-54.

research. But they also deserve to be placed into perspective by the study of the Greek and Latin fathers.

A study of the Catholic tradition can also help to guard Protestant theology against another besetting vice, that of parochialism.[1] Some heirs of the Reformation have manifested a parochialism of taste in their theological study that may have been insulated against the passing fad, but only at the cost of large portions of the Catholic tradition. Then the term 'fathers' or 'our fathers' became the designation for the linear ancestors of the theological *Tendenz* of a particular denomination—the theological fad lengthened in time but not deepened in perception and catholicity. And if the fathers of the whole church were studied at all, they were immediately hailed before the bar of denominational judgment.[2] The combination of Catholic substance and Protestant principle in Luther's Reformation suggests that a theology which is deaf to the testimony of Catholic substance, even if this deafness is rationalized by an appeal to the Protestant principle of 'Scripture alone', tends to be deaf as well to anything in Scripture that challenges its conventional exegesis. The eclipse of the doctrine of the Trinity in the Protestant theology of the nineteenth century on almost all sides was due, in so-called 'liberal' theology, to a moralistic and idealistic reading of Scripture; and in so-called 'evangelical' theology, to a preoccupation with the divinity of Christ at the expense of the doctrine of the Trinity.[3] In both cases, a parochial interpretation of the Protestant principle impoverished itself by failing to pay attention to the context supplied by the Catholic tradition, which was not merely spinning exegetical fancies when it set forth the doctrine of the Trinity as the summary of the witness of the Scriptures to the being and the revelation of God.

[1] It would be highly instructive to study the courses in church history offered at both Protestant and Roman Catholic seminaries in the past century, to determine which of them actually dealt with the whole of the history of the church and which with the history of their own denomination—plus the history of the early church as the origin of their own denomination.

[2] In the words of the pedantic prig, Wagner, in Goethe's *Faust* (Part One, lines 57off.; translation by George Madison Priest):

> It is a great delight
> To enter in the spirit of the ages and to see
> How once a sage before us thought and then how we
> Have brought things on at last to such a splendid height.

[3] Cf. H. Richard Niebuhr, *The Purpose of the Church and Its Ministry* (New York and London, 1956), pp. 44-47; *Radical Monotheism and Western Culture* (New York, 1960; London, 1961), pp. 59-60; and Claude Welch, *In This Name*, pp. 3-41.

In the same way, the heirs of Luther's Reformation during the past two centuries have sometimes concentrated upon an elaboration of the Christology of Martin Chemnitz in opposition to various modern doctrines of Christ, rather than upon an explication of the decree of the Council of Chalcedon, which would have provided a more effective answer to those doctrines.[1] Behind this posture was a definition of theological orthodoxy as dogmatic precision, which is only half of the definition; for orthodoxy implies exegetical amplitude as well as doctrinal precision. And it was characteristic of the Catholic orthodoxy of the ancient church, and of all authentic orthodoxy since, that when it formulated its propositions with dogmatic precision, it did not do so by sacrificing exegetical amplitude. The decree of Chalcedon fixed the limits of orthodox language, worship, and speculation about the person of Jesus Christ. Within these limits, which circumscribe the Christology of Chemnitz, the variety and the richness of biblical language about Christ could all find a place. Not the orthodox but the heretics were generally the ones who fastened upon a single idea, which may perhaps have been correct enough in itself, but which blocked the rest of the teaching of Scripture out of view.[2] To be rescued from the error of theological overemphasis, Protestant theology needs the passion of the Catholic tradition for *plērōma*, plenitude.

The career of one of the most eminent modern interpreters of Luther's Reformation, Werner Elert, is an illustration of this priority.[3] Elert's historical research and literary production moved backwards through the centuries. Beginning with a book on the theology and philosophy of the nineteenth century, Elert proceeded to the classical period of Lutheran dogmatics and to the thought of Luther himself. From there he was driven to the early church, particularly to the Greek fathers; and his last two books dealt with early Christian thought. Elert's experience and that of other Reformation scholars corroborates the judgment of the greatest

[1] On the embarrassments of Christological conservatism during the nineteenth century, cf. Horst Stephan, *Geschichte der deutschen evangelischen Theologie seit dem deutschen Idealismus*, revised by Martin Schmidt (Berlin, 1960), pp. 172ff.

[2] As G. L. Prestige puts it, 'It was the heretics that relied most on isolated texts, and the Catholics who paid more attention on the whole to scriptural principles', *Fathers and Heretics* (London, 1948), p. 21.

[3] Cf. the comments in my 'Foreword' to Elert, *The Structure of Lutheranism*, pp. vii-xi.

historian of Christianity in our century, upon whose scholarship modern historical theologians are still forced to depend, Adolf von Harnack:

> The centre of gravity in the discipline of church history lies in the church history and historical theology of the first six centuries. I am not speaking *pro domo* here. Rather, it is already acknowledged in wide circles and will, I hope, become universally recognized, that without a thorough knowledge of early church history a man is no more a real church historian than he would be a classical philologist without a knowledge of the golden age of Greek and Roman literature. . . . Only that scholar is eligible to be a church historian . . . who has a command of early church history.[1]

Harnack was also one of the first to insist that it is a distortion of the fathers to read them otherwise than they wanted to be read, namely, as interpreters of the Bible.[2] In the same direction, Elert urged that the 'dogma of Christ' of a theologian or period has to be seen in the light of its 'picture of Christ', which emerges from its exposition of the Scriptures, above all of the Gospels.[3] With the help of the Catholic substance of patristic exegesis, as set forth, for example, in Jean Daniélou's *Sacramentum futuri*, the Protestant exposition of Scripture can follow Luther in interpreting the story of the Flood, the account of the binding of Isaac, and the history of the Exodus as a witness to the promising and fulfilling faithfulness of God.[4] It remains to be seen whether a Protestant exegesis that neglects this Catholic substance can penetrate to the renewing message of the Scriptures. The context of theological research is, in the first place, the context of the fathers, studied with a deep regard for theological tradition.

THE PLACE OF CURRENT THEOLOGICAL TRENDS

Nevertheless, a truly Catholic regard for tradition does not mean antiquarianism. According to a *bon mot* of theology, whose origins remain obscure, the difference between tradition and traditionalism is the difference between the living faith of the dead and

[1] Memorandum of September 27, 1888, cited at length in Agnes von Zahn-Harnack, *Adolf von Harnack* (2nd. ed.; Berlin, 1951), pp. 128-131.
[2] Adolf Harnack, *Der kirchengeschichtliche Ertrag der exegetischen Arbeiten des Origenes* (Leipzig, 1919).
[3] Werner Elert, *Der Augang der altkirchlichen Christologie* (Berlin, 1957), pp. 71ff.
[4] See p. 180, note 1 above on the English translation.

the dead faith of the living. Theological Catholicity is not a wine cellar, in which only certain vintage years are to be permitted. To hear and hearken to revelation in a way that is truly Catholic Protestant theology needs not only to show a deep regard for the theological tradition, but also to give fraternal consideration to theological contemporaries; not only the fathers, but also the brethren must be given an opportunity to speak. For one cannot predict, and hence one dare not prescribe, the channels through which the Holy Spirit will shed illumination upon the word and so upon the church.

To the historian of the church and of its theology, there is, of course, considerable irritation in the ceaseless proliferation of theological print. But even the historian's scrutiny of the development of Catholic substance often owes its most penetrating insights to current trends, understanding the fathers better because of the brethren. For the present revival of research on the history of the doctrine of the Trinity, as Chapter XII has noted, theological scholarship is indebted not solely to historians like G. L. Prestige and Jacques Lebreton, but above all to the dogmatics of Karl Barth.[1] And so the theological descendants of the Reformation have reason to heed the warning of the apostle to the Corinthians: 'Therefore do not pronounce judgment before the time' (II Cor. 4. 5). Those who are fathers to this generation were once brethren to another generation. Antiquarianism is the deadly enemy both of living Catholic tradition and of truly Protestant faithfulness to the Scriptures.

Here it is necessary to clarify the meaning and scope of the word 'brethren'. As 'fathers' can become the term for a small and select group who, like the founders of the Gnostic sects, have handed on a private version of apostolic truth, so 'brethren' can be used to designate a closed corporation of theologians. Or a concern for ecumenicity may manoeuvre a theologian into the position of taking every tradition seriously except his own, and of hearkening to every brother except the brother at hand. How can the theologian listen to the brother whom he has not seen if he spurns the brother whom he has seen? 'Brethren', therefore, are not the members of a private club, but members of one family who are devoted to one Father—not indeed as they ought to be but as they are able to be,

[1] See p. 181, note 1 above.

with that fragmentary obedience that characterizes all children of that Father. As the hymnal and the liturgy of every segment of Christendom testify, better perhaps than its theology and life, all Christians have much to learn and to receive from Christian brethren on both sides of all the various borders that separate them. And both the hymnal and the liturgy must help to assure that when the theologians or the bishops forget this, as they some-times do, the church will still be able to learn it.

When the context of Christian theology includes contemporary theology, this ensures that Christian communication will always be a two-way street. In faithful obedience, the church in every generation is obliged to stand up and be counted, to bear witness to the faith and to denounce error. But if this cuts Christian brethren off from one another and from the witness to the truth that even an erring brother may bring,[1] what is called loyalty to truth may neglect the full implications of fidelity. One example from the history of theology since the Reformation is the complex interrelation between the textual criticism of the Bible and loyalty to the authority of the Bible. It is possible to argue in favour of the thesis that loyalty to biblical truth is the best doctrinal ground for scrupulous attention to variant readings; the rabbinical tradition shows that reverence for the letter of the Bible can motivate a meticulous campaign to keep all adulterations out of the text.[2] But the history of the textual study of the New Testament since Johann Albrecht Bengel certainly gives very little comfort to this thesis. For example, the authenticity of the disputed passage, I John 5. 7, was questioned by Erasmus and was attacked, for both theological and textual reasons, by the critical scholarship of the eighteenth and nineteenth centuries.[3] It was defended—more, it must be admitted, for dogmatic than for textual reasons—by the champions of biblical inspiration.[4] Not until 1927 did the Pontifical Biblical Commission grant scholars the right to 'incline toward

[1] Karl Barth, *Die protestantische Theologie im 19. Jahrhundert* (Zurich, 1947), pp. 1-6.
[2] Cf. Frederic Kenyon, *Our Bible and the Ancient Manuscripts* (2nd ed.; London and New York, 1958), pp. 78-79.
[3] Cf. Preserved Smith, *Erasmus. A Study of His Life, Ideals, and Place in History* (New York and London, 1962), pp. 165-166.
[4] On the history of the *comma Johanneum*, see the materials collected in the excursus on 'The Text of 1 John v. 7, 8' in A. E. Brooke, *A Critical and Exegetical Commentary on the Johannine Epistles*, 'The International Critical Commentary' (New York, 1912), pp. 154-165.

an opinion in opposition to its authenticity'; and the most defensive and anxious chapters in the dogmatics of conservative Protestant theologians were those devoted to 'the newer textual criticism' of passages like this one.[1]

Nor is it only in the area of technical textual and historical scholarship that the witness of 'separated brethren' may promote a deeper loyalty to the Catholic substance of tradition. For example, the history of Pietism in the eighteenth century compels the conclusion that it was, at least in part, the work and thought of Reformed and Arminian churches that led the heirs of Luther's Reformation to discover the fuller meaning of the missionary imperative in the New Testament. Proponents of Lutheran missions were denounced as Pietists and Crypto-Calvinists, which is exactly what many of them were; but to their urging, more than to Luther's Reformation itself, can be traced the origins of modern Protestant missions.[2] Thus when theology forgot a part of the Catholic substance, those who were less Catholic in their theology came along to remind it, and they deserved an audience. For, as Luther said, 'now that God has today so graciously bestowed upon us an abundance of arts, scholars, and books, it is time to reap and gather in the best as well as we can, and lay up treasure in order to preserve for the future something from these years of jubilee, and not lose this bountiful harvest.'

CHRISTIANS AND PAGANS REGARDLESS

Martin Luther was, however, too honest a theological scholar to restrict his study exclusively to books by theologians, whether Protestant or Catholic, or even to books by Christians. On the contrary, the context of theological study is not really Catholic unless it includes 'books that would be helpful in learning the languages, such as the poets and orators, regardless of whether they were pagan or Christian . . . books on the liberal arts, and . . . among the foremost the chronicles and histories.' To find a Catholic context Protestant theology needs to give appreciative attention also to non-theological thought. The theological scholar is in constant danger of concentrating upon his speciality as though other

---

[1] Joseph Chaine, *Les épitres catholiques* (2nd ed.; Paris, 1939), pp. 134-136.
[2] Cf. Kenneth Scott Latourette, *A History of the Expansion of Christianity* (7 vols.; New York and London, 1937ff.), III, 46-48.

disciplines did not exist. All the talk in the universities about the 'cross-fertilization of knowledge' is, like so much of the modern literature on marriage, more an evidence of a breakdown than a testimony to renewal. In the same way, what has somewhat awkwardly been called 'Christomonism'[1] is, despite its hostility to secularism, a capitulation to it, an unwillingness to admit that the non-theologian or even the non-Christian may have been granted insights into the nature of being and the meaning of language that will help the theologian to hear the voice of revelation more faithfully and to respond to it more completely.

To be truly Catholic, Protestant theology needs to pay appreciative attention to non-theological thought for a number of reasons. The first and most basic is the humanizing influence that only such thought can bring into theological discourse. 'First a human being, then a Christian'—whatever may be the various rights and wrongs of this formula of N. F. S. Grundtvig, it is correct in its insistence, reinforced by both the precept and the example of Luther, that in trying to be more than a natural human being, a Christian (and therefore a theologian) must be careful not to be less than a natural human being.[2] The preaching of the church can address itself to thoughtful men only if it takes seriously and appreciatively what the human spirit is able to accomplish by the sheer gift of divine creation. When a theology is informed by a sensitive study of non-theological thought, it will not dismiss the power of God in the natural order with the condescension—indeed, the slander—that has often marked evangelical thought. Despite the common caricature of Luther, the Reformers and the fathers of the church knew what later theology has often forgotten, that the human possibilities of the reason and of the natural man do not have to be denigrated to let the grace of God shine.[3] On this account it is certainly consistent with Reformation thought to urge that the theologian learn through the study of non-theological and even non-Christian thought that he belongs not only to the communion of saints, but also to the communion of the created.

In addition, theology needs non-theological thought also for its

---

[1] See p. 185, note 3 above.
[2] Cf. Johannes Knudsen, *Danish Rebel*. The Life of N. F. S. Grundtvig (Philadelphia, 1955), pp. 195-218.
[3] See the recent discussion by B. A. Gerrish, *Grace and Reason*. A Study of the Theology of Luther (Oxford, 1962), pp. 10-27 and *passim*.

own distinctive assignment of interpreting the Scriptures. If
'theology must be grammatical' then Luther was right in insisting
that the theologian consult works of grammar, rhetoric, and history that would help theology to be truly grammatical in the fullest
possible sense; for the ultimate context of any grammar, and therefore of any passage, is the history of an entire culture. Grammar is,
as Luther knew, a matter not of revelation but of research. Earlier
centuries may have been justified by their research in assuming
that the New Testament was written in a special Greek dialect
invented for the purpose,[1] but today's scholarship is obliged to set
the language of the New Testament into the history of spoken
Greek. And although it has been fashionable in recent years to
emphasize the distinctiveness of the language of the Bible, it seems
that the contemporary study of grammar is leading to a recovery
of the principle for which Luther stood: that ancient writers,
'regardless of whether they are pagan or Christian', are essential
for the theological and historical study of Scripture.[2]

So it is that the many books may illumine the one Book, and that
the Catholic substance of tradition in its fullest and broadest sense
can provide the context for the Protestant principle of critical
reverence. The example of Luther's own theology illustrates this
interaction. Only when the three sources we have been discussing
in this chapter—tradition, contemporary theology, and pagan
thought—have been identified in his work, will its true lineaments
emerge. Modern study of Luther's Reformation and modern
editions of his works are beginning to make these identifications.
The fathers, the late medieval doctors, and the pagan authors are
all represented in his works far more fully than previous editors
and previous scholars recognized. Nor was this Catholic substance
merely a straw man against which the Protestant principle of
Luther's Reformation declared its freedom. On the contrary, as
this chapter and earlier chapters have argued, the Catholic substance was the context of the Protestant principle. The heritage of
the Reformation, then, must include both Catholic substance and
Protestant principle, or it will not preserve either one.

[1] See the remarkable statement quoted in James Hope Moulton and George
Milligan, *The Vocabulary of the Greek New Testament* (London, 1952), p. XI,
note 2.
[2] Cf. James Barr, *The Semantics of Biblical Language* (Oxford, 1961), esp. pp.
288-296.

XIV

EVANGELICAL CATHOLICITY AND ITS THEOLOGICAL TASKS

THE faithful administration of the heritage of the Reformation today is a task for the entire life of the church, not only for its theology. Nevertheless, as Part One of this book has shown, the combination of Catholic substance and Protestant principle in Luther's Reformation was fundamentally a theological achievement. Hence its restatement must also take theological form. In this final chapter we shall attempt to delineate the dimensions of an evangelical Catholicity and to describe some of its theological tasks.

THE CONFESSIONAL TASK

The only empirical church in whose life an evangelical Catholicity can be achieved is a church that is empirically divided, however 'one in hope and doctrine' it may or may not be. An evangelically Catholic theology must serve a concrete church or denomination: this is one of the facts of life. What such a church or denomination has a right to expect of its theologians is usually less than it does expect of them in actual practice. Usually it expects of them that they parrot, or provide learned footnotes in support of, the current party line of the denomination; more of this later on. But the denomination does have the right to ask of the theologian as teacher and scholar that he deepen his own response to its confessional heritage, and that he help the denomination to respond more profoundly to its tradition. The basis of this right is not merely the economic reality that the denomination pays the bill for his groceries, but the psychological and theological reality that no one can jump out of his own skin or pretend that he belongs to the whole church in general while he ignores his responsibilities to one church in particular.

In the history of the confessions that have arisen since the Reformation, this insistence upon the confessional task of theology has not always taken the same form or been enforced with the same seriousness.[1] Where it has been ignored, however, there not merely denominational loyalty, but true evangelical Catholicity has suffered. For, as Part One of this book has pointed out, we have access to the Catholic tradition only through particular traditions; and while it is only the tradition itself, i.e., the revelation given in Christ and communicated to and through the apostles, that we are to take with utmost earnestness, we take the tradition with such earnestness when we listen gratefully to the specific traditions out of which we have come. When a denomination asks its theologians to be loyal to its traditions, therefore, it asks this in the name of the one tradition by which it and they want to be judged. The term 'confessional' has both a descriptive and a normative meaning here. Theology is confessional when it uses the particular confessions of its tradition to describe itself and to give an account of the way it has heard the Word of God through these confessions. But 'confessional' is also normative, because the theologian is asked to make this confession his own confession—not in addition to, nor yet in competition with, but as an interpretation of the word of God in the Bible.

When the confessions of Luther's Reformation say, 'We believe, teach, and confess', however, they are bearing witness for something (*pro-testantes*) and against something. In an age of simpleminded interconfessional toleration it needs to be pointed out that evangelical Catholicity is by definition polemical. What must separate the confessional polemics of our day from its forms in the age of the Reformation is a greater willingness to listen before we speak and to understand before we criticize. This willingness to listen, born of historical study and of Christian charity, acknowledges that from Christian sources all over the ecclesiastical map we can learn much about the meaning of our common faith. It acknowledges, too, that our sins and shortcomings as individuals

[1] See the detailed survey of materials in A. G. Rudelbach, *Historisch-kritische Einleitung in die Augsburgische Confession* (Dresden, 1841), pp. 169-252; also Otto Ritschl, *Dogmengeschichte des Protestantismus*, I, 212-267, and p. 43 above.

and as a church have often prevented us from listening and learning. Nevertheless, amid such acknowledgement a confessional theology is still obliged to 'confess'. 'To confess', in both its Greek and its Latin forms, means two things: to acknowledge one's sin before God and the church; and to bear witness to one's faith, likewise before God and the church, as well as before the world.[1] Because previous generations often appeared to speak the truth without love, it is understandable that many theologians are reluctant to engage in polemics. The very word 'polemics', like the words 'pious' and 'sermon' and 'preaching', has almost lost its usefulness because of past abuses. The restoration of fraternal polemics to its rightful role in theological discourse is one of the assignments facing a truly evangelical Catholicity.

Another assignment facing evangelical Catholicity as it attempts to define its theological task is the realization that a theology in the tradition of the Reformation is not, and should not be, merely biblical theology. So long has the Protestant principle been equated with the famous motto of William Chillingworth, 'the Bible, and the Bible only, is the religion of Protestants',[2] that Protestants have claimed to find in the formal acceptance of this motto the guarantee that their theology is indeed biblical, and neither more nor less than biblical. To the charge, summarized in Chapter XII, that the history of Protestantism since the Reformation has introduced an additional criterion into theology they indignantly replied that since the Reformation confessions merely summarized the teachings of the Bible, the single principle of 'Scripture alone' still prevailed. An evangelical Catholicity is more sensitive than is much 'biblical theology' to the forms and traditions of interpretation through which it both hears and speaks the biblical message. Instead of ignoring these forms and traditions as though they did not exist, a theology that is evangelically Catholic includes them in its purview, not idolatrously nor yet superciliously, but with what Part One of this book has called critical reverence.

[1] Cf. Otto Michel, *s. v.* 'homologeo' in Gerhard Kittel (ed.), *Theologisches Wörterbuch zum Neuen Testament* (Stuttgart, 1933ff.), v, 199-220, especially pp. 209-213 and p. 215.
[2] William Chillingworth, *The Religion of Protestants, A Safe Way to Salvation* in *The Works of William Chillingworth* (Oxford, 1838), I, 157-280.

N*

THE CONSERVING TASK

Yet there is practically no Reformation confession that claims to stand alone. Almost all of them refer at least to the ancient creeds, and most of them mention one or another church father or church tradition. Theology has not discharged its responsibility, therefore, when it has described the polemical stance of its particular confession; for beyond and beneath this confession is the wealth of the Christian tradition. Conserving this wealth is also a task of theology. The church needs a theology that will remind it of the hidden treasures in Christian history and thus deliver it from the tyranny of the here and now. And the church needs a theology that will do this even when—indeed, especially when—the church does not want such a theology.

Theology performs its conserving function when it reminds the church of neglected issues in the Catholic substance of its message and thought. There is, for example, considerable evidence to support the generalization that 'in theology since the beginning of the nineteenth century the doctrine of creation has taken second place to the doctrine of redemption'.[1] When theology permitted this to happen, it was neglecting its conserving task and simply taking its cue from the empirical church. For in the life of the church since the beginning of the nineteenth century the importance of creation has truly taken second place—or last place—behind the doctrine of redemption. For a variety of reasons too complex to sketch here, ranging from the impact of modern science to the 'Jesus-centred' piety of the evangelical movements in the Protestantism of the past century, the life and message of the church have lost a dynamic awareness of the meaning of creation. The recovery of that meaning, which appears to be a feature of contemporary Christian life, is due at least in part to the new emphasis upon creation in Christian theology. And this new emphasis, in turn, is due at least in part to the historical discovery that creation has occupied a more central place in the mainstream of the Catholic tradition than it occupied in evangelical Protestantism.[2] When it assumed once more its responsibility for conser-

[1] Wilhelm Lütgert, *Schöpfung und Offenbarung.* Eine Theologie des ersten Artikels (Gütersloh, 1934), p. 27.
[2] J. N. D. Kelly, *Early Christian Doctrines* (London and New York, 1958), pp. 83-87.

ving the treasure of the church's past, Protestant theology helped to enrich the thought and life of the church by reviving one of the most vital and most neglected issues in the Catholic substance of its tradition.

Sometimes the life of the church tends to neglect not so much the doctrines of the Catholic substance as some of its resources. As Chapter XII has pointed out, theology meets this neglect by dusting off those shelves in the ecclesiastical library to which the church has forgotten to turn. For example, it seems that contemporary Protestant theology is paying more attention to the theological implications of liturgy than it has for centuries. A concentration upon the Protestant principles summarized in Chapter VI, without the Catholic substance of the Reformation described in Chapter V, has caused many Protestants, including many Protestant theologians, to look upon liturgy as 'trappings', the multiplication of unnecessary ceremonies, 'merely symbols', and the last place in the church to look for theological resources. Theology, then, would have to control liturgy and to demand that the gestures, postures, actions, and formulas of worship correspond to the rules of clarity and meaning that systematic theology has established. Today theologians are beginning to realize that the relation between theology and liturgy is a reciprocal one, and the principle of *lex orandi, lex credendi* has achieved currency in many sections of Christendom.[1] Students of the Scriptures have discovered the elements of cult and ritual in both the Old and the New Testament; students of the history of theology have seen that, for example, worship of Christ as divine preceded the elaboration of precise theological formulas about the divinity of Christ.[2] When the church neglects such a resource as the liturgy, it is the task of true evangelical Catholicity to call this theological resource to the church's remembrance.

A related neglect is the preoccupation of a denomination with its own parochial history at the expense of the rest of the church's history. Theology performs its conserving task when it demands

---

[1] On this motto see the comment of Hermann Sasse, *This Is My Body* (Minneapolis, 1959), p. 13, note 1.

[2] In G. L. Prestige's words, 'the doctrine of the Trinity sprang from the inherent necessity to account for the religious data of Christianity, not from the importation of pagan metaphysical presuppositions', *God in Patristic Thought* (London, 1956), p. xxii.

that the church of today listen not only to the church of yesterday, but to the church of last week and last month, even though that church may speak in a strange accent. As previous chapters in Part Three have suggested, deliverance from traditionalism can come through the broadening and liberating power of tradition. Perhaps the best illustration of such deliverance is the study of the church fathers. Chapter XI has mentioned that this study has fallen upon bad days in much of Protestantism, even as a new and exciting era of patristic study has begun in Roman Catholicism. It seems clear that Protestant theology neglects this aspect of church history at its peril. Now that the focus of attention in patristic study has shifted from the dependence of the fathers upon Greek and Roman thought to their exegesis of the Scriptures,[1] Protestant theology should be able to discover its affinities with and its derivation from the evangelical Catholicity of the church fathers. In doing so, it can discover also the vitality of faith and confession which each generation of the church has had to redis-cover in the fathers. From this vitality can come new life in the church of today, as it is delivered from slavery to the recent past and reintroduced to the great conversation with the Catholic substance of the Christian centuries. A genuinely 'conservative' and evangelically Catholic theology is one which recognizes this as its assignment: to make the church of this generation sensitive to the great conversation.

THE CATHOLIC TASK

The great conversation is still going on in the Christian Church, and theology is one of its principal subjects. In the life of the church, theology has the Catholic task of reflecting and carrying on the continuing conversation. The institutional church can often be the victim of its own successes and be tempted by them to forget its needs and responsibilities beyond its own organizational boundaries. When it succumbs to this temptation, it confines theology to its own boundaries; or if it does go beyond them, it is only with the purpose of demonstrating the correctness of its own theological position. To such a limitation of its scope theology

---

[1] Cf. Robert M. Grant, *The Letter and the Spirit* (New York and London, 1957); R. P. C. Hanson, *Allegory and Event* (London, 1959); Henri de Lubac, *Histoire et esprit* (Paris, 1950).

must object, not alone for its own sake, but for the sake of the life of the church. If 'Catholicity' mean 'identity plus universality',[1] theology has the twofold Catholic function of directing the life of the church to its specific identity and of pointing the vision of the church to its inclusive universality.

The theology of the church is living proof that the interdependence of Christians always crosses denominational lines. It is simply impossible for a theologian, whether Roman Catholic or Protestant, to carry on his work without the support of men and movements that do not belong to his own tradition. To study the church fathers one needs the great edition of their writings by the French Benedictines, the critical studies of their thought by the German Lutherans of the Ritschlian school, and the standard translation by the Reformed divines of Britain and America. From all indications the theological thought and research of the next generation will give even more evidence of such dependence upon the entire community of Christian scholarship. Already the results of scholarly co-operation are evident in the consensus on the doctrine of the church summarized in Chapter XII, as well as in the area of biblical study, where Roman Catholics and various kinds of Protestants have also been working and conversing long enough to have achieved a degree of consensus, however limited and tentative that consensus may be.[2] The day of a theology written of a denomination, by a denomination, and for a denomination is happily past. Theologians have no alternative but to learn from one another and to bear one another's burdens.

Theologians are obliged to point out that the church has no other alternative either. As the theology of past generations simultaneously echoed and commanded the limited loyalties of its denomination, so the theology of this generation must in its own work display its Catholic character and by its insights remind the church of its Catholic obligations. Too often, the case for Christian unity beyond separation is put on the pragmatic grounds of efficiency, on the relativistic grounds of doctrinal indifference,

---

[1] Jaroslav Pelikan, *The Riddle of Roman Catholicism*, pp. 21-22.

[2] It is instructive to compare the discussion between Oscar Cullmann, *Peter. Disciple—Apostle—Martyr*, tr. Floyd V. Filson (London and Philadelphia, 1953 revised edn., 1962), and Charles Journet, *The Primacy of Peter from the Protestant and from the Catholic Point of View*, tr. John Chapin (Westminster, Md., 1954), with the Reformation debates on the primacy of Peter and the exegesis of Matt. 16. 18; cf. Jaroslav Pelikan, *Luther the Expositor*, pp. 113-118.

or on the sociological grounds of greater corporate consciousness. Each of these certainly has its role to play, and we do need a theological interpretation of 'non-theological factors'.[1] But we also need a theological interpretation of the Catholic responsibility of the church. Those denominations which have gone into ecumenical alliances or mergers without attention to basic theology need to hear the Reformation insistence, summarized in Chapters VIII and IX, that Catholicity means identity as well as universality. Those denominations which refuse to enter any alliance or merger which they cannot dominate must learn the lesson which, as Chapter X has shown, Luther's Reformation had to learn: that identity without universality is a sectarianism that corrodes identity itself. And theologians need to invest their theological definitions of both Catholic substance and Protestant principle with such clarity and urgency that the churches will hear them and heed them.

The place for the theologians to begin this is their own work. As Chapter XIII has said, a theologian must depend upon the whole community of Christian scholarship as well as upon scholars outside the Christian community; nevertheless, theology still has a long way to go before it outgrows its own parochialism. The writings of John Wesley seem to be the private preserve of Methodist scholars; very few Lutherans have written so much as an article about John Calvin; and the Anabaptist Reformers, once the victims of right-wing persecution, are now the victims of left-wing patriotism. Theology cannot summon the churches to a deeper Catholicity unless the range of its own concerns and sources is broadened. We may contemplate with amusement the prospect of Luther research amplified by the unique contributions of Roman Catholic scholars or of Thomistic studies carried on by Protestants, but just such mutual concern is what theology will have to discover. When theology takes up this Catholic task, it uncovers implications in the several Christian traditions that reach directly into the contemporary life of the church. No doctrine of the Lord's Supper, be it Roman Catholic or Reformed or Lutheran, can afford to ignore the radical consequences of the biblical and historical research of the past fifty years.[2] That

[1] H. Richard Niebuhr, *The Social Sources of Denominationalism* (New York and London, 1957).

[2] Cf. Ernst Käsemann, *Leib und Leib Christi* (Tübingen, 1933); Joachim Jeremias, *The Eucharistic Words of Jesus*, tr. Arnold Ehrhardt (Oxford and New

research makes some fundamental discussion of the sacrament within and among the traditions both possible and necessary. Thus theology is performing its Catholic task of working within the context of the entire church and of calling upon the entire church to recognize that this is likewise the context of its own life and work.

THE CRITICAL TASK

The churches are not always ready to hear this reminder from their theologians, just as the theologians are not always ready to issue the reminder. When the Protestant principle is distorted into partisan loyalty, it ceases to be the Protestant principle.[1] Because the Protestant principle defines itself in relation to Catholic substance, an evangelically Catholic theology must erect within its own life the agencies that will keep it conscious of that Catholic substance. But to be confessional rather than merely denominational in its service to the church, such a theology must exercise a critical function. The measure of true churchmanship is the willingness of ecclesiastical administrators to encourage and support this critical function of theology, even when the theology is critical of the current party line of the denomination.

The obligation of the theologian to exercise this critical function provided Luther's Reformation with justification for its work. Discussing his attacks upon Rome, Luther said:

> I have never wanted to do it and do not want to do it now. I was forced and driven into this position in the first place when I had to become Doctor of Holy Scripture against my will. Then as a doctor in a general free university, I began, at the command of pope and emperor, to do what such a doctor is sworn to do, expounding the Scriptures for all the world and teaching everybody. Once in this position, I have had to stay in it, and I cannot give it up or leave it yet with a good conscience.[2]

During the four centuries since the Reformation, Continental

York, 1955); Henri de Lubac, *Corpus mysticum. L'eucharistie et l'église au moyen age* (Paris, 1949). Even Professor Sasse, for all his zeal to restore the confessionally Lutheran doctrine of the Lord's Supper, must concede that there have been significant changes in the interpretation of the New Testament since the Reformation, *op. cit.*, pp. 351-359.

[1] Cf. Paul Tillich, 'The End of the Protestant Era?' *The Protestant Era*, ed. James Luther Adams (Chicago and London, 1951), pp. 222-233.

[2] *Commentary on Psalm 82*, *WA* 31-I, 212 (*LW* 13, 66).

Protestantism has entrusted a large part of the responsibility for theological teaching and research to the theological faculties of universities over which ecclesiastical authorities had little or no control. Those faculties often lost any sense of loyalty to the empirical church, to the distress of all concerned;[1] but they also provided the churches with a constant critical voice that troubled the easy conscience of church leaders. In this way the university faculties of theology performed a role somewhat analogous to that of the teaching orders within Roman Catholicism. At their best, these faculties were close enough to the churches to speak to them, yet far enough to be more than an echo. The founders of the American denominations had often experienced the estrangement of such theological faculties from the churches; therefore much, though not all, theological education in the United States has been more closely tied to the organizational life of the churches.[2] Nevertheless, it has not altogether lost its sensitivity to the critical task without which theology is not truly loyal either to its Catholic substance or to its Protestant principle.

Like the Catholic task of theology, the critical task must be applied first of all to theology itself. For this reason, among other reasons, theology dare not become the exclusive prerogative of the theological professors; its place in the life of the church requires that the academic theologians be summoned to relevance and responsibility by the theologians whose ministry expresses itself chiefly through preaching, teaching, and administering the sacraments. Augustine, after all, was not a theological professor, but, in Luther's phrase, 'the poor, insignificant pastor of Hippo,[3] Indeed, it is often the critical task of theology that is itself most deserving of criticism. When it becomes the carping of the academician or the snobbishness of the pedant, critical theology must hear a critical word from the 'men of action' whom it claims to despise. On the other hand, the situation receives little help from those 'men of action' in the church who insist upon perpetuating the dubious distinction between 'men of ideas' and 'men of action' and whose only weapon in combating the academic theologians is a homely illustration or pious epigram drawn from

[1] See Agnes von Zahn-Harnack, *Adolf von Harnack*, pp. 115-127.
[2] H. Richard Niebuhr, Daniel Day Williams, and James M. Gustafson, *The Advancement of Theological Education*, (New York, 1957), pp. 42-53.
[3] Cf. p. 62, note 5 above.

last week's instruction of the catechumens. The history of the church is littered with the corpses of such churchmen and of the theologians whom they opposed; neither group comprehended the critical task of theology in the life of the church.

Because 'the church interprets Scripture, and Scripture judges the church', as one Roman Catholic theologian has put it,[1] theology exercises its critical function within the bi-polarity of church and Scripture, described in Chapter III and developed in Chapters XII and XIII. The interpretation of Scripture is certainly the duty of the entire church, not only of its theologians; yet much of that duty falls upon the theologians, and it should. After subordinating itself to the word of God in Scripture, the church asks its theologians to do the same; then it asks them to interpret the word to the church, so that Scripture may judge the church, including the theologians. It would be too neat a formulation to speak in this connection about a 'balance of powers', for the history of the church manifests many cases of imbalance. As often as not, moreover, this imbalance has been more characteristic of the theologians than it has of the church in general. Overemphasis upon one favourite theological point is an occupational disease of theology. When a theology afflicted with this disease summons the church to share this affliction, the health of the church requires that the church refuse. Therefore the theological faculty must not be permitted to become the corporate pope of the church. Having said that, however, one must go on to say that often the church has been most defensive and deaf on the very issues where it needed the critical function of theology most.

Then theology has the duty to speak out critically, even though it knows that it may possibly be mistaken. Few documents in the history of theology are more moving than the personal statements of theologians whose conscience forced them to oppose the public teaching of the church they loved.[2] Like Jeremiah, they have known the loneliness and doubt of being misunderstood. Yet the burden of their duty to the church as God intended the church

---

[1] Edmund Ortigues, 'Écritures et traditions apostoliques au Concile de Trente', *Recherches de science religieuse*, XXXVI (1949), 296.
[2] On Archbishop Peter Richard Kenrick at the Vatican Council, see the documents cited in John Rothensteiner, *History of the Archdiocese of St Louis* (Saint Louis, 1928), II, 303-318. Cf. also Karl Adam, *The Spirit of Catholicism*, tr. Justin McCann (New York, 1954; London, 1959), pp. 230ff.

to be forced them to denounce the church as men had deformed it. The Reformation doctrine of justification by faith, when applied to the empirical church,[1] means that in the name of the church as church it is sometimes necessary to attack the church as Christendom. Chapter II has pointed out that when this distinction is taken to mean that there is a permanent dichotomy between church and Christendom, the result is sectarianism. But when the distinction is forgotten, as it sometimes is in both Roman Catholicism and Protestantism, the result is idolatry. For the church to be the church and for Christendom to become the church, theology must both hear and speak a critical word.

THE CORRELATING TASK OF THEOLOGY

Probably the most telling critical words being spoken to the church and about the church today are coming not from theologians, but from 'the world'. Church leaders may permit the external successes and internal enthusiasms of the church to beguile them into ignoring these words, or they may simply dismiss them on the grounds that the cross has always been foolishness to the Greeks. Theologians may commit the same fallacy; but when they do, they neglect a task that theology has claimed at least since the days of the apologists, the function of correlating Christian and 'secular' thought.

As Chapter XIII has argued, evangelical Catholicity assumes this task both for its own sake and for the sake of the church, because both the church and its theology need the enrichment and the criticism that can come only from life and thought beyond the walls of the church. The basis of this need is not only that theologians must study non-Christian thought in order to refute its errors, but also that they must learn from non-Christian thought what only it can teach them about man and his situation. Where but from the novels and drama of the past two generations can theologians and churchmen learn to be sensitive to the new seriousness about death and fate that characterizes our age? From whom can theology hear about present images of the cosmos if it refuses to listen to modern physics? Surely the preaching of the church has a stake in what men today believe about death or about man's place in a cooling universe. Indeed, the precedents

[1] See pp. 35-36 above.

of Luther's Reformation would suggest that the preaching of the church must take its start from what men today know about death or about the cosmos—which is not always identical with what they believe—and must attach its message to these known quantities. If the preaching of the church has any such assignment, it would seem impossible for the theology of the church to evade its assignment of correlating the thought of the church with current trends in the interpretation of man and the world.

Sometimes this will mean that theology has to side with 'the world' against the empirical church. Sometimes it will mean that theology has to interpret 'the world' sympathetically to a church whose traditional ears are unaccustomed to modern accents. And sometimes it will mean that, in the name of the church, theology has to raise fundamental questions about the secular thought it is trying to correlate with its message. Into the vacuum created by the secularization of thought during the past several centuries have crept pseudo-theologies of various sorts. Usually their dogmas are implicit and therefore seem obvious to everyone. Such a dogma was the doctrine of progress, so widespread during the nineteenth century. Ironically, the church succumbed to this dogma almost as uncritically as did 'the world'; and it is still an unsolved question whether the force that destroyed the doctrine of progress in the church was the biblical message or the realities of the twentieth century.[1] The task of theology in the presence of such secular dogmas is, first of all, to point out that they are indeed dogmas, and that the Christian faith has no monopoly on unexamined presuppositions. Then theology has the responsibility of raising basic questions about these dogmas and of asking whether these dogmas really do make better sense of life and reality than the dogmas and faith of the Christian Church. Beyond this, no theology that takes the Catholic substance and Protestant principle of the Reformation seriously can be permitted to go. It can only show that Christian faith is a possibility.

Evangelical Catholicity is impossible without this correlating task, for the church faces a culture in which its traditional answers are meaningless because its traditional questions are irrelevant. If theology takes the Catholic substance to mean that these are the

---

[1] See the wry comments of Karl Barth, *Church Dogmatics*, III-2, edd. G. W. Bromiley and T. F. Torrance (Edinburgh, 1960), 115.

right questions simply because they are the questions to which the church has become accustomed, the task of the church will shrivel still more into the cultivation of private inner piety among those who find the modern world too much to stand.[1] But this is the abdication of theology, as both the Reformation and the Catholic tradition have understood theology from the beginning. The problem of correlation is, to a considerable degree, a problem of logistics. Can the church sustain a theological enterprise comprehensive enough to exercise this function of correlation? Can it afford it? To this the only answer an evangelical Catholicity can make is: Can the church afford anything less?

For theology has a task in the life of the church more profound than any of those outlined above, the function of carrying on the love of God with the mind. As the late H. Richard Niebuhr once noted, 'Though intellectual love of God and neighbour is not the supreme exercise of love, yet it is required and possible since the man is also mind and does not wholly love his loves if his mind does not move toward them. . . . When the whole man is active the mind is also active; when the whole church is at work it thinks and considers no less than it worships, proclaims, suffers, rejoices, and fights.'[2] To carry on this function, evangelical Catholicity needs to be confessional, conserving, Catholic, critical, and correlating—all of these, and no one of them without all the others. Only thus can both the Catholic substance and the Protestant principle of Luther's Reformation be heard in the life and thought of the church today. Only thus can an evangelically Catholic theology assume its share of the church's fragmentary yet faithful obedience to the greatest of all commandments: 'Thou shalt love the Lord thy God with all thy heart, and with all thy soul, and with all thy mind.'

[1] In Reinhold Niebuhr's epigram, 'Nothing is so incredible as an answer to an unasked question', *The Nature and Destiny of Man*, II (New York and London, 1943), 6.
[2] H. Richard Niebuhr, *The Purpose of the Church and its Ministry*, p. 111.

INDEX OF NAMES